OLD ENGLISH POETRY

OLD ENGLISH POETRY

TRANSLATIONS INTO ALLITERATIVE VERSE

WITH

INTRODUCTIONS AND NOTES

BY

J. DUNCAN SPAETH

PROFESSOR OF ENGLISH IN PRINCETON UNIVERSITY

PRINCETON UNIVERSITY PRESS

PRINCETON

LONDON: HUMPHREY MILFORD
OXFORD UNIVERSITY PRESS

1922

PR
1508
S6

Pub. Sept. 34 1.95

PRINCETON
UNIVERSITY
PRESS

Committing Random acts of
Kindness everyday is
beneficial to everyone. So do it!

PREFACE

In this book of Old English poetry an effort has been made to bring together and reproduce in modern English alliterative verse, the best and most representative portions of the considerable body of extant poetry produced in England between the time of the Anglo-Saxon invasion and the Norman conquest. The classification of this poetry into the main types of Epic, Lyric, Gnomic and Historic Poetry, while necessarily formal, does no real violence to the principle of historic continuity. *Widsith* and *Beowulf* belong to the earlier period, *Brunnanburg* and *Maldon* to the later, and to this extent the arrangement is chronological as well as topical. The conditions under which this early poetry was produced and transmitted render exact dating extremely difficult or impossible and in view of the comparative fixity of form throughout the whole period, the division according to genre is not only the most convenient but the most natural. While designed chiefly for use in College and High-School in connection with survey courses in English literature, it is hoped that the general reader and student of English literature and history may find more than mere text-book matter in the volume. The brief general introductions to the various types, Heroic Epic, Biblical Epic, Saints' Legends, etc., if read through consecutively, will give a fair survey of the field of Old English poetry, and the selected bibliography will orient the student who wishes to pursue further his reading in this field.

In the epic and narrative divisions, complete poems or

pieces of narrative have so far as possible been given. In the *Beowulf,* the first 2000 lines are practically complete with only the omission of the episodes; and the last adventure is also practically complete. Of the 3182 lines of the *Beowulf* Ms. our translation gives 2125, just two-thirds of the whole. Where, as in *Elene* and *Guthlac,* larger portions have been omitted, the danger is not that the selection will appear fragmentary, but rather that an effect of greater unity will be produced than is present in the original. Throughout the book the line-numbers in parentheses on the right hand margin indicate the line-numbers of the original. Where lines or passages have been omitted, the omission is indicated by the marginal line-numbers, which will facilitate comparison with the Old English text for those who care to make it. In general, the translation follows the original line by line, but in *Guthlac,* the *Phoenix,* and some of the lyrics there has been more fusion than in *Beowulf* and the historic narratives.

As a translator of poetry I have kept in mind Rossetti's canon of translation: "The life-blood of rhythmical translation is this commandment that a good poem shall not be turned into a bad one. The only true motive for putting poetry into fresh language must be to endow a fresh nation as far as possible with one more possession of beauty. Poetry not being an exact science, literality of rendering is altogether secondary to this chief law. I say *literality,* not *fidelity,* which is not the same thing." A faithful translation must be faithful to the language into which the translation is made, as well as to the one out of which it is made. Theodore Roosevelt once said of a translation of *Beowulf:* "This poem has undoubtedly been translated out of Anglo-Saxon, but it has undoubtedly not been translated into English." Wherever faithfulness to the spirit of a line or passage has seemed to come into conflict with faithfulness to the letter, a literal translation, and in some cases the Old English passage, has been given in the notes, and the general reader is in this way provided with a check on the translator that the scholar possesses by his reference to the original Old English text.

In the preface to the volume of *Early English Poems* (1910) in which many of these translations first appeared, the writer said: "These renderings represent at least an attempt to make English poetry out of Anglo-Saxon poetry. Many of them were made years ago for use in the class-room with my students. Like the poems they aim to reproduce, they led a mouth-to-ear existence long before they were elevated to the dignity of 'letters.' Even now the translator would wish to have them judged chiefly by their effect when read aloud. The older the poetry, the more vocal it is. Versions of Old English poetry that fail to make their appeal through the living rhythm of the living voice, fail not only in an essential of all poetry but in a quintessential of Anglo-Saxon poetry." In the special note on the Old English Alliterative Metre, I have discussed the principles followed in rendering the Germanic alliterative verse in modern English.

My obligations to the scholars whose labors have made possible the interpretation of Old English life and literature to the modern mind, have been acknowledged in the notes wherever I was conscious of them. The best payment in this kind is faithful use. So far as possible within the special scope of this little book, I have tried to bring to bear on the body of Old English poetry here presented, the best results both of older and of contemporary scholarship. For the translator and interpreter of Old English poetry, Grein's *Sprach-schatz* is still an indispensable and inexhaustible treasury. It is not only a dictionary, but a concordance of Old English Poetry, and when used together with the Grein-Wuelker *Bibliothek,* it unlocks the meaning of many an obscure passage. Wherever special editions of Old English poems were available, they have been used. Among the editions to which the renderings are especially indebted, are the admirable revision of the Wyatt edition of *Beowulf* by R. W. Chambers (1914), every page of which throws light upon the text,[1] the scholarly editions of *Crist* and the *Dream of the Rood* by Professor Cook, and the excellent edition of the *Riddles* by Professor Tupper. Where I have been conscious of dependence on previous translators for words, phrases, or lines not directly suggested by the original, I have indicated the fact in the notes, generally with a reference to the Old English. The select bibliography and the many references in the notes will indicate the sources on which I have chiefly drawn for the matter in introduction and notes.

My thanks are due to Henry Holt and Co. for permitting the use of the translations and notes that had previously appeared in *Early English Poems* (Henry Holt and Co., N. Y., 1910), and to my colleagues in the English Department at Princeton, without whose encouragement this volume would not have been undertaken.

We need not fall into what Matthew Arnold called the

---

[1] Prof. Chambers' *Introduction to Beowulf* 1921 did not come to hand until after my Beowulf translation and notes had gone through the press.

fallacy of the historic estimate, in judging of the value and interest of these beginnings of English poetry for the student and lover of English literature. The significance of that literature lies in the fact that more completely than any of the national literatures produced by Western Civilization it has, like the language that is its form, achieved a union of the Northern, Germanic, and the Greco-Latin, Classic spirit.

In its beginnings, in the Epic poetry of the Heroic Age, we witness the response of the Northern Spirit, as embodied in the Germanic tribes that settled England, to the challenge of life, scarcely touched by the spirit of older civilizations. The conversion of the Old English to Christianity first brought them into the main stream of the cultural inheritance of the West. In the Christian literature of the Anglo-Saxons we witness the beginnings of that capacity for absorption and assimilation of foreign cultural influences without loss of native bent and vigor, which has been characteristic of the later and greater periods of English literature. The increasing responsibility thrown upon the peoples who are the inheritors of this great tradition in the task of saving and perpetuating a civilization whose final worth will not be estimated in political, economic, industrial, or commercial achievement, but in the contribution of ideal values it has made to the progress of the human race, renders it especially fitting that in these days we reinforce our consciousness of a common destiny by turning back to our common origins and remembering afresh the rock whence we were hewn, and the hole of the pit whence we were digged.

J. D. S.

Princeton, September 1921.

TABLE OF CONTENTS

I. Epic Poetry

1. HEROIC EPIC

BEOWULF

THE MYTH OF THE SHEAF-CHILD

List to an old-time lay of the Spear-Danes,
Full of the prowess of famous kings,
Deeds of renown that were done by the heroes;
Scyld the Sheaf-Child from scourging foemen,
5 From raiders a-many their mead-halls wrested.
He lived to be feared, though first as a waif,
Puny and frail he was found on the shore.
He grew to be great, and was girt with power
Till the border-tribes all obeyed his rule,
10 And sea-folk hardy that sit by the whale-path
Gave him tribute, a good king was he.
Many years after, an heir was born to him,
A goodly youth, whom God had sent
To stay and support his people in need.
15 (Long time leaderless living in woe,
The sorrow they suffered He saw full well.)
The Lord of Glory did lend him honor,
Beowulf's fame afar was borne,
Son of old Scyld in the Scandian lands.
20 A youthful heir must be open-handed,
Furnish the friends of his father with plenty,
That thus in his age, in the hour of battle,

Willing comrades may crowd around him   (*23*)
Eager and true.   In every tribe
Honorable deeds shall adorn an earl.
The aged Scyld, when his hour had come,
5 Famous and praised, departed to God.
His faithful comrades carried him down
To the brink of the sea, as himself had bidden,
The Scyldings' friend, before he fell silent,
Their lord beloved who long had ruled them.
10 Out in the bay a boat was waiting
Coated with ice, 'twas the king's own barge.
They lifted aboard their bracelet-bestower,
And down on the deck their dear lord laid,
Hard by the mast.   Heaped-up treasure
15 Gathered from far they gave him along.
Never was ship more nobly laden
With wondrous weapons and warlike gear.
Swords and corslets covered his breast
Floating riches to ride afar with him
20 Out o'er the waves at the will of the sea.
No less they dowered their lord with treasure,
Things of price, than those who at first
Had launched him forth as a little child
Alone on the deep to drift o'er the billows.
25 They gave him to boot a gilded banner,
High o'er his head they hung it aloft.
Then set him adrift, let the surges bear him.
Sad were their hearts, their spirits mournful;
Man hath not heard, no mortal can say
30 Who found that barge's floating burden.

I

THE LINE OF THE DANISH KINGS AND THE BUILDING OF HEOROT

Now Beowulf was king in the burgs of the Scyldings,
Famed among folk. (His father had left   (*54*)
The land of the living). From his loins was sprung
Healfdene the royal, who ruled to old age,
5 Gray and battlegrim, the bold-hearted Scyldings.
Children four to this chief of the people
Woke unto life, one after another;
Heorogar and Hrothgar, and Halga the brave,
And winsome Sigeneow, a Scylfing she wedded;
10 Saewela's queen they say she became.
To Hrothgar was given such glory in battle,
Such fame he won, that his faithful band
Of youthful warriors waxed amain.
So great had grown his guard of kinsmen,
15 That it came in his mind to call on his people
To build a mead-hall, mightier far
Than any e'er seen by the sons of men,
Wherein to bestow upon old and young,
Gifts and rewards, as God vouchsafed them,
20 Save folk-share lands and freemen's lives.
Far and wide the work was published;
Many a tribe, the mid-earth round,
Helped to fashion the folk-stead fair.
With speed they built it, and soon 'twas finished,
25 Greatest of halls. Heorot he named it,
Whose word was law o'er lands afar;
Nor failed in his promise, but freely dealt
Gifts at the feast. The fair hall towered

Wide-gabled and high, awaiting its doom,   (82)
The sweep of fire; not far was the time
That ancient feuds should open afresh,
And sword-hate sunder sons from fathers.

5 In the darkness dwelt a demon-sprite,
Whose heart was filled with fury and hate,
When he heard each night the noise of revel
Loud in the hall, laughter and song.
To the sound of the harp the singer chanted
10 Lays he had learned, of long ago;
How the Almighty had made the earth,
Wonder-bright lands, washed by the ocean;
How he set triumphant, sun and moon
To lighten all men that live on the earth.
15 He brightened the land with leaves and branches;
Life he created for every being,
Each in its kind, that moves upon earth.
So, happy in hall, the heroes lived,
Wanting naught, till one began
20 To work them woe, a wicked fiend.
The demon grim was Grendel called,
March-stalker huge, the moors he roamed.
The joyless creature had kept long time
The lonely fen, the lairs of monsters,
25 Cast out from men, an exile accurst.
The killing of Abel, on offspring of Cain
Was justly avenged by the Judge Eternal.
Nought gained by the feud the faithless murderer;
He was banished unblest from abode of men.
30 And hence arose the host of miscreants,
Monsters and elves and eldritch sprites,

Warlocks and giants, that warred against God; (*113*)
Jotuns and goblins; He gave them their due.

II

The Ravaging of Heorot Hall by the Monster Grendel

When night had fallen, the fiend crept near
To the lofty hall, to learn how the Danes
5 In Heorot fared, when the feasting was done.
The aethelings all within he saw
Asleep after revel, not recking of danger,
And free from care. The fiend accurst,
Grim and greedy, his grip made ready;
10 Snatched in their sleep, with savage fury,
Thirty warriors; away he sprang
Proud of his prey, to repair to his home,
His blood-dripping booty to bring to his lair.
At early dawn, when day-break came,
15 The vengeance of Grendel was revealed to all;
Their wails after wassail were widely heard,
Their morning-woe. The mighty ruler,
The aetheling brave, sat bowed with grief.
The fate of his followers filled him with sorrow,
20 When they traced the tracks of the treacherous foe,
Fiend accurst. Too fierce was that onset,
Too loathsome and long, nor left them respite.
The very next night, anew he began
To maim and to murder, nor was minded to slacken
25 His fury of hate, too hardened in crime.
'Twas easy to find then earls who preferred

A room elsewhere, for rest at night,   (*139*)
A bed in the bowers, when they brought this news
Of the hall-foe's hate; and henceforth all
Who escaped the demon, kept distance safe.

 5 So Grendel wrongfully ruled the hall,
One against all till empty stood
That lordly mansion, and long remained so.
For the space of twelve winters the Scyldings' Friend
Bore in his breast the brunt of this sorrow,
10 Measureless woe. In mournful lays
The tale became known; 'twas told abroad
In gleemen's songs, how Grendel had warred
Long against Hrothgar, and wreaked his hate
With murderous fury through many a year,
15 Refusing to end the feud perpetual,
Or decently deal with the Danes in parley,
Take their tribute for treaty of peace;
Nor could their leaders look to receive
Pay from his hands for the harm that he wrought.
20 The fell destroyer kept feeding his rage
On young and old. So all night long
He prowled o'er the fen and surprised his victims,
Death-shadow dark. (The dusky realms
Where the hell-runes haunt are hidden from men.)
25 So the exiled roamer his raids continued;
Wrong upon wrong in his wrath he heaped.
In midnights dark he dwelt alone
'Mongst Heorot's trophies and treasures rich.
Great was the grief of the gold-friend of Scyldings,
30 Vexed was his mood that he might not visit
His goodly throne, his gift-seat proud,

Deprived of joy by the judgment of God (*169*)
Many the wise men that met to discover
Ways of escape from the scourge of affliction.
Often they came for counsel together;
5 Often at heathen altars they made
Sacrifice-offerings, beseeching their idols
To send them deliverance from assault of the foe.
Such was their practice, they prayed to the Devil;
The hope of the heathen on hell was fixed,
10 The mood of their mind. Their Maker they knew
    not,
The righteous Judge and Ruler on high.
The Wielder of Glory they worshipped not,
The Warden of Heaven. Woe be to him
Whose soul is doomed through spite and envy,
15 In utter despair and agony hopeless
Forever to burn. But blessed is he
Who, after this life, the Lord shall seek,
Eager for peace in the arms of the Father.

III

THE VOYAGE OF BEOWULF TO THE HALL OF HROTHGAR

Thus boiled with care the breast of Hrothgar; (*189*)
20 Ceaselessly sorrowed the son of Healfdene,
None of his chieftains might change his lot.
Too fell was the foe that afflicted the people
With wrongs unnumbered, and nightly horrors.
Then heard in his home king Hygelac's thane,
25 The dauntless Jute, of the doings of Grendel.
In strength he outstripped the strongest of men

That dwell in the earth in the days of this life.
Gallant and bold, he gave command (*198*)
To get him a boat, a good wave-skimmer.
O'er the swan-road, he said, he would seek the king
5 Noble and famous, who needed men.
Though dear to his kin, they discouraged him not;
The prudent in counsel praised the adventure,
Whetted his valor, awaiting good omens.

So Beowulf chose from the band of the Jutes
10 Heroes brave, the best he could find;
He with fourteen followers hardy,
Went to embark; he was wise in seamanship,
Showed them the landmarks, leading the way.
Soon they descried their craft in the water,
15 At the foot of the cliff. Then climbed aboard
The chosen troop; the tide was churning
Sea against sand; they stowed away
In the hold of the ship their shining armor,
War-gear and weapons; the warriors launched
20 Their well-braced boat on her welcome voyage.

Swift o'er the waves with a wind that favored,
Foam on her breast, like a bird she flew.
A day and a night they drove to seaward,
Cut the waves with the curving prow,
25 Till the seamen that sailed her sighted the land,
Shining cliffs and coast-wise hills,
Headlands bold. The harbor opened,
Their cruise was ended. Then quickly the sailors,
The crew of Weder-folk clambered ashore,

Moored their craft with clank of chain-mail, (*226*)
And goodly war-gear. God they thanked
That their way was smooth o'er the surging waves.

High on the shore, the Scylding coast-guard
5 Saw from the cliff where he kept his watch,
Glittering shields o'er the gunwale carried,
Polished weapons. It puzzled him sore,
He wondered in mind who the men might be.
Down to the strand on his steed came riding
10 Hrothgar's thane, with threatening arm
Shook his war-spear and shouted this challenge:
"Who are ye, men, all mailed and harnessed,
That brought yon ship o'er the broad sea-ways,
And hither have come across the water,
15 To land on our shores? Long have I stood
As coast-guard here, and kept my sea-watch,
Lest harrying foe with hostile fleet
Should dare to damage our Danish land.
Armed men never from overseas came
20 More openly hither. But how do ye know
That law of the land doth give ye leave
To come thus near. I never have seen
Statelier earl upon earth than him,—
Yon hero in harness. No house-carl he,
25 In lordly array, if looks speak true,
And noble bearing. But now I must learn
Your names and country, ere nearer ye come,
Underhand spies, for aught I know,
In Danish land. Now listen ye strangers,
30 In from the sea, to my open challenge:
Heed ye my words and haste me to know
What your errand and whence ye have come."

IV

Beowulf's Words With the Coast-Guard

Him the hero hailed with an answer,   (258)
The war-troop's leader, his word-hoard unlocked:
"In truth we belong to the tribe of the Jutes;
We are Hygelac's own hearth-companions.
5 Far among folk my father was known,
A noble chieftain; his name was Ecgtheow
Honored by all, he ended his days
Full of winters and famed in the land.
Wise men everywhere well remember him.
10 Hither we fare with friendly purpose
To seek thy lord, the son of Healfdene,
The land-protector. Instruct us kindly.
Bound on adventure we visit thy lord,
The prince of the Danes. Our purpose is open;
15 Nought keep we secret; thou surely wilt know
If the tale we were told is true or not:
That among the Scyldings a monster strange
A nameless demon, when nights are dark,
With cruel cunning, for cause unknown,
20 Works havoc and slaughter. I have in mind
A way to help your wise king Hrothgar,
Your ruler to rid of the ravening foe,
If ever his tide of troubles shall turn,
The billows of care that boil in his breast
25 Shall cool and subside, and his sorrow be cured;
Else, failing my purpose, forever hereafter
He shall suffer distress, while stands on its hill,
Mounting on high, his matchless hall."
Straight answered the coast-guard, astride his horse,
30 The warrior brave: "Twixt words and deeds
A keen-witted thane, if he thinks aright,

Must well distinguish and weigh the difference. (*289*)
Your words I believe, that you wish no evil
To the Scylding lord. I will let you bring
Your shields ashore and show you the way.
5 My comrades here shall keep the watch,
From meddling foe defend your craft,
Your fresh-tarred boat, fast by the beach,
And faithfully guard her till again she bear
With curving bow, o'er the bounding main,
10 Her master well-loved to the Wedermark.
Fortune oft favors the fighter who yields not;
Hero unflinching comes unhurt from the fray."
Landward they hastened, leaving behind them
Fast at her moorings the full-bosomed boat,
15 The ship at anchor. Shone the boar-heads
Gleaming with gold, o'er the guards of their helmets;
Bright and fire-forged the beast kept watch.
Forward they pressed, proud and adventurous,
Fit for the fight, till afar they descried
20 The high-peaked radiant roof of the hall.
Of houses far-praised 'neath heaven by the people
That inhabit the earth, this house was most famous,
The seat of king Hrothgar; its splendor gleamed
    bright
O'er many a land. Their leader well-armed
25 Showed them the shining shield-burg of heroes,
And set them right on the road to their goal.
Then, wheeling his steed, he wished them farewell:

" 'Tis time that I leave you; the Lord of Heaven,
The Father Almighty in mercy keep you
30 Safe on your journey; seaward I turn,
Watch to keep and ward against foe."

V

BEOWULF'S ARRIVAL AT THE HALL AND THE MANNER
OF HIS RECEPTION

The street was stone-paved; straight it led   *(320)*
To the goal of their journey. Glistened their byrnies
Stout and strong-linked; sang the rings
Of their iron mail as they marched along,
5 In armor and helmet right up to the hall.
Sea-voyage-sated, they set their shields,
Their linden-woods broad, along the wall.
As they bent to the bench, their byrnies clattered.
They stacked their spears that stood in a row,
10 Ashwood tipped with iron above;
Well-equipped was the warlike band.
A stately Dane the strangers addressed,
Asked who they were and whence they had come:
"Whence do ye bear your burnished shields,
15 Your visored helmets and harness gray
Your heap of spear-shafts? A servant of Hrothgar's
His herald, am I. Hardier strangers,
Nobler in mien, have I never seen.
'Tis clear you come to the court of Hrothgar,
20 Not outlaws and beggars, but bent on adventure."
To him gave answer the hero brave,
The lord of the Weders these words returned,
Bold 'neath his helmet: "We are Hygelac's men,
His board-companions. I am Beowulf called.
25 Ready am I the ruler to answer,

To say to thy lord, the son of Healfdene,   (*345*)
Why we have come his court to seek,
If he will graciously grant us a hearing."
Wulfgar replied (he was prince of the Wendles,
5 His noble renown was known to many,
His courage in war, and wisdom in counsel):
"I will carry thy quest to the king of the Danes,
And ask him whether he wishes to grant
The boon thou dost ask of the breaker-of-rings,
10 To speak to himself concerning thy journey;
And straight will I bring thee the answer he sends."
Swiftly he hied him where Hrothgar sat,
White-haired and old, his earls around him.
Stately he strode, till he stood in the presence
15 Of the king of the Danes,—in courtly ways
Was Wulfgar skilled; he spoke to his lord:
"Hither have fared from a far country,
A band of Jutes o'er the bounding sea.
Their leader and chief by his chosen comrades
20 Is Beowulf called; this boon they ask:
That they may find with thee, my lord,
Favor of speech; refuse them not,
But grant them, Hrothgar, gracious hearing.
In armor clad, they claim respect
25 Of choicest earls; but chiefly their lord
Who lately hither hath led his comrades."

VI

Hrothgar's Welcome to Beowulf

Hrothgar spoke, the Scyldings' protector:
"Beowulf I knew in his boyhood days;
His aged father was Ecgtheow named.

To him, to take home, did Hrethel give (*374*)
His only daughter. Their dauntless son
Now comes to my court in quest of a friend.
My sea-faring men whom I sent afar
5 To the land of the Jutes, with generous gifts,
In token of friendship, have told me this,
That the power of his grip was so great it equalled
The strength of thirty stout-armed thanes.
Him bold in battle, the blessed God
10 Hath sent in his mercy, to save our people
—So I hope in my heart—from the horror of Grendel.
I shall offer him gold for his gallant spirit.
Go now in haste, and greet the strangers;
Bid to the hall the whole of the company;
15 Welcome with words the warrior band,
To the home of the Danes." To the hall door went
Wulfgar the courtly, and called them in:
"My master commands me this message to give you,
The lord of the Danes your lineage knows;
20 Bids me to welcome you, brave-hearted warriors,
Bound on adventure o'er the billowy main.
Ye may rise now and enter, arrayed in your armor,
Covered with helmets, the king to greet.
But leave your shields, and your shafts of slaughter,
25 Here by the wall to await the issue."
Then rose the leader, around him his comrades,
Sturdy war-band; some waited without,
Bid by the bold one their battle-gear to guard.
Together they hastened where the herald led them,
30 Under Heorot's roof. The hero went first,

Strode under helmet, till he stood by the hearth. (*404*)
Beowulf spoke, his byrnie glistened,
His corslet chain-linked by cunning of smithcraft:
"Hail, king Hrothgar! Hygelac's thane
5 And kinsman am I. Known is the record
Of deeds of renown I have done in my youth.
Far in my home, I heard of this Grendel;
Sea-farers tell the tale of the hall:
How bare of warriors, this best of buildings
10 Deserted stands, when the sun goes down
And twilight deepens to dark in the sky.
By comrades encouraged, I come on this journey.
The best of them bade me, the bravest and wisest,
To go to thy succor, O good king Hrothgar;
15 For well they approved my prowess in battle,
They saw me themselves come safe from the conflict
When five of my foes I defeated and bound,
Beating in battle the brood of the monsters.
At night on the sea with nicors I wrestled,
20 Avenging the Weders, survived the sea-peril,
And crushed in my grip the grim sea-monsters
That harried my neighbors. Now I am come
To cope with Grendel in combat single,
And match my might against the monster, alone.
25 I pray thee therefore, prince of the Scyldings,
Not to refuse the favor I ask,
Having come so far, O friend of the Shield-Danes,
That I alone with my loyal comrades,
My hardy companions, may Heorot purge.
30 Moreover they say that the slaughterous fiend
In wanton mood all weapons despises.
Hence,—as I hope that Hygelac may,

My lord and king, be kind to me,— (436)
Sword and buckler I scorn to bear,
Gold-adorned shield, as I go to the conflict.
With my grip will I grapple the gruesome fiend,
5 Foe against foe, to fight for our life.
And he that shall fall his faith must put
In the judgment of God. If Grendel wins
He is minded to make his meal in the hall
Untroubled by fear, on the folk of the Jutes,
10 As often before he fed on the Danes.
No need for thee then to think of my burial.
If I lose my life, the lonely prowler
My blood-stained body will bear to his den,
Swallow me greedily, and splash with my gore
15 His lair in the marsh; no longer wilt then
Have need to find me food and sustenance.
To Hygelac send, if I sink in the battle,
This best of corslets that covers my breast,
Heirloom of Hrethel, rarest of byrnies,
20 The work of Weland. So Wyrd will be done."

VII

THE FEASTING IN HEOROT AND THE CUSTOMS OF THE HALL

Hrothgar spoke, the Scyldings' defender:
"Thou hast come, dear Beowulf, to bring us help,
For the sake of friendship to fight our battles. (458)

(Hrothgar recounts the exploits of Beowulf's father.)

Sad is my spirit and sore it grieves me (473)

To tell to any the trouble and shame (474)
That Grendel hath brought me with bitter hate,
The havoc he wrought in my ranks in the hall.
My war-band dwindles, driven by Wyrd
5 Into Grendel's grasp; but God may easily
End this monster's mad career.
Full often they boasted, my beer-bold warriors,
Brave o'er their ale-cups, the best of my fighters,
They'd meet in the mead-hall the mighty Grendel,
10 End his orgies with edge of the sword.
But always the mead-hall, the morning after,
The splendid building, was blood-bespattered;
Daylight dawned on the drippings of swords,
Soiled with slaughter were sills and benches.
15 My liege-men perished, and left me poor.
Sit down to the board; unbend thy thoughts;
Speak to my men as thy mood shall prompt."
For the band of the Jutes a bench was cleared;
Room in the mead-hall was made for them all.
20 Then strode to their seats the strong-hearted heroes.
The warriors' wants a waiting-thane served;
Held in his hand the highly-wrought ale-cup,
Poured sparkling mead, while the minstrel sang
Gaily in Heorot. There was gladness of heroes,
25 A joyous company of Jutes and of Danes.

VIII

UNFERTH TAUNTS BEOWULF

Then up spoke Unferth, Ecglaf's son,
Who sat at the feet of the Scylding ruler;

He vented his jealousy. The journey of Beowulf,
His sea-adventure, sorely displeased him.   (502)
It filled him with envy that any other
Should win among men more war-like glory,
5 More fame under heaven than he himself:
"Art thou the Beowulf that battled with Brecca,
Far out at sea, when ye swam together,
What time you two made trial of the billows,
Risking your lives in reckless folly,
10 On the open sea? None might dissuade you,
Friend nor foe, from the fool-hardy venture,
When straight from the shore you struck for the open,
Breasted the waves and beat with your arms
The mounting billows, measured the sea-paths
15 With lusty strokes. Stirred was the ocean
By wintry storms. Seven days and nights
Your sea-strife lasted; at length he beat you;
His strength was the better; at break of day
He made the beach where the Battle-Reamas
20 Dwell by the shore; and straightway returned
To his people beloved in the land of the Brondings,
Where liegemen and towns and treasure were his.
In sooth I say, the son of Beanstan
His boast against thee made good to the full.
25 But now I ween a worse fate awaits thee
Though thy mettle be proved in many a battle
And grim encounter, if the coming of Grendel
Thou darest abide, in the dead of the night."
Beowulf spoke, the son of Ecgtheow:
30 "What a deal of stuff thou hast talked about Brecca,
Garrulous with drink, my good friend Unferth.
Thou hast lauded his deeds. Now listen to me!

More sea-strength had I, more ocean-endurance
Than any man else, the wide earth round.   (*534*)
'Tis true we planned in the pride of our youth
This ocean-adventure, and vowed we would risk
5 Our lives in the deep, each daring the other.
We were both of us boys, but our boast we fulfilled.
Our naked swords as we swam from the land,
We held in our grasp, to guard against whales.
Not a stroke could he gain on me, strive as he would,
10 Make swifter speed through the swelling waves,
Nor could I in swimming o'ercome him at sea.
Side by side in the surge we labored
Five nights long.   At last we were parted
By furious seas and a freezing gale.
15 Night fell black; the norther wild
Rushed on us ruthless and roughened the sea.
Now was aroused the wrath of the monsters,
But my war-proof ring-mail, woven and hand-locked,
Served me well 'gainst the sea beasts' fury;
20 The close-linked battle-net covered my breast.
I was dragged to the bottom by a bloody-thirsty mon-
          ster,
Firm in his clutch the furious sea-beast
Helpless held me.   But my hand came free,
And my foe I pierced with point of my sword.
25 With my battle-blade good 'twas given me to kill
The dragon of the deep, by dint of my blow."

IX

BEOWULF COMPLETES THE STORY OF HIS SWIMMING
ADVENTURE WITH BRECCA.   HROTHGAR'S DE-
PARTURE FROM THE HALL

"Thus sore beset me sea-beasts thronging,   (559)
Murderous man-eaters. I met their charges,
Gave them their due with my goodly blade.
They failed of their fill, the feast they expected
5 In circle sitting on the sea-floor together
With me for their meal. I marred their pleasure.
When morning came, they were cast ashore
By the wash of the waves; their wounds proved fatal;
Bloated and dead on the beach they lay.
10 No more would they cross the course of the ships
In the chop of the channel charge the sailors.
Day broke in the east, bright beacon of God;
The sea fell smooth. I saw bold headlands,
Windy walls; for Wyrd oft saveth
15 A man not doomed, if he dauntless prove.
My luck did not fail me, my long sword finished
Nine of the nicors. Ne'er have I heard
Of fiercer battle fought in the night,
Of hero more harried by horrors at sea.
20 Yet I saved my life from the sea-beasts' clutch.
Worn with the struggle, I was washed ashore
In the realm of the Finns by the run of the tide,
The heave of the flood. I have failed to hear
Of like adventure laid to thee,
25 Battle so bitter. Brecca did never,—
Neither of you was known to achieve
Deed so valiant, adventure so daring,

Sword-play so nimble; not that I boast of it,   (586)
But mark me, Unferth, you murdered your brothers,
Your closest of kin. The curse of hell
For this you will suffer, though sharp be your wit.
5 In sooth I say to you, son of Ecglaf,
Never had Grendel such grim deeds wrought,
Such havoc in Heorot, so harried your king
With bestial fury, if your boasted courage
In deeds as well as in words you had proved.
10 But now he has found he need not fear
Vengeance fierce from the Victory-Scyldings,
Ruthless attack in return for his raids.
He takes his toll of your tribe as he pleases,
Sparing none of your spearmen proud.
15 He ravens and rages and recks not the Dane folk,
Safe from their sword-play. But soon I will teach him
How the Jute-folk fight. Then freely may go
To the mead-hall who likes, when the light of morn-
         ing,
The next day's dawn, the dark shall dispel,
20 And the heaven-bright sun from the south shall
         shine."

Glad in his heart was the giver of rings,
Hoped to have help, the hoar-headed king;
The Shield-Danes' shepherd was sure of relief,
When he found in Beowulf so firm a resolve.
25 There was laughter of heroes. Loud was their
         revelry,
Words were winsome as Wealhtheow rose,
Queen of Hrothgar, heedful of courtesy,
Gold-adorned greeted the guests in the hall.

First to her lord, the land-defender,   (615)
The high-born lady handed the cup;
Bade him be gleeful and gay at the board,
And good to his people. Gladly he took it,
5 Quaffed from the beaker, the battle-famed king.
Then leaving her lord, the lady of the Helmings
Passed among her people in each part of the hall,
Offered the ale-cup to old and young,
Till she came to the bench where Beowulf sat.
10 The jewel-laden queen in courteous manner
Beowulf greeted; to God gave thanks,
Wise in her words, that her wish was granted,
That at last in her trouble a trusted hero
Had come for comfort. The cup received
15 From Wealhtheow's hand the hardy warrior,
And made this reply, his mind on the battle;
Beowulf spoke, the son of Ecgtheow:
"I made up my mind when my mates and I
Embarked in our boat, outbound on the sea,
20 That fully I'd work the will of thy people,
Or fall in the fight, in the clutch of the fiend.
I surely shall do a deed of glory,
Worthy an earl, or end my days,
My morning of life, in the mead hall here."
25 His words pleased well the wife of Hrothgar,
The Jutish lord's boast. The jewelled queen
Went to sit by the side of her lord.

Renewed was the sound of noisy revel,
Wassail of warriors. Brave words were spoken.
30 Mirth in the mead-hall mounted high,
Till Healfdene's son the sign did give

That he wished to retire. Full well he knew   (*646*)
The fiend would find a fight awaiting him,
When the light of the sun had left the hall,
And creeping night should close upon them,
5 And shadowy shapes come striding on
Dim through the dark. The Danes arose.
Hrothgar again gave greeting to Beowulf,
Wished him farewell; the wine-hall lofty
He left in his charge. These last words spoke he:
10 "Never before have I fully entrusted
To mortal man this mighty hall,
Since arm and shield I was able to lift.
To thee alone I leave it now,
To have and to hold it. Thy hardihood prove!
15 Be mindful of glory; keep watch for the foe!
No reward shalt thou lack if thou live through this
    fight.

X

Beowulf's Watch in Heorot

Then Hrothgar went with his warrior-band,
The Arm-of-the-Scyldings, out of the hall.
Would the war-lord Wealhtheow seek,
20 The queen for his bed-mate. The best of kings
Had placed in the hall, so heroes report,
A watch against Grendel, to guard his house,
Deliverance bring to the land of the Danes.
But the lord of the Jutes joyfully trusted
25 In the might of his arm and the mercy of God.
Off he stripped his iron byrnie,

Helmet from head, and handed his sword,   (*672*)
Choicest of blades, to his body-thane,
And bade him keep the battle armor.
Then made his boast once more the warrior,
5 Beowulf the bold, ere his bed he sought,
Summoned his spirit; "Not second to Grendel
In combat I count me and courage of war.
But not with the sword will I slay this foeman,
Though light were the task to take his life.
10 Nothing at all does he know of such fighting,
Of hewing of shields, though shrewd be his malice
Ill deeds to contrive. We two in the night
Shall do without swords, if he dare to meet me
In hand to hand battle. May the holy Lord
15 To one or the other award the victory,
As it seems to Him right, Ruler all-wise."
Then he sought his bed. The bolster received
The head of the hero. In the hall about him,
Stretched in sleep, his sailormen lay.
20 Not one of them thought he would ever return
Home to his country, nor hoped to see
His people again, and the place of his birth.
They had heard of too many men of the Danes
O'ertaken suddenly, slain without warning,
25 In the royal hall. But the Ruler on High
Through the woof of fate to the Wederfolk gave
Friendship and help, their foes to o'ercome,
By a single man's strength to slay the destroyer.
Thus all may learn that the Lord Almighty
30 Wields for aye the Wyrds of men.   (*702*)

.   .   .   .

XI

BEOWULF'S FIGHT WITH GRENDEL

Now Grendel came, from his crags of mist   (710)
Across the moor; he was curst of God.
The murderous prowler meant to surprise
In the high-built hall his human prey.
5 He stalked 'neath the clouds, till steep before him
The house of revelry rose in his path,
The gold-hall of heroes, the gaily adorned.
Hrothgar's home he had hunted full often,
But never before had he found to receive him
10 So hardy a hero, such hall-guards there.
Close to the building crept the slayer,
Doomed to misery. The door gave way,
Though fastened with bolts, when his fist fell on it.
Maddened he broke through the breach he had made;
15 Swoln with anger and eager to slay,
The ravening fiend o'er the bright-paved floor
Furious ran, while flashed from his eyes
An ugly glare like embers aglow.
He saw in the hall, all huddled together,
20 The heroes asleep. Then laughed in his heart
The hideous fiend; he hoped ere dawn
To sunder body from soul of each;
He looked to appease his lust of blood,
Glut his maw with the men he would slay.
25 But Wyrd had otherwise willed his doom;
Never again should he get a victim
After that night. Narrowly watched
Hygelac's thane how the horrible slayer
Forward should charge in fierce attack.

Nor was the monster minded to wait: (739)
Sudden he sprang on a sleeping thane,
Ere he could stir, he slit him open;
Bit through the bone-joints, gulped the blood,
5 Greedily bolted the body piecemeal.
Soon he had swallowed the slain man wholly,
Hands and feet. Then forward he hastened,
Sprang at the hero, and seized him at rest;
Fiercely clutched him with fiendish claw.
10 But quickly Beowulf caught his forearm,
And threw himself on it with all his weight.
Straight discovered that crafty plotter,
That never in all midearth had he met
In any man a mightier grip.
15 Gone was his courage, and craven fear
Sat in his heart, yet helped him no sooner.
Fain would he hide in his hole in the fenland,
His devil's den. A different welcome
From former days he found that night!
20 Now Hygelac's thane, the hardy, remembered
His evening's boast, and bounding up,
Grendel he clenched, and cracked his fingers;
The monster tried flight, but the man pursued;
The ravager hoped to wrench himself free,
25 And gain the fen, for he felt his fingers
Helpless and limp in the hold of his foe.
'Twas a sorry visit the man-devourer
Made to the Hall of the Hart that night.
Dread was the din, the Danes were frighted
30 By the uproar wild of the ale-spilling fray.
The hardiest blenched as the hall-foes wrestled
In terrible rage. The rafters groaned;

'Twas wonder great that the wine-hall stood,   (771)
Firm 'gainst the fighters' furious onslaught,
Nor fell to the ground, that glorious building.
With bands of iron 'twas braced and stiffened
5 Within and without. But off from the sill
Many a mead-bench mounted with gold
Was wrung where they wrestled in wrath together.
The Scylding nobles never imagined
That open attack, or treacherous cunning,
10 Could wreck or ruin their royal hall,
The lofty and antlered, unless the flames
Should some day swallow it up in smoke.
The din was renewed, the noise redoubled;
Each man of the Danes was mute with dread,
15 That heard from the wall the horrible wail,
The gruesome song of the godless foe,
His howl of defeat, as the fiend of hell
Bemoaned his hurt. The man held fast;
Greatest he was in grip of strength,
20 Of all that dwelt upon earth that day.

XII

THE DEFEAT OF GRENDEL

Loath in his heart was the hero-deliverer
To let escape his slaughterous guest.
Of little use that life he deemed
To human kind. The comrades of Beowulf
25 Unsheathed their weapons to ward their leader,
Eagerly brandished their ancient blades,
The life of their peerless lord to defend.

Little they deemed, those dauntless warriors, (798)
As they leaped to the fray, those lusty fighters,
Laying on boldly to left and to right,
Eager to slay, that no sword upon earth
5 No keenest weapon could wound that monster:
Point would not pierce, he was proof against iron;
'Gainst victory-blades the devourer was charmed.
But a woful end awaited the wretch,
That very day he was doomed to depart,
10 And fare afar to the fiends' domain.

Now Grendel found, who in former days
So many a warrior had wantonly slain,
In brutish lust, abandoned of God,
That the frame of his body was breaking at last.
15 Keen of courage, the kinsman of Hygelac
Held him grimly gripped in his hands.
Loath was each to the other alive.
The grisly monster got his death-wound:
A huge split opened under his shoulder;
20 Crunched the socket, cracked the sinews.
Glory great was given to Beowulf.
But Grendel escaped with his gaping wound,
O'er the dreary moor his dark den sought,
Crawled to his lair. 'Twas clear to him then,
25 The count of his hours to end had come,
Done were his days. The Danes were glad,
The hard fight was over, they had their desire.
Cleared was the hall, 'twas cleansed by the hero
With keen heart and courage, who came from afar.
30 The lord of the Jutes rejoiced in his work,
The deed of renown he had done that night.

His boast to the Danes he bravely fulfilled;   *(829)*
From lingering woe delivered them all;
From heavy sorrow they suffered in heart;
From dire distress they endured so long;
5 From toil and from trouble. This token they saw:
The hero had laid the hand of Grendel
Both arm and claws, the whole forequarter
With clutches huge, 'neath the high-peaked roof.

XIII

The Celebration of the Victory and the Song of the Gleeman

When morning arrived, so runs the report,
10 Around the gift-hall gathered the warriors;
The folk-leaders fared from far and near,
The wide ways o'er, the wonder to view,
The wild beast's foot-prints. Not one of them felt
Regret that the creature had come to grief,
15 When they traced his retreat by the tracks on the
          moor;
Marked where he wearily made his way,
Harried and beaten, to the haunt of the nicors,
Slunk to the water, to save his life.
There they beheld the heaving surges,
20 Billows abrim with bloody froth,
Dyed with gore, where the gruesome fiend,
Stricken and doomed, in the struggle of death
Gave up his ghost in the gloom of the mere,
His heathen soul for hell to receive it.
25 Then from the mere the thanes turned back,

Men and youths from the merry hunt,   *(854)*
Home they rode on their horses gray,
Proudly sitting their prancing steeds.
Beowulf's prowess was praised by all.
5 They all agreed that go where you will,
'Twixt sea and sea, at the south or the north,
None better than he, no braver hero,
None worthier honor could ever be found.
(They meant no slight to their master and lord
10 The good king Hrothgar, their ruler kind.)

Now and again the noble chiefs
Gave rein to their steeds, and spurred them to race,
Galloped their grays where the ground was smooth.
Now and again a gallant thane,
15 Whose mind was stored with many a lay,
With songs of battle and sagas old,
Bound new words in well-knit bars,
Told in verse the valor of Beowulf,
Matched his lines and moulded his lay.   *(872)*

Here is introduced an episode of the Nibelungen Legend. The
gleeman tells how Sigmund the Volsung with his son and nephew
Fitela ranged the forests and slew wild beasts. Later when Fitela
was no longer with him, Sigmund killed a dragon and won a
great treasure.

20 When the lay was ended they urged once more *(916)*
Their racers fleet to fly o'er the plain.
As the morning sped, and the sun climbed higher,
Many went in, the marvellous sight
More closely to scan. The king himself

With a troop of trusty retainers about him   (*921*)
Strode from his bower; the bestower-of-rings
Came, and with him the queen, in state,
The meadow-path trod, by her maidens attended.

XIV

HROTHGAR'S PRAISE OF BEOWULF, AND BEOWULF'S REPLY

5 Hrothgar spoke when he reached the hall,
  Stood on the step, and stared at the roof
  Adorned with gold, and Grendel's hand:
  "Prompt be my heart to praise the Almighty
  For the sight I behold. Much harm have I suffered,
10 And grief from Grendel, but God still works
  Wonder on wonder, the Warden of Glory.
  But a little while since, I scarcely dared,
  As long as I lived, to look for escape
  From my burden of sorrow, when blood-stained stood
15 And dripping with slaughter, this stately hall.
  Wide-spread woe my warriors scattered;
  They never hoped this house to rid,
  While life should last, this land-mark of people,
  Of demons and devils. 'Tis done by the hero.
20 By the might of the Lord this man has finished
  The feat that all of us failed to achieve
  By wit or by war. And well may she say,
  —Whoever she be,—that bore this son,
  That the Ancient of Days dealt with her graciously,
25 And blest her in child-birth. Now Beowulf, hear!
  I shall henceforth hold thee, hero beloved,

As child of my own, and cherish thee fondly   (948)
In kinship new. Thou shalt never lack
Meed of reward that is mine to give.
For deeds less mighty have I many times granted
5 Fullest reward to warriors feebler,
In battle less brave. Thy boldness and valor
Afar shall be known; thy fame shall live
To be great among men. Now God the Almighty
With honor reward thee, as ever he doth."

10 Beowulf spoke, the son of Ecgtheow:
"Gladly we fought this good fight through,
Fearlessly faced the foe inhuman,
Grappled him gruesome; it grieves me sore
That the man-beast himself you may not see,
15 Dead in the hall, fordone in the fray.
I meant to master the monster quickly,
To his death-bed pin him by power of my grip,
Hold him hard till my hand could strangle him,
Bringing him low, but he broke away.
20 In vain I tried to prevent his escape.
The Lord was unwilling; I lost my hold
On the man-destroyer; too strong was the monster,
Too swift on his feet. But to save his life
He left behind him the whole of his fore-paw,
25 Arm and shoulder. 'Twas a useless shift,
Profiting nothing. He ne'er will prolong
His life by the loss, the loathly slayer,
Sunk in sin; but sorrow holds him,
Caught in the grasp of its grip relentless,
30 In woful bonds to await in anguish,
Guilty wretch, the rest of his doom,

As the Lord Almighty shall mete it to him." (*979*)

More silent seemed the son of Ecglaf
Less boastful in bragging of brave deeds done
When all of them, looking aloft, beheld
5 The hand on high, where it hung 'neath the roof,
The claw of the fiend; each finger was armed
With a steel-like spur instead of a nail,
The heathen's handspikes, the horrible paw
Of the evil fiend. They all declared
10 No iron blade could e'er have bit
On the monstrous bulk of the man beast's hide,
Or hewn away that woful talon.

XV

The Feasting and Giving of Treasure In the Hall

Now orders were given the guest-hall to cleanse,
And furnish it fresh. Forth went hurrying
15 Men and maids. To the mead-hall they went
And busily worked. Woven tapestries,
Glinting with gold, hung gay on the walls,
Marvellous wonders for men to look upon.
Ruin and wreck had been wrought in the building,
20 Though braced within by iron bands,
The hinges were wrenched, the roof alone stood
Undamaged and sound, when the sin-spotted wretch
The demon destroyer, in despair of his life,
Turned and made off,—not easy it is
25 To escape from death, essay it who will.

(So each of us all to his end must come   (*1004*)
Forced by fate to his final abode
Where his body, stretched on the bier of death,
Shall rest after revel.)   Now right was the hour
5 For Healfdene's heir to enter the hall;
The king himself would come to the feast.
I never have heard of nobler bearing
'Mongst ranks of liegemen surrounding their lord
As they took their seats, the trusty comrades,
10 And fell to feasting.   Freely quaffed
Many a mead-cup the mighty kinsmen
Hrothgar and Hrothulf, the high hall within.
Heorot was filled with a friendly host.
(Far was the day when the Scylding host
15 Should treachery plot, betraying each other.)
Then Healfdene's son bestowed on Beowulf
A gold-adorned banner for battle-reward,
A rich-broidered standard, breast-plate and helmet.
The swordmen assembled saw the treasures
20 Borne before the hero.   Beowulf drank
The health of Hrothgar, nor had reason to feel
Ashamed before shieldmen to show his reward.
Never were offered by earls that I heard of,
In token of friendship four such treasures,
25 Never was equalled such ale-bench bounty.
Round the ridge of the helmet a rim of iron
Wound with wire, warded the head,
That the offspring of files, with fearful stroke,
The hard-tempered sword-blade, might harm it not,
30 When fierce in the battle the foemen should join.
At a sign from the king, eight stallions proud
Bitted and bridled were brought into hall.

On the back of one was a wondrous saddle,   (*1037*)
Bravely wrought and bordered with jewels,
The battle-seat bold of the best of kings
When Hrothgar himself would ride to the sword-play.
5 (Nor flinched from the foe the famous warrior
In the front of the fight where fell the slain.)
To the hero delivered the lord of the Scyldings
The heir of Ing, both armor and horses,
Gave them to Beowulf, and bade him enjoy them.
10 Thus royally, the ruler famous,
The heroes' hoard-guard, heaped his bounty;
Repaid the struggle with steeds and trophies,
Praised by all singers who speak the truth.

XVI

THE KING'S GIFTS TO BEOWULF'S MEN, AND THE GLEEMAN'S LAY OF FINN

The Lord of the earls then added gifts,
15 At the mead-bench remembered the men, each one,
That Beowulf brought o'er the briny deep,
With ancient heirlooms and offered to pay
In gold for the man that Grendel had slain,
As more of them surely the monster had killed
20 Had not holy God and the hero's courage
Averted their doom.   (So daily o'errules
The Father Almighty the fortunes of men.
Therefore is insight ever the best,
And prudence of mind; for much shall suffer
25 Of lief and of loath who long endures
The days of his life in labor and toil.)

Now music and song were mingled together, (*1063*)
In the presence of Hrothgar, ruler in war.
Harp was struck and hero-lays told.
Along the mead-bench the minstrel spread
5 Cheer in hall when he chanted the lay
Of the sudden assault on the sons of Finn.   (*1068*)

The episode which follows, alludes obscurely to details of a feud
between Frisians and Danes. The Finnsburg fragment contains
a portion of the same story and one of the heroes, Hnaef, is also
mentioned in Widsith.

XVII

THE LAY OF FINN ENDED. THE SPEECH OF THE QUEEN

The lay was ended, (*1159*)
The gleeman's song.   Sound of revelry
Rose again.   Gladness spread
10 Along bench and board.   Beer-thanes poured
From flagons old the flowing wine.
Wealhtheow the queen walked in state,
Under her crown, where uncle and nephew
Together sat,—they still were friends.
15 There too sat Unferth, trusted counsellor,
At Hrothgar's feet; though faith he had broken
With his kinsmen in battle, his courage was proved.
Then the queen of the Scyldings spoke these words:
"Quaff of this cup my king and my lord,
20 Gold-friend of men.   To thy guests be kind,
To the men of the Jutes be generous with gifts.
Far and near thou now hast peace.
I have heard thou dost wish the hero for son

To hold as thy own, now Heorot is cleansed, (*1176*)
The jewel-bright hall. Enjoy while thou mayest,
Allotment of wealth, and leave to thy heirs
Kingdom and rule when arrives the hour
5 That hence thou shalt pass to thy place appointed.
Well I know that my nephew Hrothulf
Will cherish in honor our children dear
If thou leavest before him this life upon earth;
He will surely requite the kindness we showed him,
10 Faithfully tend our two young sons,
When to mind he recalls our care and affection
How we helped him and housed him when *he* was a
    child."
She turned to the bench where her two boys sat
Hrethric and Hrothmund, and the rest of the youth,
15 A riotous band, and right in their midst,
Between the two brothers, Beowulf sat.

XVIII

The Queen's Gifts to Beowulf

With courteous bow the cup she offered,
Greeted him graciously and gave him to boot
Two armlets rare of twisted gold,
20 A robe and rings, and the rarest collar;
A better was never known among men,
Since Hama brought to his bright-built hall
The jewelled necklace, the gem of the Brisings.

(*1199*)

Lines 1190-1215 interrupt the narrative to tell of the subsequent
history of Wealhtheow's gift; how Beowulf gave it to Hygelac, who
wore it on his famous raid against the Frisians, in which he was
slain by the Franks.

Before the warriors Wealhtheow spoke: (*1215*)
"Accept dear Beowulf, this bright-gemmed collar;
Make happy use of this heirloom jewelled,
This ring and robe and royal treasure;
5 Be brave and bold.   My boys instruct
In gentle manners; mine be the praise.
Thou hast done such a deed that in days to come
Men will proclaim thy might and valor
To the ends of the earth where the ocean-wave
10 Washes the windy walls of the land.
I wish thee joy of thy jewelled treasure,
Long be thy life; enlarge thy prosperity,
Show thee a friend to my sons in deed.
Here each earl to the other is faithful,
15 True to his liege-lord, loyal and kind.
My warriors obey me, willing and prompt.
The Danes carousing, do as I bid."
She went to her seat, the wine flowed free;
'Twas a glorious feast.   The fate that impended,
20 None of them knew, though near to them all.

When darkness came, the king of the Danes
Went to his rest in the royal bower;
But a throng of his kinsmen kept the hall
As they used to do in the days of old.
25 They cleared the boards and covered the floor
With beds and bolsters.   One beer-thane there
Lay down to sleep with his doom upon him.
They placed by their heads their polished shields,
Their battle-boards bright, on the bench nearby.

Above each earl, within easy reach,   (*1244*)
Was his helmet high and his harness of mail
And the spear-shaft keen. 'Twas their custom so,
That always at rest they were ready for war
5 At home or abroad, where'er they might be,
At what hour soever for aid might call
Their lord and king; they were comrades true.

END OF THE FIRST ADVENTURE

XIX

The Coming of Grendel's Dam to Avenge Her Son

Then sank they to sleep, but sorely paid
One poor wretch for his rest that night.
10 The same thing fell, as in former days
When Grendel his raids on the gold-hall made,
Before the fiend had found his match,
Caught in his sins. 'Twas seen that night
An avenger survived the villainous fiend
15 Although they had ceased from their sorrow and care.
'Twas Grendel's mother, a monstrous hag.
She remembered her loss. She had lived in the deep,
In a water-hell cold since Cain had become
The evil slayer of his only brother,
20 His kin by blood; accursed he fled
Marked by murder from men's delights,
Haunted the wilds; from him there sprung
Ghastly demon-shapes, Grendel was one.   (*1266*)

The omitted lines break the narrative to turn back to the
Grendel fight.

Now grim and vengeful   (1276)
His mother set out on her errand of woe,
Damage to wreak for the death of her son.
Arrived at Heorot, the Ring-Danes she found
5 Asleep in the hall.   Soon was to come
Surprise to the earls when into the hall
Burst Grendel's dam.   (Less grim was the terror
As terror of woman in war is less,
— The fury of maidens, than full-armed men's,
10 When the blood-stained war-blade with wire-bound
        hilt,
Hard and hammer-forged, hurtling through air,
Hews the boar from the helmet's crest.)
Many the swords that were suddenly drawn,
Blades from the benches; buckler and shield
15 Were tightly grasped; no time for the helmet,
For harness of mail, when the horror was on them.
The monster was minded to make for the open;
Soon as discovered, she sought to escape.
Quickly she seized a sleeping warrior,
20 Fast in her clutch to the fens she dragged him.
He was to Hrothgar of heroes the dearest,
Most trusted of liegemen between the two seas,
Comrade the nearest, killed in his sleep,
The bravest in battle.   Nor was Beowulf there;
25 They had elsewhere quartered the earl that night,
After the giving of gifts in the hall.
There was shouting in Heorot; the hand she seized,
The bloody talon, she took away.

Sorrow was renewed in the nearby dwellings, (*1304*)
Bad was the bargain that both had made
To pay for their friends with further lives lost.
With grief overcome was the gray-haired king
5 When he learned that his thane was alive no more,
His dearest comrade by death o'ertaken,
Quick from his bower was Beowulf fetched,
The hero brave.   At break of dawn
He with his comrades came to the place
10 Where the king in sorrow was waiting to see
Whether God the Wielder of All would grant him
A turn in his tide of trouble and woe.
Then entered the room the ready hero;
With his band of brave men the boards resounded.
15 He eagerly greeted the aged ruler,
Delayed not to ask the lord of the Ingwines
If his night had passed in peace and quiet.

XX

HROTHGAR DESCRIBES THE HAUNT OF THE MONSTER
AND ASKS BEOWULF TO UNDERTAKE
A SECOND ADVENTURE

Hrothgar spoke, the Scylding defender:
"Speak not of peace, for pain is renewed
20 'Mongst all the Danes.   Dead is Æschere,
Elder brother of Irmenlaf,
My comrade true and counsellor trusted,
My right-hand friend when in front of the combat
We stood shoulder to shoulder, when shield-burg
broke,

And boar-crests crashed in battle together.   (*1328*)
Earls should ever like Æschere be.
On Heorot's floor he was foully slain
By warlock wild.   I wot not whither
5 The prey-proud fury hath fled to cover,
Glutted and gorged.   With gruesome claws
And violence fierce she avenged thy deed,
The slaying of Grendel her son last night,
Because too long my loyal thanes
10 He had hunted and hurt.   In the hall he fell;
His life was forfeit.   To the fray returned
Another as cruel, her kin to avenge;
Faring from far, the feud re-opened.
Hence many a thane shall mourn and think
15 Of the giver of gifts with grief renewed
And heart-woe heavy.   The hand lies low
That fain would have helped and defended you all.
I have heard my people, the peasant folk
Who house by the border and hold the fens,
20 Say they have seen two creatures strange,
Huge march-stalkers, haunting the moorland,
Wanderers outcast.   One of the two
Seemed to their sight to resemble a woman;
The other manlike, a monster misshapen,
25 But huger in bulk than human kind,
Trod an exile's track of woe.
The folk of the fen in former days
Named him Grendel.   Unknown his father,
Or what his descent from demons obscure.
30 Lonely and waste is the land they inhabit,
Wolf-cliffs wild and windy headlands,
Ledges of mist, where mountain torrents

Downward plunge to dark abysses,   (*1360*)
And flow unseen. Not far from here
O'er the moorland in miles, a mere expands:
Spray-frosted trees o'erspread it, and hang
5 O'er the water with roots fast wedged in the rocks.
There nightly is seen, beneath the flood,
A marvellous light. There lives not the man
Has fathomed the depth of the dismal mere.
Though the heather-stepper, the strong-horned stag,
10 Seek this cover, forspent with the chase,
Tracked by the hounds, he will turn at bay,
To die on the brink ere he brave the plunge,
Hide his head in the haunted pool.
Wan from its depths the waves are dashed,
15 When wicked storms are stirred by the wind,
And from sullen skies descends the rain.
In thee is our hope of help once more.
Not yet thou hast learned where leads the way
To the lurking-hole of this hatcher of outrage.
20 Seek, if thou dare, the dreaded spot!
Richly I pay thee for risking this fight,
With heirlooms golden and ancient rings,
As I paid thee before, if thou come back alive."

XXI

THE ARRIVAL OF HROTHGAR AND BEOWULF AT GRENDEL'S MERE

Beowulf spoke, the son of Ecgtheow:
25 "Sorrow not gray-beard, nor grieve o'er thy friend!
Vengeance is better than bootless mourning.

To each of us here the end must come   (*1386*)
Of life upon earth: let him who may
Win glory ere death. I deem that best,
The lot of the brave, when life is over.
5 Rise, O realm-ward, ride we in haste,
To track the hag that whelped this Grendel.
I tell thee in truth, she may turn where she will,
No cave of ocean nor cover of wood,
No hole in the ground shall hide her from me.
10 But one day more thy woe endure,
And nurse thy hope as I know thou wilt."
Sprang to his feet the sage old king,
Gave praise to God for the promise spoken.
And now for Hrothgar a horse was bridled,
15 A curly-maned steed. The king rode on,
Bold on his charger. A band of shield-men
Followed on foot. Afar they saw
Footprints leading along the forest.
They followed the tracks, and found she had crossed
20 Over the dark moor, dragging the body
Of the goodliest thane that guarded with Hrothgar
Heorot Hall, and the home of the king.
The well-born hero held the trail;
Up rugged paths, o'er perilous ridges,
25 Through passes narrow, an unknown way,
By beetling crags, and caves of the nicors.
With a chosen few he forged ahead,
Warriors skilled, to scan the way.
Sudden they came on a cluster of trees
30 Overhanging a hoary rock,
A gloomy grove; and gurgling below,
A stir of waters all stained with blood.

Sick at heart were the Scylding chiefs,   (*1418*)
Many a thane was thrilled with woe,
For there they beheld the head of Æschere
Far beneath at the foot of the cliff.
5 They leaned and watched the waters boil
With bloody froth. The band sat down,
While the war-horn sang its summons to battle.
They saw in the water sea-snakes a many,
Wave-monsters weird, that wallowed about.
10 At the base of the cliff lay basking the nicors,
Who oft at sunrise ply seaward their journey,
To hunt on the ship-trails and scour the main,
Sea-beasts and serpents. Sudden they fled,
Wrathful and grim, aroused by the hail
15 Of the battle-horn shrill. The chief of the Jutes,
With a bolt from his bow a beast did sunder
From life and sea-frolic; sent the keen shaft
Straight to his vitals. Slow he floated,
Upturned and dead at the top of the waves.
20 Eager they boarded their ocean-quarry;
With barb-hooked boar-spears the beast they gaffed,
Savagely broached him and brought him to shore,
Wave-plunger weird. The warriors viewed
The grisly stranger. But straightway Beowulf
25 Donned his corslet nor cared for his life. . . . (*1442*)

Lines 1442-1473 break the narrative with a description of Beowulf's armor and the sword Hrunting, lent him by Unferth.

XXII

Beowulf's Fight With Grendel's Dam

To Hrothgar spoke the son of Ecgtheow: (*1473*)
"Remember O honored heir of Healfdene,
Now that I go, thou noble king,
Warriors' gold-friend, what we agreed on,
5 If I my life should lose in thy cause,
That thou wouldst stand in stead of my father,
Fulfil his office when I was gone.
Be guardian thou, to my thanes and kinsmen,
My faithful friends, if I fail to return.
10 To Hygelac send, Hrothgar beloved,
The goodly gifts thou gavest to me.
May the lord of the Jutes, when he looks on this
    treasure,
May Hrethel's son, when he sees these gifts,
Know that I found a noble giver,
15 And joyed while I lived, in a generous lord.
This ancient heirloom to Unferth give,
To the far-famed warrior, my wondrous sword
Of matchless metal. I must with Hrunting
Glory gain, or go to my death."

20 After these words the Weder-Jute lord
Sprang to his task, nor staid for an answer.
Swiftly he sank 'neath the swirling flood;
'Twas an hour's time ere he touched the bottom.
Soon the sea-hag, savage and wild,
25 Who had roamed through her watery realms at will
For winters a hundred, was 'ware from below,
An earthling had entered her ocean domain.

Quickly she reached and caught the hero; (*1500*)
Grappled him grimly with gruesome claws.
Yet he got no scratch, his skin was whole;
His battle-sark shielded his body from harm.
5 In vain she tried, with her crooked fingers,
To tear the links of his close-locked mail.
Away to her den the wolf-slut dragged
Beowulf the bold, o'er the bottom ooze.
Though eager to smite her, his arm was helpless.
10 Swimming monsters swarmed about him,
Dented his mail with dreadful tusks.
Sudden the warrior was 'ware they had come
To a sea-hall strange and seeming hostile,
Where water was not nor waves oppressed,
15 For the caverned rock all round kept back
The swallowing sea. He saw a light,
A flicker of flame that flashed and shone.
Now first he discerned the sea-hag monstrous,
The water-wife wolfish. His weapon he raised,
20 And struck with his sword a swinging blow.
Sang on her head the hard-forged blade
Its war-song wild. But the warrior found
That his battle-flasher refused to bite,
Or maim the foe. It failed its master
25 In the hour of need, though oft it had cloven
Helmets, and carved the casques of the doomed
In combats fierce. For the first time now
That treasure failed him, fallen from honor.
But Hygelac's earl took heart of courage;
30 In mood defiant he fronted his foe.
The angry hero hurled to the ground,
In high disdain, the hilt of the sword,

The gaudy and jewelled; rejoiced in the strength
Of his arm unaided. So all should do   (*1534*)
Who glory would find and fame abiding,
In the crash of conflict, nor care for their lives.
5 The Lord of the Battle-Jutes braved the encounter;
The murderous hag by the hair he caught;
Down he dragged the dam of Grendel
In his swelling rage, till she sprawled on the floor.
Quick to repay in kind what she got,
10 On her foe she fastened her fearful clutches;
Enfolded the warrior weary with fighting;
The sure-footed hero stumbled and fell.
As helpless he lay, she leapt on him fiercely;
Unsheathed her hip-knife, shining and broad,
15 Her son to avenge, her offspring sole.
But the close-linked corslet covered his breast,
Foiled the stroke and saved his life.
All had been over with Ecgtheow's son,
Under the depths of the ocean vast,
20 Had not his harness availed to help him,
His battle-net stiff, and the strength of God.
The Ruler of battles aright decided it;
The Wielder all-wise awarded the victory:
Lightly the hero leaped to his feet.

XXIII

Beowulf's Victory and Return to Heorot

25 He spied 'mongst the arms a sword surpassing,
Huge and ancient, a hard-forged slayer,
Weapon matchless and warriors' delight,

Save that its weight was more than another   (*1560*)
Might bear into battle or brandish in war;
Giants had forged that finest of blades.
Then seized its chain-hilt the chief of the Scyldings;
5 His wrath was aroused, reckless his mood,
As he brandished the sword for a savage blow.
Bit the blade in the back of her neck,
Cut the neck-bone, and cleft its way
Clean through her flesh; to the floor she sank;
10 The sword was gory; glad was the hero.
A light flashed out from the inmost den,
Like heaven's candle, when clear it shines
From cloudless skies. He scanned the cave,
Walked by the wall, his weapon upraised;
15 Grim in his hand the hilt he gripped.
Well that sword had served him in battle.
Steadily onward he strode through the cave,
Ready to wreak the wrongs untold,
That the man-beast had wrought in the realm of
       Danes. . . .   (*1578*)
20 He gave him his due when Grendel he found   (*1584*)
Stretched as in sleep, and spent with the battle.
But dead was the fiend, the fight at Heorot
Had laid him low. The lifeless body
Sprang from the blows of Beowulf's sword,
25 As fiercely he hacked the head from the carcass.

But the men who were watching the water with
       Hrothgar
Suddenly saw a stir in the waves,
The chop of the sea all churned up with blood
And bubbling gore. The gray-haired chiefs

For Beowulf grieved, agreeing together   (1595)
That hope there was none of his home-returning,
With victory crowned, to revisit his lord.
Most of them feared he had fallen prey
5 To the mere-wolf dread in the depths of the sea.
When evening came, the Scyldings all
Forsook the headland, and Hrothgar himself
Turned homeward his steps. But sick at heart
The strangers sat and stared at the sea,
10 Hoped against hope to behold their comrade
And leader again.

              Now that goodly sword
Began to melt with the gore of the monster;
In bloody drippings it dwindled away.
15 'Twas a marvellous sight: it melted like ice,
When fetters of frost the Father unlocks,
Unravels the ropes of the wrinkled ice,
Lord and Master of months and seasons.
Beheld in the hall the hero from Juteland
20 Treasures unnumbered, but naught he took,
Save Grendel's head, and the hilt of the sword,
Bright and jewelled,—the blade had melted,
Its metal had vanished, so venomous hot
Was the blood of the demon-brute dead in the cave.

25 Soon was in the sea the slayer of monsters;
Upward he shot through the shimmer of waves;
Cleared was the ocean, cleansed were its waters,
The wolfish water-hag wallowed no more;
The mere-wife had yielded her miserable life.
30 Swift to the shore the sailors' deliverer
Came lustily swimming, with sea-spoil laden;

Rejoiced in the burden he bore to the land.   (*1625*)
Ran to meet him his mailéd comrades,
With thanks to God who gave them their leader
Safe again back and sound from the deep.
5 Quickly their hero's helmet they loosened,
Unbuckled his breastplate.   The blood-stained waves
Fell to a calm 'neath the quiet sky.
Back they returned o'er the tracks with the footprints,
Merrily measured the miles o'er the fen,
10 Way they knew well, those warriors brave;
Brought from the holm-cliff the head of the monster;
'Twas toil and labor to lift the burden,
Four of their stoutest scarce could carry it
Swung from a spear-pole, a staggering load. . . .
                                              (*1638*)
15 Thus the fourteen of them, thanes adventurous,
Marched o'er the moor to the mead-hall of Hrothgar.
Tall in the midst of them towered the hero;
Strode among his comrades, till they came to the hall.
In went Beowulf, the brave and victorious,
20 Battle-beast hardy, Hrothgar to greet.
Lifting by the hair the head of Grendel,
They laid it in the hall, where the heroes were carous-
      ing,
Right before the king, and right before the queen;
Gruesome was the sight that greeted the Danes.

XXIV XXV

Beowulf's Story of His Fight, and Hrothgar's Counsel

Beowulf spoke, the son of Ecgtheow: (*1651*)
"Gladly we offer this ocean-booty,
That here thou lookest on, lord of the Scyldings,
For sign of victory, son of Healfdene.
5 Hard was the fight I fought under water;
That combat nearly cost me my life.
Soon had been ended the ocean-encounter,
Had God in his mercy not given me aid.
No help I got from the good blade Hrunting,
10 The well-tried weapon worthless proved.
By the grace of God, who guided me friendless,
A splendid old sword I spied on the wall,
Hanging there, huge; by the hilt I grasped it,
And seeing my chance, I struck amain
15 At the sea-cave's wardens, when sudden the blade
Melted and burned, as the blood gushed out,
The battle-gore hot. The hilt I saved
From the villainous fiends, and avenged their crimes,
The murder of the Danes, as was meet and due.
20 I promise thee now, in peace thou shalt sleep
In Heorot hall, with the whole of thy band.
Thou and thy thanes may throng within
As ye used of yore, both young and old.
Thou need'st not fear renewal of strife,
25 Harm to thy folk at the hands of the fiends."
The golden hilt was given to the king;
The jewelled work of the giants of old
Came into hand of the hoary warrior.

On the death of the demons, the Danish lord kept it,
Wondersmiths' work. When the world was rid
Of the evil fiend, the enemy of God,   (*1681*)
Guilty of murder, and his mother too,
5 The trophy passed to the peerless lord,
The goodliest king, that gave out treasure
Between the two seas on Scandia's isle.
Hrothgar gazed on the golden hilt,
Relic of old, where was writ the tale
10 Of a far-off fight, when the flood o'erwhelmed,
The raging sea, the race of the giants
(They wantonly dared to war against God;
Then rose in his wrath the Ruler Eternal,
'Neath the heaving billows buried them all.)
15 On the polished gold of the guard of the hilt,
Runes were writ that rightly told,
To him that read them, for whom that weapon,
Finest of sword-blades, first was made,
The splendid hilt with serpents entwined.
20 All were silent, when the son of Healfdene,
The wise king spoke: "Well may he say,
The aged ruler, who aye upholds
Truth and right, 'mid the ranks of his people,
Whose mind runs back to by-gone days,
25 This guest is born of a goodly breed.
Thy fame shall fly afar among men,
Beowulf my friend, firmly thou holdest
Both wisdom and might. My word will I keep,
The love that I proffered. Thou shalt prove a de-
      liverer
30 To thy folk and followers in far-off years,
A help to the heroes. Not Heremod thus

Ecgwela's heir, did offer at need   (*1710*)
His strength to the Scyldings; instead, he brought
Slaughter and death on the sons of the Danes.
Swoln with wrath he slew his comrades,
5 His friends at the board and fled alone,
Ill-famed earl, an outcast from men.
Though God endowed him with gifts of strength,
With boldness and might above all men,
And prospered him greatly, yet he grew to be
10 Blood-thirsty and cruel. No bracelets he gave
To the Danes as was due, but dwelt in gloom
Reaped the reward of the woful strife,
And wearisome feud. Take warning from him.
                                                    (*1722*)

.   .   .   .

Hrothgar now delivers a long sermon to Beowulf on the dangers
of pride, the fickleness of fortune, and the brevity of life, and ends
by asking him to sit down to the feast, promising more gifts on
the morrow.

Beowulf hastened, happy in mood,   (*1785*)
15 To seek his bench as bid by the king.
Once more, as of old, for the earls in hall,
The famous in battle, the board was set
For feasting anew. When night with its shadows
O'erwhelmed the world, the heroes arose.
20 The gray-haired ruler his rest would seek,
The Scylding his bed; and Beowulf too,
The lusty warrior, longed for his sleep.
Soon an attendant showed the way
To the stranger from far, spent with his faring.
25 With courtly custom, he cared for his needs.
All that to warriors, overseas wandering,
Was due in those days, he did for the guest.

High-gabled and gold-decked, the gift-hall towered;
The stout-hearted hero slept soundly within,   (*1800*)
Till the raven black, with blithe heart hailed
The bliss of heaven, and bright the sun
5 Came gliding o'er earth. Then, eager to start,
The warriors wakened; they wished to set out
On their homeward journey. The hero brave
Would board his ship, and back again sail.
The hardy one bade that Hrunting be brought
10 To the son of Ecglaf: the sword he offered him;
Thanked him for lending the lovely weapon;
Called it a war-friend, keen in the battle;
Not a word in blame of the blade he uttered,
Great-hearted hero. Now hastened the guests,
15 Eager to part, and armed for their voyage.
Their dauntless leader, beloved of the Danes,
Came to the high-seat, and to Hrothgar the king
The bold-in-battle now bade farewell.   (*1816*)

XXVI

Beowulf's Leave-Taking of Hrothgar

Beowulf spoke, the son of Ecgtheow:
20 "Now we sea-farers would make known our desire;
Far-travelled wanderers, we wish to return
To Hygelac now. A hearty welcome
We here have found, thou hast harbored us well.
If ever on earth I may anywise win,
25 Master of men, more of thy love
Than now I have won, for another adventure
Of arms and war I am eager and willing.

If ever I hear, o'er the ocean-ways   (*1826*)
That neighbor-tribes threaten annoyance or war,
As feud-seeking foemen aforetime assailed thee,
A thousand thanes to thee will I bring,
5 Heroes to help thee. For Hygelac, I know,
Though young in years will yield me aid;
The people's Shepherd will surely help me
By word and deed to do thee service,
And bring thee spear-shafts to speed thee in battle,
10 Thy might to strengthen when men thou needest.
If ever Hrethric, heir of thy line,
Should come to sojourn at the court of the Jutes,
A host of friends he will find awaiting him.
Who boasts himself brave, abroad should travel."
15 The aged Hrothgar answering spoke:
"To utter these words, the All-wise Lord
Hath prompted thy heart; more prudent counsel
From one in years so young as thou,
I never have heard. Thou art hardy in strength,
20 And sage in spirit, and speakest well.
If ever it happen that Hrethel's heir
Be stricken by spear and slain in battle,
If sickness or sword assail thy lord,
And thou survive him, I think it likely
25 The Sea-Jutes in vain will seek for a better
As choice for their king, their chief to become
And rule o'er the thanes, if thou be willing
The lordship to hold. The longer I know thee
The better I like thee, Beowulf my friend.
30 Thou hast brought it about that both our peoples
Jutes and the Spear-Danes shall be joined in peace.
They shall cease from war, the strife shall be ended

The feuds of aforetime, so fiercely waged.   (*1858*)
While I rule this realm, our riches we share;
Many shall travel with treasure laden,
Each other to greet, o'er the gannet's bath;
5 O'er the rolling waves the ringéd prow
Tokens of friendship shall freely bring
And bind our people in peace together,
Toward friend and foe, in faith as of old."

Still other treasures, twelve in all,
10 Healfdene's heir in the hall bestowed
On Beowulf brave, and bade him take them
And seek his people, and soon return.
Then kissed the king, of kin renowned,
The thane beloved. The lord of the Scyldings
15 Fell on his neck. Fast flowed the tears
Of the warrior gray; he weighed both chances,
But held to the hope, though hoary with years,
That each should see the other again,
And meet in the mead-hall. The man was so dear
20 That he could not restrain the storm in his breast.
Locked in his heart, a hidden longing
For the man he loved so, left him no peace,
And burnt in his blood. But Beowulf went;
The gold-decked hero the grass-way trod
25 Proud of his booty. The boat awaited
Its owner and master, where at anchor it rode.
As they went on their way, the warriors praised
The bounty of Hrothgar, the blameless king.
None was his equal till age snatched away
30 The joy of his manhood,—no mortal it spares.

XXVII

Beowulf's Return Voyage to Hygelac

Then came to the coast the comrades brave   (*1888*)
The lusty warriors, wearing their ring-nets,
Their chain linked corslets. The coast-guard saw
    them,
The same that at first had spied them coming;
5 This time he chose not to challenge them harshly,
But gave them his greeting, galloping toward them.
Said the Weder-folk would welcome the sight of them
Boarding their ship in shining armor.
Then by the sands, the seaworthy craft,
10 The iron-ringed keel, with arms was laden,
With horses and treasure. On high the mast
Towered above the treasures of Hrothgar.
To the man who had waited as watchman aboard,
Beowulf gave a gold-bound sword.
15 (Oft on the mead-bench that heirloom precious
Its owner would honor.) When all had embarked,
They drove for the deep, from Daneland's shore.
Then soon did the mast its sea-suit wear,
A sail was unfurled, made fast with ropes,
20 The sea-wood sang as she sped o'er the ocean
No baffling head-wind hindered her course;
The foamy-necked floater flew o'er the billows,
The sea-craft staunch o'er the salt-sea waves,
Till they came in sight of the cliffs of Jutland
25 The well known capes, and the wind-driven keel
Grating the sand, stood still on the shore.
Soon was at hand the harbor-watch eager.
Long had he looked for his loved companions

Scanning the sea for their safe return.   (*1916*)
The broad-bosomed boat to the beach he moored
With anchor-ropes fast, lest the force of the waves
That comely craft should cast adrift.

5 Then Beowulf bade them bring ashore
His treasure-cargo of costly gold
And weapons fine; not far was the way
To Hygelac's hall, where at home he dwelt
The king and his comrades, close by the sea.   (*1940*)

END OF THE SECOND ADVENTURE

After the death of Hygelac and his son, Beowulf became king of
the Jutes, and ruled over them fifty years. In his old age his
people were harried by a fire-dragon whom the hero went out to
fight. It seems that an outlaw, banished and flying for shelter, had
come upon a treasure hid in a deep cave or barrow, guarded by a
dragon. Long years before, an earl, the last of his race, had buried
the treasure. After his death the dragon, sniffing about the stones,
had found it and guarded it three hundred years, until the banished
man discovered the place, and carried off one of the golden goblets.
In revenge the dragon made nightly raids on Beowulf's realm, flying
through the air, spitting fire, burning houses and villages, even
Beowulf's hall, the "gift-stool" of the Jutes. Beowulf had an iron
shield made against the dragon's fiery breath, and with eleven companions, sought out the hill-vault near the sea. These events are
related in Sections XXVIII-XXXV of the Beowulf MS.

XXXV

BEOWULF'S FIGHT WITH THE FIRE DRAGON

Before attacking the fire-dragon Beowulf once more and for the
last time makes his "battle-boast" in the presence of his followers.

10 Beowulf said to them, brave words spoke he: (*2510*)
"Brunt of battles I bore in my youth;

One fight more I make this day.   *(2512)*
I mean to win fame defending my people,
If the grim destroyer will seek me out,
Come at my call from his cavern dark."
5 Then he greeted his thanes each one,
For the last time hailed his helmeted warriors,
His comrades dear. "I should carry no sword,
No weapon of war 'gainst the worm should bear,
If the foe I might slay by strength of my arm,
10 As Grendel I slew long since by my hand.
But I look to fight a fiery battle,
With scorching puffs of poisonous breath.
For this I bear both breastplate and shield;
No foot will I flinch from the foe of the barrow.
15 Wyrd is over us, each shall meet
His doom ordained at the dragon-cliff!
Bold is my mood, but my boast I omit
'Gainst the battle-flier. Abide ye here,
Heroes in harness, hard by the barrow,
20 Cased in your armor the issue await:
Which of us two his wounds shall survive.
Not yours the attempt, the task is mine.
'Tis meant for no man but me alone
To measure his might 'gainst the monster fierce.
25 I get you the gold in glorious fight,
Or battle-death bitter shall bear off your lord."
    Uprose with his shield the shining hero,
Bold 'neath his helmet. He bore his harness
In under the cliff; alone he went,
30 Himself he trusted; no task for faint-heart.
Then saw by the wall the warrior brave,

Hero of many a hard-fought battle,   (*2543*)
Arches of stone that opened a way;
From the rocky gate there gushed a stream,
Bubbling and boiling with battle-fire.
5 So great the heat no hope was there
To come at the hoard in the cavern's depth,
Unscathed by the blast of the scorching dragon.
He let from his breast his battle-cry leap;
Swoln with rage was the royal Jute,
10 Stormed the stout-heart; strong and clear
Through the gloom of the cave his cry went ringing.
Hate was aroused, the hoard-ward knew
The leader's hail. Too late 'twas now
To parley for peace. The poisonous breath
15 Of the monster shot from the mouth of the cave,
Reeking hot. The hollow earth rumbled.
The man by the rock upraised his shield,
The lord of the Jutes, 'gainst the loathly dragon.
Now kindled for battle the curled-up beast;
20 The king undaunted with drawn sword stood,
'Twas an heirloom olden with edge of lightning.
Each was so fierce he affrighted the other.
Towering tall 'neath tilted shield,
Waited the king as the worm coiled back,
25 Sudden to spring: so stood he and waited.
Blazing he came in coils of fire
Swift to his doom. The shield of iron
Sheltered the hero too short a while,—
Life and limb it less protected
30 Than he hoped it would, for the weapon he held
First time that day he tried in battle;

Wyrd had not willed he should win the fight.   (*2575*)
But the lord of the Jutes uplifted his arm,
Smote the scaly worm, struck him so fierce
That his ancient bright-edged blade gave way,
5 Bent on the bone, and bit less sure
Than its owner had need in his hour of peril.
That sword-stroke roused the wrath of the cave-
          guard;
Fire and flame afar he spirted,
Blaze of battle; but Beowulf there
10 No victory boasted: his blade had failed him,
Naked in battle, as never it should have,
Well-tempered iron.   Nor easy it was
For Ecgtheow's heir, honored and famous,
This earth to forsake, forever to leave it;
15 Yet he must go, against his will
Elsewhere to dwell.   So we all must leave
This fleeting life.—Erelong the foes
Bursting with wrath the battle renewed.
The hoard-ward took heart, and with heaving breast
20 Came charging amain.   The champion brave,
Strength of his people, was sore oppressed,
Enfolded by flame.   No faithful comrades
Crowded about him, his chosen band,
All æthelings' sons, to save their lives,
25 Fled to the wood.   One of them only
Felt surging sorrow; for nought can stifle
Call of kin in a comrade true;

XXXVI

WIGLAF'S REPROACH TO HIS COMRADES. BEOWULF MORTALLY WOUNDED.

The shield-thane beloved, lord of the Scylfings,
Wiglaf was called; 'twas Weohstan's son   (*2603*)
Ælfheré's kinsman.   When his king he saw
Hard by the heat under helmet oppressed,
He remembered the gifts he had got of old,
Lands and wealth of the Wægmunding line,
The folk-rights all that his father's had been;
He could hold no longer, but hard he gripped
Linden shield yellow and ancient sword. . . . (*2610*)

The intervening lines tell the history of the sword and the feuds
which it has participated.

For the first time there the faithful thane,   (*2625*)
Youthful and stalwart, stood with his leader,
Shoulder to shoulder in shock of battle.
Nor melted his courage, nor cracked his blade,
His war-sword true, as the worm found out
When together they got in grim encounter.

Wiglaf in wrath upbraided his comrades,
Sore was his heart as he spake these words:
"Well I mind when our mead we drank
In the princely hall, how we promised our lord
Who gave us these rings and golden armlets,
That we would repay his war-gifts rich,
Helmets and armor, if haply should come
His hour of peril; us hath he made
Thanes of his choice for this adventure;
Spurred us to glory, and gave us these treasures

Because he deemed us doughty spearmen,   *(2641)*
Helmeted warriors, hardy and brave.
Yet all the while, unhelped and alone,
He meant to finish this feat of strength,
5 Shepherd of men and mightiest lord
Of daring deeds. The day is come,—
Now is the hour he needs the aid
Of spearmen good. Let us go to him now,
Help our hero while hard bestead
10 By the nimble flames. God knows that I
Had rather the fire should ruthlessly fold
My body with his, than harbor me safe.
Shame it were surely our shields to carry
Home to our lands, unless we first
15 Slay this foe and save the life
Of the Weder-king. Full well I know
To leave him thus, alone to endure,
Bereft of aid, breaks ancient right.
My helmet and sword shall serve for us both;
20 Shield and armor we share to-day."

Waded the warrior through welter and reek;
Buckler and helmet he bore to his leader;
Heartened the hero with words of hope:
"Do thy best now, dearest Beowulf.
25 Years ago, in youth, thou vowedst
Living, ne'er to lose thine honor,
Shield thy life and show thy valor.
I stand by thee to the end!"
After these words the worm came on,
30 Snorting with rage, for a second charge;
All mottled with fire his foes he sought,

The warriors hated. But Wiglaf's shield   (*2672*)
Was burnt to the boss by the billows of fire;
His harness helped not the hero young.
Shelter he found 'neath the shield of his kinsman,
5 When the crackling blaze had crumbled his own.
But mindful of glory, the mighty hero
Smote amain with his matchless sword.
Down it hurtled, driven by anger,
Till it stuck in the skull; then snapped the blade,
10 Broken was Nægling, Beowulf's sword,
Ancient and gray. 'Twas granted him never
To count on edge of iron in battle;
His hand was too heavy, too hard his strokes,
As I have heard tell, for every blade
15 He brandished in battle: the best gave way,
And left him helpless and hard bestead.
Now for a third time neared the destroyer;
The fire-drake fierce, old feuds remembering,
Charged the warrior who wavered an instant;
20 Blazing he came and closed his fangs
On Beowulf's throat; and throbbing spirts
Of life-blood dark o'erdrenched the hero.

XXXVII

The Slaying of the Dragon

Then in the hour of utmost peril,
The stripling proved what stock he came of;
25 Showed his endurance and dauntless courage.
Though burnt was his hand when he backed his kinsman,

With head unguarded the good thane charged,
Thrust from below at the loathly dragon,   (2699
Pierced with the point and plunged the blade in,
The gleaming-bright, till the glow abated
5 Waning low. Ere long the king
Came to himself, and swiftly drew
The warknife that hung at his harness' side,
And cut in two the coiléd monster.
So felled they the foe and finished him bravely,
10 Together they killed him, the kinsmen two,
A noble pair. So needs must do
Comrades in peril. For the king it proved
His uttermost triumph, the end of his deeds
And work in the world. The wound began,
15 Where the cave-dragon savage had sunk his teeth
To swell and fever, and soon he felt
The baleful poison pulse through his blood,
And burn in his breast. The brave old warrior
Sat by the wall and summoned his thoughts,
20 Gazed on the wondrous work of the giants:
Arches of stone, firm-set on their pillars,
Upheld that hill-vault hoar and ancient.

Now Beowulf's thane, the brave and faithful,
Dashed with water his darling lord,
25 His comrade and king all covered with blood
And faint with the fight; unfastened his helmet.
Beowulf spoke despite his hurt,
His piteous wound; full well he knew
His years on earth were ended now,
30 His hours of glad life gone for aye
His days allotted, and death was near:

"Now would I gladly give to a son   (2729)
These weapons of war, had Wyrd but granted
That heir of my own should after me come,
Sprung from my loins. This land have I ruled
5 Fifty winters. No folk-king dared,
None of the chiefs of the neighboring tribes,
To touch me with sword or assail me with terror
Of battle-threats. I bided at home,
Held my peace and my heritage kept,
10 Seeking no feuds nor swearing false oaths.
This gives me comfort, and gladdens me now,
Though wounded sore and sick unto death.
As I leave my life, the Lord may not charge me
With killing of kinsmen. Now quickly go,
15 Wiglaf beloved, to look at the hoard,
Where hidden it rests 'neath the hoary rock.
For the worm lies still, put asleep by his wound,
Robbed of his riches. Then rise and haste!
Give me to see that golden hoard,
20 To gaze on the store of glorious gems,
The easier then I may end my life,
Leave my lordship that long I held."

XXXVIII

The Rescue of the Hoard and the Death of Beowulf

Swiftly, 'tis said, the son of Weohstan
Obeyed the words of his bleeding lord,
25 Maimed in the battle. Through the mouth of the cave
Boldly he bore his battle-net in.

Glad of the victory, he gazed about him;　　(*2756*
Many a sun-bright jewel he saw,
Glittering gold, strewn on the ground,
Heaped in the den of the dragon hoary,
5　Old twilight-flier,—flagons once bright,
Wassail cups wondrous of warriors departed
Stript of their mountings, many a helmet
Ancient and rusted, armlets a many,
Curiously woven.　(Wealth so hoarded,
10　Buried treasure, will taint with pride
Him that hides it, whoever it be.)
Towering high o'er the hoard he saw
A gleaming banner with gold inwoven,
Of broidure rare; its radiance streamed
15　So bright, he could peer to the bounds of the cave,
Survey its wonders; no worm was seen.
Edge of the sword had ended his life.
Then, as they say, that single adventurer
Plundered the hoard that was piled by the giants;
20　Gathered together old goblets and platters,
Took what he liked; the towering banner
Brightest of beacons he brought likewise.
The blade of Beowulf, his brave old chief,
With edge of iron had ended the life
25　Of him that had guarded the golden hoard
For many a year, and at midnight hour
Had spread the terror of surging flames
In front of the den, till death o'ertook him.
So Wiglaf returned with treasure laden.
30　The high-souled hero hastened his steps,
Anxiously wondered if he should find
The lord of the Weders alive where he left him

Sapped of his strength and stretched on the ground.
As he came from the hill he beheld his comrade,
His lord of bounty, bleeding and faint,   (*2789*)
Near unto death. He dashed him once more
5 Bravely with water, till burden of speech
Broke from his breast, and Beowulf spoke,
Gazing sad at the gold before him:
"For the harvest of gold that here I look on,
To the God of Glory I give my thanks.
10 To the Ruler Eternal I render praise
That ere I must go, he granted me this,
To leave to my people this priceless hoard.
'Twas bought with my life; now look ye well
To my people's need when I have departed.
15 No more I may bide among ye here.
Bid the battle-famed build on the foreland
A far-seen barrow when flames have burnt me.
High o'er the headland of whales it shall tower,
A beacon and mark to remind my people.
20 And sailors shall call it in years to come
Beowulf's Barrow, as bound from afar
Their tall ships stem the storm-dark seas.

The great-hearted king unclasped from his neck
A collar of gold and gave to his thane,
25 The brave young warrior, his bright-gilt helmet,
Breastplate and ring. So bade him farewell:
"Thou art the last to be left of our house.
Wyrd hath o'erwhelmed our Wægmunding line,
Swept my kinsmen swift to their doom.
30 Earls in their prime. I must follow them."
These words were the last that the warrior gray
Found, ere the funeral-flames he chose.

Swift from his bosom his soul departed
To find the reward of the faithful and true.   *(2820)*

In lines 2821-2891, Section XXXIX of the MS., the narrative
doubles back upon itself to repeat the description of Beowulf and
the dragon lying dead before the cave, and to report Wiglaf's reproach to the returning deserters.

XL

BEOWULF'S DEATH ANNOUNCED TO THE PEOPLE. THE SPEECH OF THE HERALD.

Then Wiglaf bade the battle-work tell   *(2892)*
To the sorrowful troop that had sat all day
5 At the sea-cliff's edge, their shields in hand,
In dread and in hope, yet doubtful of either:
Their dear lord's return, or his death in the fight.
The herald that came to the headland riding,
Nought kept back of the news that befell,
10 But truthfully told them the tidings all:
"Now lies low the lord of the Weders;
The generous giver of gifts to the Jutes,
Sleeps his battle-sleep, slain by the worm.
At his side lies stretched his slaughterous foe,
15 Fordone by the dagger. The dragon fierce
Would take no wound from touch of sword;
Its blade would not bite. At Beowulf's side
Wiglaf sits, the son of Weohstan;
By the hero dead, the hero living
20 At his head keeps watch with woful heart
O'er friend and foe.   *(2910)*

    .   .   .   .

The Herald now warns of renewed attacks on the Jutes by Franks and Frisians, and alludes to the origin of the feud in the famous raid in which Hygelac was slain. He further warns of renewed attacks by the Swedes, now that Beowulf is dead, and refers to the origin of the wars between Swedes and Jutes and to a famous battle at "Ravenswood." The episodic digression over, the herald returns to present events.

XLI

The Herald's Speech Concluded

'Tis time we hasten (*3007*)
To see where lies our lord and king,
Our giver of bounty, and bear him away
To the funeral pyre; of precious gems
5 Not a few shall melt in the fire with him.
The hoard he won, the wealth untold,
The priceless treasure he purchased so dear,
And bought with his life at the bitter end,
The flame shall enfold it, the fire consume.
10 No warrior one keepsake shall carry away,
No necklace be worn by winsome maid.
In sorrow rather, and reft of her gold,
Alone she shall tread the track of an exile,
Now our lord lies low, his laughter stilled,
15 His mirth and revel. Now many a spear
Shall morning-cold be clasped in the hand
And held on high. No harp shall sound
The warriors to wake, but the wan-hued raven
Shall croak o'er the carcass and call to the eagle,
20 To tell how he fared at the feast after battle
When he and the gray wolf gorged on the slain."

Thus ended his tale, his tidings of woe, (3028)
The faithful thane, nor falsely reported
Wyrd or word. The warriors rose;
To the Eagles' Cliff they came in sadness,
5 With welling tears, the wonder to see.
Lying helpless, their lord they found
Stretched on the ground, the giver of rings.
The end had come to him, open-handed
King of the Weders, warrior brave.
10 That day a fearful death he had found.
A stranger thing they saw near by:
The loathsome monster lying dead
On the field where they fought, the fiery dragon,
The gruesome beast was burnt and charred.
15 Fifty feet in full he measured
In length, as he lay, along the ground.
'Twas his wont at night to wing aloft
And dip to earth as his den he sought;
Now he lay dead, his night-revels over.
20 Scattered about were bowls and flagons,
Golden platters, and priceless swords,
With rust eaten through, as though they had lain
Winters a thousand in the womb of the earth.
O'er that heritage huge, the hoard of afore-time,
25 A spell had been woven to ward off despoilers,
And none might touch the treasure-vault hidden;
Save that God alone, the Lord of victory,
The Guardian of men, might grant the power
To unlock the hoard, and lift the treasure,
30 To such a hero as to Him seemed meet. (3057)

.   .   .   .

XLII

Beowulf's Body Carried to the Funeral Pyre and the Dragon Cast into the Sea.

Wiglaf spoke, the son of Weohstan: (3076)
"Let us go once more to gaze at the marvels (3101)
Still left 'neath the rock; I will lead you in
Where your hands may touch great heaps of gold,
5 Bracelets and rings. Let the bier be ready
When out of the cave we come again,
To bear away the warrior brave,
Our lord beloved, where long he shall bide,
Kept in the sheltering care of God."
10 The son of Weohstan, warrior brave,
Called on the folk-men, far and wide,
From house and home to hasten and bring
Wood for the pyre of the peerless man,
His funeral pile. "Now fire shall consume,
15 The wan flame wax o'er the warrior strong,
Who oft stood firm in the iron shower
When the storm of arrows, sent from the bow-string,
Flew o'er the shield-wall, and the fleet-winged shaft,
Feathered behind, pushed home the barb."
20 Now the wise young warrior, Weohstan's son,
Seven men called, of the king's own thanes,
The best of the band; the bravest he gathered;
Himself the eighth, they sought the den
Of the hateful beast; one bore in his hand
25 A lighted torch and led the way.
No lots were drawn for the dragon's hoard
When they saw it lying, loose in the cave,
Uncared for, unguarded, unclaimed by a soul;

There was none to hinder as they hurried away,
Laden with spoils and splendid heirlooms.   (*3130*)
O'er the edge of the cliff they cast the dragon,
Into the sea, the scaly worm;
5 Let the waves engulf the gold-hoard's keeper.
On a wagon they loaded the wondrous treasure,
Gold past counting.   The gray-haired king
They bore to the pyre, on the Point of Whales.

XLIII

The Burning of Beowulf's Body

Then built for Beowulf the band of the Jutes
10 A funeral pyre; 'twas firmly based.
They hung it with helmets as he had bidden,
With shining byrnies and battle-shields.
In the midst they laid, with loud lament,
Their lord beloved, their leader brave.
15 On the brow of the cliff they kindled the blaze,
Black o'er the flames the smoke shot up;
Cries of woe, in the windless air,
Rose and blent with the roar of the blast,
Till the frame of the body burst with the heat
20 Of the seething heart.   In sorrowing mood
They mourned aloud their leader dead.
Joined in the wail a woman old,
With hair upbound for Beowulf grieved,
Chanted a dreary dirge of woe,
25 Dark forebodings of days to come,
Thick with slaughter and throes of battle,
Bondage and shame.   The black smoke rose.

High on the headland they heaped a barrow, *(3156)*
Lofty and broad 'twas built by the Weders,
Far to be seen by sea-faring men.
Ten days long they toiled to raise it,
5 The battle-king's beacon. They built a wall
To fence the brands of the funeral burning,
The choicest and best their chiefs could devise.
In the barrow they buried the bracelets and rings,
All those pieces of precious treasure
10 That bold-hearted men had brought from the cave,
Returned to earth the heirloom of heroes,
The gold to the ground, again to become
As useless to men as of yore it had been.

Around the barrow the battle-brave rode,
15 Twelve in the troop, all true-born æthelings,
To make their lament and mourn for the king;
To chant a lay their lord to honor.
They praised his daring; his deeds of prowess
They mentioned in song. For meet it is
20 That men should publish their master's praise,
Honor their chieftain, and cherish him dearly
When he leaves this life, released from the body.

Thus joined the men of the Jutes in mourning
Their hero's end. His hearth-companions
25 Called him the best among kings of the earth,
Mildest of men, and most beloved,
Kindest to kinsmen, and keenest for fame.

END OF BEOWULF

THE LIFE OF THE GLEEMAN

(From the *Widsith*)

Widsith unlocked his store of lays. (*1*)
Farthest he fared among folk on earth
Through sundry lands receiving gifts
In many a mead-hall. From Myrgings sprung
5 His ancient line. With Alhild beloved
Weaver of peace he went at the first
From Angles to east of us, to Ermanric's home,
King of the Hreth-Goths, the ruthless traitor
And treaty-breaker. Much-travelled he sang:—

. . . .

10 I was with Ermanric all that time (*88*)
But the king of the Goths proved kind to me
Gave me a ring that royal giver,
Of gold-work pure, worth good six hundred
Shining shillings, as shown by scale.
15 When home I returned, my treasure I gave
To Edgils my lord, my beloved protector,
In lieu of the lands he let me hold,
The ruler of Myrgings, in right of my father.
Alhild my lady, Edwin's daughter,
20 Queen of the daring, bequeathed me another;
Praise of her bounty was published abroad,
When I made my lays through many a land;
Told of the goodliest gold-decked queen
Known among men for making of gifts.
25 Then Scilling and I our song uplifted;
Before our ruler with ringing voice,

Loud to the harp our lay we chanted;   (*105*)
Many there were, warriors mighty,
Skilled in our art who openly said
They never heard singing of songs that was better.
5 Far I roamed o'er the realm of the Goths,
Seeking for comrades the strongest and bravest:
Ever the first were Ermanric's followers. . . .(*111*)
Many a spear, sped from the midst of them,   (*127*)
Yelling aloud as it leaped at the foe.
10 Wudga and Hama took women and men;
The banished comrades won booty of gold.
In all my faring I found it true:
He to whom God hath given the power
To be lord of men, is most beloved,
15 Who holds his kingdom while here he lives.

Thus fated to wander, wayfaring gleemen
Make their songs in many a land,
Ask their need and utter their thanks.
North or south, ever some one they meet,
20 A judge of songs or a generous giver,
Proud to be praised in presence of liegemen,
Honored in lays till all is fled,
Life and light together. Who lives for glory
Holds under heaven the height of fame.

2. BIBLICAL EPIC

THE FALL OF MAN

(*Younger Genesis, lines 246-764*)

The Ruler of hosts, in the realms of heaven,　(*246*)
By the strength of his arm established on high
Ten angel tribes: he trusted them well
To serve their leader and loyally work
5 The will of God, who gave them their reason,
Whose hand had shaped them, their Holy Lord.
He dowered them all with wealth; but one He made
　　so great,
Such wisdom He gave him of mind, such might to
　　wield,
In heaven he was next to God; so glorious He made
　　him,
10 So gleaming his hue on high, that he had from his
　　maker,
He was like unto shining stars.　His lord he was
　　bound to serve,
Hold dear the bliss of heaven; he was bound to thank
　　his lord
For the bounteous gift of light that so long He let
　　him enjoy.
But he turned it all to evil, and openly stirred up strife
15 Gainst Heaven's highest Ruler, who sitteth on His
　　holy throne.

Dear had he been to our King, nor could it be kept
    from the Lord   (*261*)
That His angel proud, was plotting rebellion.
He rose 'gainst his ruler, and railed against God.
He uttered defiance, refused to serve Him;
5 Said that his body was bright and gleaming,
Wondrous and fair, nor would he further
Give obedience to God in heaven,
Or serve him longer. It seemed to himself
That his power and might were more than God's,
10 His followers firmer in fealty bound.
Many things uttered the angel in pride;
By the power of his single strength he planned
To make for himself a mightier throne,
A higher in heaven. His haughty mood
15 Stirred him to build a stately hall
And strong, in the north and west. He said he
    doubted
Whether he further would follow God.
"Why should I toil?" said he; "I need acknowledge
No man for my master; I may with these hands
20 Work marvels as many. Mine is the power
To rear a throne more royal than His,
A higher in heaven. Then why should I grovel to
    win His grace,
Bow in obedience to Him, when I may be Highest
    myself?
Faithful followers back me, unfailing in battle;
25 Those hardy heroes have chosen me for their chief,
Sturdy warriors; with such 'tis well wars to plan,
Battles to fight, with friends like these, faithful and
    true.
Loyal their hearts, their leader I'll be,

Rule in this realm; not right I think it   (289)
To fawn upon God for favor and gifts.
Henceforth his liegeman no longer am I!"
When the Almighty heard this boast,
5 How his angel on high with haughty lips
Defiance uttered, and foolishly strove
To rise against God, . . . He was wroth in His
    heart,   (295)
And cast him down from his seat on high,   (300)
Hurled him to hell; from heaven banished,
10 Down in those deeps he was changed to a devil.
Thus fell the fiend with his followers all;
Three days and nights they downward fell.
Those angels of light the Lord did change
To devils dark. For His deeds and words
15 They failed to honor, wherefore the Lord
Deprived them of light, and placed them, lost
Deep under earth in darkest hell.

There through the night immeasurably long,
Fire unflagging they feel, each one;
20 Then comes with the dawn an eastern wind,
And bitter-cold frost,—ever fire or frost.
Throes and hardship are theirs to endure,
Banished from heaven. Their home was changed.
Then first the hollow of hell was filled
25 With fallen fiends. But the faithful angels
Held the heights of heaven above,
While the fiends below in fire lay,
The foes who in folly fought against God.
They have their reward in the womb of hell,
30 Blaze and broad flames, and bitter smoke,

Glare and gloom.   Beguiled by their pride
The service of God they despised and forgot. . *(326)*
Then spoke the insolent foe who once was fairest of
    angels,   *(338)*
Most dazzling in heaven, and dear to his lord;
5 Within him sorrow seethed round his heart;   *(353)*
Without was the reek of the rolling flames,
The welter of fire—such words he spake;
"This narrow place is nothing like
That other world that once we knew,
10 Where high in heaven our homes were set
Though God who gave, would not grant us to hold
    them,
Rule our realm.   Unrighteous his deed,
To hurl us flying to this flaming pit,
And the heat of hell, from heaven cut off!
15 He hath planned to establish man in our place!
This is the sorest of all my sorrows,
That Adam should, who was shaped of earth,
For aye possess my stronghold there,
And live in bliss while we must endure
20 This brunt of wrath.   Ah welaway!
If but my hands were free; if but an hour I had,
One winter's hour, then would I with this band—!
But iron bonds are all about me,
The rough chain rides me hard; realmless I am.
25 Hell's strong clutches clamp me down,
Pin me fast, a prey to the flames,
Over and under me endless fire.
I have never looked on a loathlier sight,
Quenchless blaze that quickens ever.
30 Cables tough, and torturing chains

Hold me here; my hands are shackled,   (379)
My feet are fettered; fast I am bound;
I may not pass the portals of hell,
Loose my limbs from the links that hold them,
5 Hammered hard, of iron hot,
Bars and bolts. Thereby hath God
Gripped my neck. I know from this,
That the Lord of men my mind did mark;
Saw that Adam and I should quarrel
10 O'er heaven's realm, if my hands were free.
But now we endure the throes of hell, darkness and
      heat,
Grim and bottomless. God Himself
Hath swept us into swarthy gloom, though guiltless
      of sin!
No wrong we did in his realm, yet robbed He us all
      of light;
15 Cast us into cruellest woe! now may we wreak our
      wrongs,
Pay him reward of hate; because he reft us of light.
He hath marked a place called midgard, where man
      He hath wrought
After His likeness. He looks to replace us
In heaven with spotless souls! Now seek we earnestl
20 How on Adam and all his offspring,
Our wrongs we may right, and wreak our vengeance
If haply we may beguile him to go astray from God
I have no hope of the light that He will long enjoy;
Of the bliss that is His forever, 'mongst angel-host
      in heaven.
25 Nor may we hope to soften the heart of God Al
      mighty.

Then keep we that kingdom from man since we may
    come to it never;   (*404*)
Tempt them to break His word, and turn from the
    will of their Maker.
Thus shall His wrath be kindled, to cast them away
    forever.
Then shall they seek this hell, sink to these gulfs of
    horror;
5 And we shall hold them in chains, these children of
    men our vassals.
Think of this deed, ye thanes of mine!
If any there be, whom erst I favored
With gifts of price, in that goodly kingdom,
Where happy we lived and held our realm,
10 No fitter time he could find, to return
The bounty I dealt, no better way,
Than if now he were willing at need to escape;
Break through these bars, by boldness and cunning;
On feathery pinions fly through the air,
15 Wheeling aloft till he light on the spot
Where Adam and Eve on earth are standing,
With bounty blessed, while banished we are
To the dark abyss. They are dearer than we
To Heaven's Lord; they live in joy,
20 They have the wealth that once was ours,
Our realm and our right! This rueth me sore,
That they shall in heaven be happy forever!
If any of you may alter their state,
And make them transgress the command of God,
25 I shall lie at ease in my links of iron.   (*433*)
Who gaineth me this shall get his reward,

The best I can give in the bounds of this fire:
He shall sit with myself, who comes to say   *(438*
They have broken the law of the Lord of heaven."

Then girded himself a foe of God
With trappings of war, on treachery bent;
Set helmet on head, and hardily clasped it;
Firmly fastened it down.   He was fluent of speech
A master of guile.   He mounted aloft,
Swung through hell's door, the hardy adventurer,
10 Wheeling through mid-air, on mischief bent,
Cleaving the flames with his fiendish skill.
He hoped to deceive the servants of God;
Trick them with lies and lead them astray;
Tempt them to rouse the wrath of God.
15 Onward he flew, with fiendish skill
And came where Adam on earth was standing,
The work of God's hand, wondrously made;
And with him his wife, of women the fairest.   *(457*
Near by stood two stately trees,   *(460*
20 Laden all over with largess of fruit,
Bearing their bounty, as bidden by God,
Heaven's high King, whose hand had set them
For the children of men, to make their choice
Of good and of evil; for each must choose
25 'Twixt weal and woe.   Unlike was their fruit:
One was beautiful, bright and shining,
Delightful to look on; that was life's tree.
Who tasted its fruit, should flourish forever;
Life everlasting his lot should be.
30 Age might not injure nor dread disease.
His days should pass in pleasure unending,

High in the favor of heaven's King.   (474)
And rich reward awaits him hereafter,
In heaven above when hence he departs.

The second tree all swart uptowered,
5 Dark and dismal: that was Death's tree.
Bitter the fruit it bore unto men!
Both good and evil should each man know.
Who tasted the fruit of that fatal tree,
His life should wane and wither away
10 In sorrow and trouble, in sweat and in toil.
Age would strip him of strength and vigor,
Gladness and glory; his goal is death.
A little while he lingers on earth,
But soon goes down to the darkest of lands,
15 To serve the fiends in fire and woe,
Hugest of tortures. The tempter knew it,
The sneaking spy with his spite against God.
In the shape of a serpent, he soon was coiled
Round the tree of death, through his devil's craft.
20 He took of the fruit, and turned to find
The handiwork of heaven's King.
With lying words, the loathly fiend
Came toward the man, and questioned him there:
"Hast thou any longing Adam, up to God?
25 I have on his errand hither fared from far.
'Twas not long since, that I sat with God himself.
He bade me come and tell thee to take of this fruit.
I heard him approve thy words and deeds,   (507)
Praise thy life, in His light above.
30 Obey the behest that His herald brings!

Boundless stretch earth's broad green plains.　　(*510*)
God sitteth on high, in heaven enthroned,
Nor deigns Himself to suffer the toil
Of this journey long.　So the Lord of hosts
5　His herald doth send, to speak His will.
He bids thee heed and obey His words.
Stretch forth thy hand, and hold this fruit;
Take it and taste it; thy heart will expand,
Thy body grow brighter; thy bounteous Lord
10　Sends thee this help from heaven above."

Adam answered, where on earth he stood,
God's handiwork: "When I heard the Lord,
The King of heaven, call me aloud,
With stern voice bid me stand on earth,
15　And obey His will,—when He brought me this
　　　　woman,
This winsome bride, and bid me beware
Lest the tree of Death should darkly deceive me,
And betray me to woe, He warned me that hell
Should hold him ever, within whose heart
20　Evil was lurking. . . . Unlike thou seemest　　(*531*)
To any angel that ever I saw!　　(*538*)
Nor dost thou offer me any token,
That truly from heaven thou hither art sent,
Come from the Lord.　I cannot obey thee!
25　But take thyself off!　My trust is in God,
My faith is in Him whose hands did fashion me,
That He may grant me each gift from on high,
Without sending His servant to speak in His place."
　　Then wrathfully turned the tempter away;
30　Went where he saw the woman standing,

Winsome and fair. The words he spake   (549)
Brought woe to the world, and worst of pangs
To all her offspring, in after years:
"I know ye will rouse the wrath of God,
5 When I tell him myself, returned from the journey,
The long hard way, that ye would not listen,
Nor heed the message that hither He sent,
Far from the east. He shall fare Himself
To make you His answer; no messenger then
10 His word will bear, for I wot He will kindle
His anger against you. But if thou, woman,
A willing ear to my words shalt lend,
His vengeance yet thou mayest avert.
Bethink thee, Eve, that through thy wit
15 Ye both may be saved from bitter woe!
Eat of the fruit, and thine eyes shall be light!
Far and wide o'er the world thou shalt look,
God himself thou shalt see on His throne,
And the favor of Heaven shalt have forever.
20 Also, dear Eve, thou may'st alter the mind
Of Adam thy husband, if thou have his goodwill,
And he trust thy words, when the truth thou reveal-
est:
How glad was thy heart when God's behest
Thou promptly didst heed: mayhap he will leave
25 His stubborn mood, and silence the answer
Of wrath in his bosom, if both of us now
Urge him together. Now earnestly ply him
To do thy bidding, lest both of ye fall
Into God's disfavor, and get you His wrath!
30 If this thou fulfillest, O fairest of women,
I shall hide from your Lord the harsh words of Adam,

The insults thy husband did heap upon me,   (580)
When he challenged my honor, charged me with
        falsehood
Said I was evil, no angel of God.
Yet well do I know all the ways of the angels,
5 The heavenly mansions.   This many a year
With loyal heart my lord I have followed,
And rendered to God, the Ruler of Heaven,
My dutiful service; no devil am I!"

So he led with his lies, and lured with his wiles
10 The woman to wrong; till the will of the serpent
Worked in her bosom; (the weaker mind
God had given her.)   She began to listen
And lean to his lore.   At last she took
From the tempter the fruit of the fatal tree,
15 Against God's word.   No worse deed ever
For man was done.   'Twas marvel great
That the Lord everlasting allowed it to happen,
Permitted so many men upon earth
By lying lore to be led astray.
20 She tasted the fruit and turned from God,
From His word and will.   Then wide was her vision
By the gift of the fiend, who beguiled her with lies,
And darkly betrayed her; his doing it was
That heaven and earth more white did seem,
25 And all the world more wondrous fair,
More glorious-great the works of God.
(She beheld them not by human power,
But the fiend had falsely feigned it before her;
Her sight deceived her, when she seemed to look
30 So far abroad.)   The fiend now spoke,

The tempter-foe,—his tale nought profited: (*610*)
"Now thou mayst see, I need not tell thee,
How altered thy form, O fairest Eve,
How beauteous thy body, since obeying my words,
5 And heeding my lore. Now light shines about thee,
Glorious and bright. I brought it from God,
So fair from Heaven, thou mayst feel it and touch it.
Reveal to Adam this vision of brightness,
Vouchsafed by me. If with simple mind
10 He agree to my wish, I will give him his fill
Of the glorious light I gave to thee,
Nor store up his insolent speeches against him,
Though scarce he deserve so swift a pardon.
Nor shall his children be charged with his fault,
15 Banished from heaven for his misdoing;
Their life shall be happy, though he hath done wrong."
    Then went to Adam of women the fairest,
The winsomest wife the world ever saw,
(Though comely her form, as she came from God's
        hand
20 Yet was she undone by darkest wiles
And won by lies), these words she spake: (*630*)
"Adam my lord, this fruit is so sweet,   (*655*)
So blithe in my breast, so bright this herald,
This angel of God so good and fair,
25 By his trappings I see he is sent from above.
'Tis wiser for us to win his favor
Than set him against us by surly words.
If today thou hast uttered aught that was harsh,
He yet will forgive, if he get our obedience.
30 What profits this strife with the spokesman of God,
Thy Lord and Master? We need his good-will,

For he may commend us to our Maker in heaven,
Our Ruler on high.   From here I can see   (666)
Where He sits himself,—'tis south and east—
Enwound with glory, the world's Creator.
5 I behold his angels hovering about Him
In winged robes, a radiant host
And choir glad.   Whence cometh this vision,
If God Himself vouchsafed it not to us,
The King of heaven?   I can hear afar,
10 And look abroad o'er the bright creation.
Joyful harping I hear in heaven!
Filled is my soul, and flooded with light,
Since first I took and tasted this fruit.
Here in my hand, dear husband, I bring it;
15 Gladly I give it; from God it hath come,
I firmly believe, as his faithful angel
Hath told us it came, in truthful words.
Nought else was ever on earth like this;
'Tis sent by God as his spokesman declares."

20   Sore she beset him, and spurred him all day
To the deed of darkness; drove him to break
The will of their Lord.   The loathly fiend
Stood near by, and subtly the while
Incited their spirits to sin and shame. . . .   (687)
25 Long she urged him, till Adam at last   (705)
Goaded by Eve, began to yield;
His mind was turned, he trusted too much
The winning words that the woman spake.
Yet did she it all in duty and love,
30 Nor weened what woe, what wailing and sorrow
Should come to mankind, because she had hearkened

To the voice of the devil. She deemed she was win-
 ning $\qquad$ (712)
God's goodwill, by giving her husband
The fruit to taste, and turning his mind
By winsome words, her wish to perform.
5 Death and the grave he got from the woman,
Though it had not that name,—'twas known as the
 fruit
Yet the devil's seduction meant death's long sleep,
Doom of hell and downfall of heroes,
Undoing of man and mortal woe,
10 Because they ate of that cursed fruit.

As soon as the evil one saw it was done,
He laughed aloud, and leapt for joy.
For the fall of them both, the bitter foe
Gave thanks to his lord, that loathly thane!
15 "Now have I got me thy grace and favor,
Worked thy will, and won my reward.
Man is betrayed for many a day;
Adam and Eve forever have lost
The love of their Lord, for leaving His word,
20 His law and command. No more they shall hold
The kingdom of heaven: to hell they shall go.
They shall make the dark journey; no more thy sor-
 row
Bear in thy breast, where bound thou liest;
Nor mourn in thy mind, that men shall inherit
25 The heights of heaven, the while we endure
Labor and throes in a land of gloom.
Because of thy pride, our cohorts fell,
Hurled from the towering halls of heaven,

Goodly abodes. For God was wroth (740)
Because we refused to fawn with his followers,
Bow our heads in obeisance to Him.
Therefore the Ruler was wroth in His heart,
5 Hurled us to hell, in the heat of His anger;
Flung to the flames the flower of His host,
And then with His hands, in heaven He raised
New seats of glory, and gave them to man.
Blithe be thy mood, and merry thy breast!
10 Double damage today is wrought!
This brood of man hath missed forever
The glory of heaven,—they go their way
To the flames and thee. And God Himself
Is made to suffer sorrow and loss.
15 On Adam's head 'tis all repaid,
With hate of his Lord and heroes' downfall,
Mortal throes of men upon earth.
Healed is my hurt, my heart expands.
Wreaked are all our ancient wrongs,
20 The lingering woe we long endured!
Back I'll haste to the blaze of hell,
Satan to seek, struck into chains."
Netherward bent his way that boder of evil,
Stooped to the gulfs of hell and the far-flung flames.

THE DROWNING OF THE EGYPTIANS

(*Exodus,* lines 447-515)

25 The host was harrowed with horror of drowning;
Sea-death menaced their miserable souls.
The slopes of the hill-sides were splashed with blood.

There was woe on the waters, the waves spat gore;
They were full of weapons, and frothed with slaugh-
ter.   (*451*)
Back were beaten the bold Egyptians,
Fled in fear; they were filled with terror.
5 Headlong they hastened their homes to seek.
Less bold were their boasts as the billows rolled o'er
them,
Dread welter of waves. Not one of that army
Went again home, but Wyrd from behind
Barred with billows their backward path.
10 Where ways had lain, now weltered the sea,
The swelling flood. The storm went up
High to the heavens; hugest of uproars
Darkened the sky; the dying shrieked
With voices doomed. The deep streamed with blood.
15 Shield-walls were shattered by shock of the tempest.
Greatest of sea-deaths engulfed the mighty,
Captains and troops. Retreat was cut off
At the ocean's brink. Their battle-shields gleamed
High o'er their heads as the heaped-up waters
20 Compassed them round, the raging flood.
Doomed was the host, by death hemmed in,
Suddenly trapped. The salty billows
Swept with their swirling the sand from their feet
As the ocean cold to its ancient bed,
25 Through winding channels the churning flood,
Came rolling back o'er the rippled bottom,
Swift avenger, naked and wild.
With slaughter was streaked the storm-dark air;
The bursting deep with blood-terror yawned,
30 When He who made it, by Moses' hand

Unbitted the wrath of the raging flood;　　　　(480)
Wide it came sweeping to swallow the foe;
Foamed the waters, the fated sank;
Earth was o'erwhelmed, the air was darkened;
5 Burst the wave-walls, the bulwarks tumbled;
The sea-towers melted, when the Mighty One smot
The pride of the host, through the pillar of fire,
With holy hand from heaven above.
The onslaught wild of the angry main
10 None might oppose. He appointed their end
In the roaring horror. Wroth was the sea:
Up it rose, down it smote, dealing destruction.
Slaughter-blood spread, the sea-wall fell,
Upreared on high, the handiwork of God,
15 When the ocean He smote with His ancient sword,
Felled the defence of the foam-breasted waves.
With that death-blow deep, the doomed men slept.
The army of sinners their souls gave up,
The sea-pale host, ensnared and surrounded,
20 When the dark upheaval o'erwhelmed them all,
Hugest of wild waves. The host sank down,
Pharaoh and his folk, the flower of Egypt
Utterly perished. The enemy of God
Soon discovered, when the sea he entered,
25 That the ocean's master was mightier than he.
By the strength of His arm He decided the battle,
Wrathful and grim. He gave the Egyptians
Thorough reward for that day's work.
Not one of that host to his home came back;
30 Of all those warriors not one returned
To bring the news of the battle's end,
To tell in the towns the tidings of woe,

Their husband's doom to the heroes' wives,   (511)
How sea-death swallowed the stately host
No messenger left.   The Lord Almighty
Confounded their boasting; they fought against God.

3. SAINTS' LEGENDS

ELENE

I

CONSTANTINE'S VISION OF THE CROSS

5 In the circle of years, in the span of time,   (1)
Two hundred and three and thirty winters
Had passed o'er the world, since the Prince of glory,
The Lord Almighty, and Light of the faithful,
Was born on earth in the image of man.
10 Constantine's reign had run six years
Since he, a hero, on high was raised
To rule o'er the Roman realm afar;
Shield-bearer strong, he sheltered his people,
Ruled in righteousness, rendered justice,
15 Defended his folk from foemen's attack,
Spread abroad the bounds of his realm.
And God was with him and gave him strength,
Glory and might.   To many on earth
The king became a comfort and help,
20 An avenger in war, when his weapons he raised,
And fell on the foe that frighted his land.

Now the king was threatened with thunder of battle;
Hordes of Huns their hosts assembled,

Hugas and Hrethgoths harnessed for war; (20
Fierce-hearted Franks were faring against him.
Their lances glittered, their linkéd mail;
Mid shouts of battle and beating of shields
5 Their banners they raised, and banded together.
They massed their ranks and marched to war.
The wolf of the weald his war-song chanted,
Howled his death-rune. Hoarsely screamed
The wet-winged eagle o'er the wake of the foe.
10 Straight through the strongholds strode the invaders
The mighty host, as many in number,
As the king of the Huns could call to his standards
From hearth and from hall. The horde pressed for
    ward;
With well-tried warriors, as they went along,
15 They swelled their ranks, and soon arrived
In a country strange, those spearmen bold.
Prepared for battle, they pitched their tents
On the Danube's strand. By the stream arose
The hue and roar of the host tumultuous.
20 They would threaten the realm of Rome with thei
    throngs,
Plunder its towns. The approach of the Huns
Was published abroad in the burgs of the people.
Then Caesar sent, and summoned his army
To gather in haste against the foe;
25 Commanded his men to muster for battle,
With bow and arrow to arm for war.

Soon were the Romans ready for combat,
The victory-famed, though fewer in numbers
Than the hordes that had come with the king of the
    Huns.

They rode round their ruler; their raised shields
  clanged,   (50)
 Their battle-boards rang. Above them the raven
 Scenting the slaughter, circled and cried.
 The king rode ahead. The host was advancing;
5 Heralds shouted, horses trampled,
 Trumpets brayed, the troop marched on,
 Swift to the combat; the king was adread,
 Stricken with fear, when he saw that host
 Of Huns outlandish and Hrethgoths wild,
o Gathered all, at the end of his realm,
 By the water's edge, and armed for war,
 A countless host. His heart was troubled;
 The ruler of Rome of his realm despaired,
 For lack of fighters; too few his warriors
5 To support him in arms 'gainst the overmight
 Of the ruthless foe. The Romans encamped,
 The earls round their lord, at the edge of the stream,
 As night came on, and near the spot
 Where first they had faced their foe's advance.

o To Caesar himself, as in slumber he lay,
 By his host surrounded, and wrapt in sleep,
 To the victory-famed, a vision appeared.
 A shining figure in shape of a man,
 Gleamed before him, more fair and glorious
5 Than any warrior that early or late
 He had seen 'neath the sun. He started up,
 And donned his helmet. The herald addressed him,
 Greeted him gladly; the glorious shape
 Named him by name,—the night was gone:
o "Constantinus; the king of angels

The Wielder of all, his aid and alliance　　　(*80*)
Bids me offer thee.　Be not afraid,
Though alien hordes o'erawe thee with terror
Of hateful war.　To heaven look up,
5　Whence comfort shall come, from the King of Glory
And a victory-sign be revealed to thee!"

His eager heart answered the angel's behest;
He gazed to heaven as the herald had bidden.
Streaming with splendor, in the sky he beheld
10　The tree of glory, o'ertopping the clouds,
With gold adorned and with gleaming jewels;
In letters of light on the lustrous beam,
Shining was writ:　"In this sign thou shalt conquer
Defeat thy foe in the fearful battle,
15　The loathsome host."　The light departed,
And with it the angel went up to heaven,
To the home of the pure.　The prince of men
Was happy in heart, and healed of his sorrow
By that vision fair of the victory-tree.

II

The Victory of Constantine

20　Now Constantine the king renowned,
The lord of bounty, and leader of armies,
Shelter of earls, gave orders to make
A standard shaped like the shining token,
The sign he had seen in the skies revealed,
25　The cross of Christ.　With the coming of dawn,
At break of day he bade them rouse,

His warriors stir to the storm of battle,   (*106*)
Raise their banners and bear before them
The beacon of God against the foe.
War trumpets blew as they went to the combat,
5 Leading the ranks.   The raven was glad.
The dewy-winged eagle eagerly watched
The warriors go.   The gray-wolf howled,
The beast of the holt.   Then came battle-terror,
The clash of hordes, the crash of boards,
10 Heavy smiting, hand-to-hand fighting,
When first they stood in the storm of the arrows
That the battle-grim haters hurled at their foe:
Showers of shafts o'er the shields of the doomed,
Sharp-tongued arrows, adders of war,
15 By the strength of their sinews they sent them hissing.
But steadily strode the stout-hearted on,
Broke the shield-hedge, buried their swords
In the breasts of their foes and bravely advanced.
Where the standard was shown there were shouts of
    victory.
20 Golden helmet and glittering spear
Flashed o'er the field where fell the pagans;
The hordes of the Huns, the heathen armies,
Fled in haste when the holy sign
Was raised at the call of the Roman king.

25 Far and wide the foe was scattered
Some had fallen on the field of battle;
Some had scarcely saved their lives
By sudden flight.   Some took refuge
In deserts wild, more dead than living,
30 And hid in caves, or crawled to the banks

Of the Danube stream. Some were drowned: (*136*

In the rushing flood they found their end.

Then the band of the brave was joyful;

From early dawn till evening light

5 The host of the Hun they hotly pursued,

Hurled their ash-spears, adders of war,

Fast diminished the foeman's might;

Few of the fiends e'er found their home.

'Twas clear to them all that Constantine

10 Was conqueror crowned by the King of Glory;

In that day's work he was worthy deemed

To win renown through the wondrous cross.   (*147*

III

The Quest of the Cross By Elene

In the heart of the prince was praise of Christ (*212*

From that time forth. The thought of the cross

15 He bore in his mind, and bade his mother

Fare abroad with a band of followers,

With her liegemen go to the land of the Jews

And seek the spot where the sign of glory,

The holy beacon was buried in earth,

20 The rood of the Lord. Not loath was Elene

To go on the quest as the king had bidden;

She was glad to obey her giver of bounty,

Her own dear son. Soon she was ready;

Heeding the words of the warden of hosts,

25 The woman prepared for the welcome voyage.

Bands of earls set out for the shore,

Went in haste where harnessed stood,

By the water's edge, the ocean-steeds, (*227*)
Sea-stallions fettered, afloat on the waves.
Elene's purpose to all was plain
When she turned with her train to the tossing sea.
5 Goodly warriors were gathered in plenty
By the wave-wet strand of the Wendel-sea,
Troop after troop, o'er the trails they hastened;
The steeds of the sea were swiftly loaded
With shield and shaft and shining corslet,
o With man and maid, and mailéd warriors.
They drove o'er the flood their foam-flecked coursers,
Their tall wave-tramplers, o'er the trails of the deep.
The tumbling seas in that tumult wild
Oft broke on board, and all about
5 Was the noise of waters. I have never heard
Of a queen that sailed with a comlier fleet
Out o'er the ways of the ocean-stream.
There might one watch the waves at the bows
As they breasted the billows, break into foam.
o Under swelling sails the swift ships ran,
The wave-skimmers plunged. The warriors were
proud;
Keen was their courage. The queen rejoiced.
So came to the roads the ring-stemmed keels,
In the land of the Greeks. They left their ships,
5 Tossed by the tide, their tight sea-homes,
Fast at anchor, afloat in the bay,
To await their errand's issue there,
When the queen with her train should return once
more,
And seek them out o'er the eastern ways.

There earls were seen in armor clad,
With choicest swords, and chain-linked mail,   (257)
With helmet visored, and haughty boar-crest,
With breast-plates burnished. About their queen
5 Ash-spear in hand, the earls were ranged,
Eager to march. On they fared,
Those heroes hardy in harness of war,
Liegemen of Caesar, to the land of the Greeks.
Their ranks were rich with radiant jewels,
10 Gold-set gems, the gift of their lord.
Elene the queen ever was faithful,
Kept in mind the command of the king,
Eager in soul to seek with her train,
Her war-troop chosen of well-tried spearmen,
15 The land of the Jews o'er the level plains.
Erelong it fell, in a little while,
The hardy band of heroes bold
Arrived at the gates of Jerusalem.
Entered the city that arméd troop
20 Of earls renowned with their noble queen.   (275)

Arrived in Jerusalem Elene questions the wise men of Judea concerning the crucifixion. They all profess ignorance. One of them,
Judas by name, is delivered over to her as a hostage. He knows
the history of the cross but refuses to divulge it. Thrown into a pit
and threatened with starvation, he suffers a change of heart and
leads the queen to Mt. Calvary. Here he falls on his knees and
prays that God may reveal to him where the cross is buried by let-
ting a smoke arise from the spot.

X

THE DISCOVERY OF THE CROSS

Then from the mount a mist arose   (802)
Like a smoke to the skies. His spirit within him

Was quickened with comfort. He clapped his hands
On high toward heaven in holy rapture.   (*805*)
Then Judas spoke in joyous mood:
"Now do I know,—I deny it no longer—
5 That Thou in sooth art the Saviour of men.
Thanks eternal be to Thee, O Lord,
Ruler of hosts, that reignest in glory,
That Thou in Thy might hast made me to know,
Though hard was my heart, Thy hidden ways." (*812*)

. . . .

0 Eager and glad he began to delve   (*827*)
In willing trust for the tree of glory
'Neath the cover of turf, 'till twenty feet down
Buried deep in darkness of earth
Crosses three he came upon;
5 Concealed they lay 'neath a lid of rock
In their gloomy fastness. He found them together
Covered with sand where the sinful Jews
Had left and forgotten them, long ago:
The souls unrighteous on the Son of God
0 Had showered their hate as they should not have done,
Had the plotter of evil not prompted their hearts
His lore to obey. Blithe was Judas,
The mind of the man was moved with joy,
His soul was inspired by the sight of the tree,
5 The sacred sign he saw in the earth;
He clasped with his hands the cross of glory,
And moved it amain from its mouldering grave.

Now all the earls went in to the city,
Carrying proudly the crosses three.
0 They set them up in sight of the queen,

Those earls renowned. The noble Elene   (848)
Kneeling before them, was filled with joy,
And wished to know on which of the three
The Hope of heroes had hangéd been.

5 "Lo, we have heard from holy books
A tale of truth that twain with Him
Suffered the throes, Himself the third,
High on the rood; the heavens darkened
In that terrible hour. Tell if thou canst

10 On which of the crosses the King of glory
And Lord of angels in agony hung."
But Judas could not clearly tell,
('Twas not revealed) the victory-tree
On which the Lord was lifted high,

15 The Son of God. He gave command
With sound of singing to set up the trees
In the city's midst, to remain in sight
'Till God before men a marvel should work,
And the might of the rood make manifest.

20 So they gathered around and raised their song,
Watching with care the crosses three,
'Till the ninth hour brought them a new delight,
A marvellous thing. A multitude came,
A crowd of folk, carrying one dead;

25 Borne on a bier they brought him nigh,
A youth he seemed, his soul had fled.
Then Judas rejoiced, ('twas just the ninth hour)
His heart within him was eager with hope;
He bade them lay the lifeless corpse,

30 The dead man's body, down on the earth,
And hold aloft o'er that house deserted
Two of the crosses. Then the counsellor wise,

The right decider, studied deeply   (*880*)
The motionless corpse; it remained as before:
Lifeless it lay, the limbs were cold
Locked in death. Then they lifted on high
5 The third of the crosses. The corpse lay still
Till above it was raised the rood of triumph,
The very cross of the King of heaven,
The victory-sign. Then sudden it rose
Endowed with spirit; soul and body
10 Were joined together. Great was their joy,
Fain was that folk the Father to praise;
And with Him the Son they worshipped aloud,
With words of thanksgiving. Glory to Him,
World without end from every creature.   (*893*)

XII

THE BUILDING OF THE TEMPLE OF THE HOLY ROOD

The marvellous story was soon made known;   (*967*)
It flew o'er the folkways far and near.
The tidings sped o'er city and town
And sea-girt shore. Shame was brought,
Confusion on all who fain would darken
20 The counsel of God. The glad news spread
That the cross of Christ, long covered with earth,
Was found again, most glorious token
Of triumph raised 'neath the roof of heaven
In the tide of time. To the tribe of the Jews
25 'Twas the bitterest fate, to that folk unblest
A cruel grief, that the Christians' joy
They might not quench. The queen commanded

That heralds should haste from her host of earls,
With eager speed o'er the ocean-stream,   (981
To seek the ruler of the Roman folk,
And bring to the brave the best of news,
5 The joyful tidings that the token of victory
By the favor of God was found at last,
Buried in earth, where ages long
Hidden it lay, a loss to saints
And Christian folk.   The king was glad,
10 His soul was merry; his spirit rejoiced
At the marvellous news; and many arrived,
Richly arrayed, in the royal city
To question the messengers come from afar.
The warrior's dearest wish was fulfilled;
15 With laughing heart he heard the news
That his heralds brave had brought from the east:
How safe and sound o'er the swan-road wide,
The queen and her comrades had come ashore
In the land of the Greeks.   Their lord commanded
20 They should hold themselves ready to hasten bac
Without delay.   They lingered not
When once they had learned the will of their lord,
The Ætheling's wish.   He asked them to greet
The lady Elene, liegemen brave,
25 When across the sea they came again safe,
Heroes haught, to the holy city.
Constantine further counselled his heralds
To bid their mistress build a church
For the sake of them both, on the sacred mount;
30 To rear on its top a temple of God,
On Calvary high, in honor of Christ
And heroes to help, where the Holy Rood

First was found, the fairest of trees   (*1012*)
Storied and sung by sons of men,
O'er the ways of the world. His will she performed,
When out of the west, from over the seas,
5 Their welcome word her warriors brought.
Then the queen commanded that men be sought,
Craftsmen skilled, in stone-work cunning,
The best to be found in that foreign land,
And bade them build on the brow of the hill
10 A temple of God, by the Guardian of spirits
Guided from heaven. The Holy Rood
She bade them cover with costly gold,
Set it with gems and jewels precious,
Secure in a shrine of silver encase it,
15 And lock it safe. There since that day
The cross of life hath lain unbroken,
Rood triumphant and incorruptible,
Solace unfailing in sore affliction,
To all who suffer anguish or pain;
20 By the holy sign they shall soon find help
And grace from God.   (*1032*)

SAINT GUTHLAC

(From Guthlac B.)

THE TEMPTATION OF GUTHLAC

Oft were the fens by foul fiends haunted;   (*866*)
Hordes of demons, dark and menacing,
Swarmed round the spot where the saint of God,
25 Dauntless of courage, kept his abode.
Filled was the air with uproar confused;

Riotous battle-din raised in the wilderness   *(871)*
The fiendish rout, bereft of all beauty,
Sundered from joy.   But the servant of God,
Hero hardy, the hellish rabble
5 Boldly defied.   They fled for a space,
Not long the delay; the loathly guests,
The trouble-smiths, quickly the turmoil renewed
With yelpings loud and long-drawn yells.
At times they would bellow like beasts of prey,
10 Or howl in troops; at times they would change
Into human form, the fierce man-haters,
With deafening clamor, or don the shape
Of creeping serpents, those spirits accurst,
Spewing venom, the vile deceivers.
15 Yet Guthlac ever on guard they found;
Watchful and wary, he waited in patience,
Though the thronging demon-bands threatened to slay
     him.

The fowls of the air would oft-times flutter
About his board, made bold by hunger,
20 Feed from his hand and fondly thank him
With happy songs; and sundry folk,
Wayfarers meek, would make his abode
Their journey's goal, and joyfully gain
Healing and help at the hands of the saint,
25 Soul and body restored by his blessing.   *(895)*

THE DEATH OF GUTHLAC

And now the end of his earthly toil,   *(904)*
Of his life of labor, at last drew near.

'Twas fifteen years since first he chose (*908*)
In the desert wild his dwelling to make,
When a spirit holy from heaven descended,
To call him hence. His heart within him
5 Burned to depart; his bodily frame
Was stricken sore with sudden fever;
His joints were loosed, his limbs grew heavy; (*927*)
Yet firm was his faith, though feeble his body,
That God Almighty was minded to try him,
10 His Maker kind. His courage he summoned,
Nor feared in his heart the foe's temptations,
Nor piercing of pain, nor pangs of anguish,
Nor parting of death; but praise of the Lord
Glowed in his breast, and burning love
15 O'er all his ills triumphant rose,
And conquered his pain. Nor prized he greatly
This fleeting life, though the friendly house-mates,
Body and soul, were soon to sever
Their union dear. So the days sped on.
20 Night-shadows fell. Near was the hour
When he must endure the mortal doom,
Death's sharp stroke, our destined lot,
Earned by our elders in ancient days. (*948*)

A youthful disciple, his serving-thane, (*972*)
25 Dwelt near by, and daily came
To visit his master. With mind devout
And pious spirit, his steps he bent
To the chapel wherein his chosen teacher,
His master in wisdom, was wont to pray.
30 Straight he entered, the saint to greet,
And open his heart to the holy lore

Of the hermit mild. His mood was sad   (980)
When he found his master with fever stricken;
Deep in his bosom, the burden of grief
Weighed on his soul, as he spoke these words:
5 "My lord beloved, how liest thou here,
Sick unto death, and sore afflicted,
Friend and protector, my father dear!
Never before have I found thee thus,
Languid and prone; hast thou power of speech?
10 Much do I fear a fever sudden
In the still night-watches hath stolen upon thee.
Sad is my spirit; vouchsafe me comfort.
Dost know what the end of this illness shall be?"
The saint made answer with utterance feeble;
15 He scarce drew breath, so baleful the stroke
Of the burning fever; yet bravely rallied
The man of God, and made reply:
"I tell thee truly the touch of this evil
In the dead of night hath darkly descended,
20 Unlocked my life-hoard. My limbs grow heavy,
Smitten with pain. My soul's habitation,
The body frail, shall be folded in earth.
My limbs shall be laid in their loamy bed,
To sleep in peace. The slayer approacheth,
25 Swift for his prey. When seven nights
In the course of time shall have come and gone,
My hours are spent, and my spirit shall pass:
When the eighth day dawns, the end shall come."

                                              (1010)

There was sound of mourning and sad lament; (1020)
30 The young thane's heart was heavy with grief
When he had heard that the holy man

Was about to depart. That bitter news (*1023*)
Of his lord beloved laid on his heart
Its burden of sorrow. His spirit was darkened;
The hot tears welled from his woe-brimmed heart.

(*1026*)

5 When the holy in spirit beheld his disciple (*1033*)
With grief o'erwhelmed, and weeping sore,
Glad and serene, he began to cheer
His well-loved comrade with words of comfort:
"Be not cast down! Though this dread disease
10 Doth harass my body, not hard I find it
Obedient to bow to the bidding of God.
No terror of death doth trouble my spirit,
In the hour of trial, with anxious thoughts.
Still less do I dread the dark battalions
15 Of the demons of hell. With deadly sin
Their chief and leader may charge me never,
With lust of the flesh. In the flame they suffer
Scalding remorse; they mourn their loss,
Their exile-journey, of joy bereft,
20 Of love and delight, and the lot of the faithful,
In death's dark hall. My dearest son,
Refuse not my comfort, I fain would depart
To my heavenly home, and have my reward
In joy everlasting, the life of the blest,
25 And see my Saviour, O son beloved.
No hardship I hold it, nor heavy toil;
The giver of glory I go to seek,
Gladness and peace and the presence of God,
Whom singly I served, with steadfast mind
30 Through all the days of this dreary life,
With heart and soul; I surely shall find

High in heaven where my hopes are set,   (*1060*)
Fair and unfading, my final reward.
My spirit is fain to fly from the body
Leave this land, to its long joy come,
5 Abode of the blest. Not bitter to me
What there shall befall; my faith is sure
After body is broken comes bliss eternal."
Stilled was the voice of the valiant saint,
Prophet renowned; he had need of rest,
10 Failing and faint. The fading twilight,
Deepened to dusk, the dark night-watches
Stalked o'er the earth and stole upon men.

Now dawned the light of the day when the Lord,
With breath of life to his body restored,
15 Radiant and glorious arose from his grave,
O'er earth triumphant, at Eastertide.
A mighty host to heaven he raised,
When his glory burst the gates of Hell.
Filled with the hope of that happy festal,
20 Day of rejoicing, the gentle saint
The strength of his spirit summoned again.
Firm was his faith, though feeble his body,
Wasted and faint with the fever's rage.
As best he could, from his bed he rose;
25 His service he said in the sacred shrine,
His holy office, with upright heart
And deep devotion, he duly performed.
Then as befits a faithful master,
Straight he bethought him his thane to instruct
30 In the word of God; by the gift of the spirit
To teach him love of the life eternal,

Wonder and glory of the world of light. (*1090*)

Now seven days' time had sped o'er the earth (*1114*)
Since the flickering flight of fiery darts
Had lodged in his side, and sought to unlock
5 With crafty keys his casket of life.
Again the disciple of Guthlac went forth
In dutiful mood his master to seek.
The saint outstretched in his cell he found,
The pure in heart in the hallowed place,
10 Wasted and weak awaiting his end.
The day was at noon, his death was near;
His breath came slow as he spoke to his thane:
"Now listen well to my last request,
My darling child, and do my bidding.
15 When the breath of life has left my body,
Haste to deliver my latest message.
The long way take, to tell my sister
Of my happy departure to heaven above,
And joy eternal. Tell her also
20 That here I refrained from beholding her face
Through all these years of our earthly life,
Because I wished that we should meet
In heaven above, in bliss eternal,
Before the face of the father of lights,
25 United in love that shall never be broken,
Sinless and stainless, possessing forever
Our hearts' desire in the heavenly city,
Midst brightest angels; bid her also
To lay in the grave my lifeless body
30 Cover my limbs with loam of earth,
Coffined in darkness to dwell for long,

Hold and inhabit the house of clay."   (*1169*)

Troubled in thought, the thane replied:
"By the grace of Him that guardeth our souls
I implore thee to answer and ease my pain.
5 Near is thy end, as I know by thy words.
Often my heart has been heavy with sorrow;
In the dark night-watches never I dared
To question or call thee, my comforter dear.
Often at eve, at the hour of twilight
10 When the gleaming light of the glorious sun,
Bright candle of day, declined in the west,
With another I heard thee holding converse;
I was 'ware of the voice of a visitor strange,
'Twixt waning of day and dark of the night.
15 And sometimes at dawn I seemed to hear,
In the morning gray, a murmur of voices.
My spirit was troubled: those strange communings
Filled me with fear, and fain would I know,
If thou, dear master, art minded to tell me,
20 Who it may be and whence he hath come."
In silence long the saint endured;
At last he answered his loved disciple,
With voice that faltered, and vanishing strength:
"The thing thou askest, my thane beloved,
25 I meant to tell to no mortal on earth;
To thee alone at last I reveal it.   (*1204*)
When the days of my sojourn, spent in the desert,
Had lengthened to years, the Lord of victory
Sent from heaven a holy spirit.
30 Often at morn that messenger fair
Like a conquerer came from the King of glory,

Or descended at eve, that angel of light,   (*1217*)
And solace sweet to my solitude brought,
Healing and hope and help in affliction,
My mind he stored with manifold wisdom,
5 Mysteries high.   No mortal may know
What hidden things that herald of God
Revealed to my heart, nor have I leave
To unseal the secret to soul alive."   (*1224*)

Then sank to the wall the weary saint,   (*1243*)
10 And bowed his head.   Yet brave was his spirit;
Calmly he breathed.   There came from his mouth
A fragrance sweet, as in summer time
The air is filled with odors rich
From fields of honey-brimmed flowers abloom.
15 So all day long, till evening fell,
This breathéd sweetness still uprose
From the lips of the saint.   When the lordly sun
Had sought his bed, and black under clouds
Of the northern skies the night came on,
20 Folding in mist the face of the earth,
Shrouding her beauty in shadows of gloom,
A sudden brightness broke from the sky,
A radiance holy, from heaven sent,
Illumined the night.   Beneath it lay
25 In blessed mood the man of God,
Awaiting his end.   So all night long,
Pure o'er the pure, the precious beam
Brightly shone.   The shadows black
Were swept from the sky.   The splendor shed
30 Its holy light round the hut of the saint,
From evening gloom, till glow of dawn

Brought up from the east, o'er ocean waves,   (*1266*)
The glorious sun. Then Guthlac rose
In the strength of his spirit, and spoke to his thane,
His comrade true: "The time has come
5 That thou must leave me. Bethink thee well
Of all that I bid thee, and bring my message
To the sister I love. My spirit yearns
To flee from my body to the bliss of heaven."
He lifted his hands, his heart refreshed
10 By the sacrament holy, the soul's pure food,
Opened his eyes, with ardor aglow,
Heavenward gazed, and gave up his spirit
Glad and rejoicing, in glory to dwell.

Then Guthlac's soul was guided to heaven;
15 Flights of angels upward bore it
To bliss eternal. His body grew cold
As it lay 'neath the sky. A light shone forth,
Brightest of beams; like a beacon it marked
The cell of the saint; the sacred glow
20 Up from the floor, like a flaming tower,
Straight arose to the roof of heaven.
More fair it showed than the shining sun,
Clear as star-light. Choirs angelic
Jubilant sang. The joyous strains
25 Of their heavenly song fell soft on the ear,
And all the space within was filled
With odors sweet and air-borne music,
And echoings far of angel voices,
More wondrous-strange and winsome-fair
30 Than tongue of man may tell on earth.
And mightier now the melody swelling

Peal on peal, the plain o'erflowed   *(1299)*
And rocked the isle. Then ran affrighted
The comrade of Guthlac, till he came to his boat.
Straight he embarked, and stricken with woe
5 His wave-steed o'er the flood he urged.
After sport on the billows the boat made land,
Grated the shingle. But grief held sway
In the heart of the thane as he thought in woe
Of the master beloved he had left behind,
10 His dearest friend, dead on the isle.
His heart was wrung, and hot tears rolled
Down o'er his cheek, as he chose his way.
So he came at last where the lady was,
The winsome maiden. Wyrd he hid not,
15 The doomed man's death. A dirge he chanted,
These words he spoke bewailing his friend:
"Endurance is best in the blows of affliction,
When the hour woven by Wyrd is come.
My lord, thy brother, the best of men
20 That ever was known in England's realm,
The bulwark of friends and defense of the needy,
Has gone to God from the gladness of life,
To seek his heavenly home above.
He told me to say that soon thou too
25 Mayest join him there in joy eternal,
And live in bliss. He bade thee also
To lay in the grave his lifeless body,
And cover his limbs with loam of earth.
And now, dear maid, thou knowest my errand.
Heavy with grief, I go from hence."

II. Lyric Poetry

1. RELIGIOUS LYRIC

Cædmon

NORTHUMBRIAN HYMN

Now hymn we aloud the Lord of Heaven,
Praise His wisdom and wonderful power,
The glorious works of the great Creator,
How the Father Eternal founded this world.
5 First He set for the sons of men,
Heaven to roof them. The Holy Ruler,
The King of mankind, then cast the foundations
Of earth in the midst, and made thereafter
Land for the living, the Lord Almighty.

Cynewulf

HYMN OF PRAISE

(From The *Crist,* lines 348-377)

Hail thou Holy One, Heaven's Ruler,
Thou of old wert equal with the Father,
God in the Highest, in Thy glorious home!
No angel was yet created in heaven,
5 None of the mighty unnumbered host,
That keep the realms of the kingdom on high,
Worshipping God the Wielder of majesty,
When Thou with the Father didst first establish
The firm foundations of the far-spread world.
10 Ye share alike the Spirit of Comfort,
Enthroned on high. We therefore pray Thee
With humble hearts, to help Thy servants.
O Saviour Christ, we call to Thee
To hear the cries of Thy captive people,
15 Woe-entangled by wayward wills,
Fettered fast by the fiends of hell,
Cast into chains by the crew accursed,
And held in bondage. Our hope is in Thee;
Thou alone canst deliver Thy people.
20 Help us miserable, by the might of Thy coming!
Comfort us who suffer, and save us disconsolate,
Though we have offended with our faults against
Thee.
Have mercy on Thy servants, remember our infirmi-
ties,

How we fail and falter with feeble hearts,
How shamefully we all have erred from Thy ways.
No longer delay, our Lord and Redeemer,
Come and deliver us, O King of Thy people!
5 We need Thy grace, and the gift of Thy salvation,
That henceforth more worthily we may worship Thy
    name,
Walk in Thy ways, and Thy will perform.

(From The *Crist,* lines 850-866)

10 Our life is likest a long sea-voyage:
O'er the water cold in our keels we glide,
O'er Ocean-streams, in our stallions of the deep
We drive afar. 'Tis a dreary waste
Of ceaseless surges we sail across,
15 In this wavering world, o'er wind-swept tracts
Of open sea. Anxious the struggle,
Ere we bring at last our barks to land,
O'er the rough sea-ridges. Our rescue is near;
The Son of God doth safely guide us,
20 Helps us in to our harbor of refuge;
Shows from the deck the sheltered waters,
Where smoothly to anchor our ancient chargers,
Hold with hawsers our horses of the deep.
Then fix we our hope on that haven of safety
25 That the Prince of Glory prepared for us all,
The Ruler on high, when He rose to heaven.

DOOMSDAY

(From The *Crist*, lines 867-1006)

Lo! on a sudden, and all unlooked for,
In the dead of the night, the day of the Lord
5 Shall break tremendous on man and beast,
O'erwhelming the world and the wide creation,
As a ruthless robber, ranging at night,
Who strides through the dark with stealthy pace,
And suddenly springs on sleep-bound heroes,
10 Greets with violence his victims unguarded.

A mighty host on the mount of Sion
Shall gather together, glad and rejoicing,
The faithful of the Lord, they shall find their reward.

With one accord from the quarters four,
15 And uttermost ends of the earth at once,
Glorious angels together shall blow
Their shattering trumpets; the trembling earth
Shall shake and sink, as they sound together,
Piercing strong to the starry track.
20 Their music swells from the South and North,
From East and from West, o'er the world's wide
round.
They wake from the dead to the day of judgment
The children of men, with their challenge dread.
Out of their ancient earth and mold,
25 Forth from their sleep profound they wake them.
Howling with fear, they shall huddle and flock,
Moaning and groaning, aghast with terror,
Bewailing the deeds that were done in the body.

Eye hath not seen a sight more awful,   (*892*)
To men shall appear no portent more dread:
Sinners and saints in strange confusion,
Mingled together shall mount from their graves,
5 The bright and the black: for both shall arise,
Some fair, some foul, as foreordained
To different home, of devils or angels.

From South and East o'er Sion's top,
In sudden radiance the sun shall flame
10 From the throne of God; more gleaming-bright,
Than man may imagine, or mind conceive.
Resplendent it shines, as the Son of God
Dazzling breaks through the dome of heaven.
Glorious appears the presence of Christ,
15 The King as He comes, through the clouds in the East,
Merciful and mild in mind, to his own;
But with altered mood of anger toward the wicked:
Unlike His looks for the lost and the blest. . . . (*909*)

The greedy spirit of consuming flame   (*972*)
20 Shall leap o'er the land, and the lofty halls;
With the terror of fire shall fill the world.
The battle-thirsty flame shall blaze afar,
Devouring the earth, and all therein.
Strong-built walls shall split and crumble;
25 Mountains shall melt, and the mighty cliffs
That buttress the earth 'gainst battering waves,
Bulwarks upreared 'gainst the rolling billows,
Shall fall on a sudden. The sweep of the fire
Shall leave no bird nor beast alive.
30 The lurid flame shall leap along the world,

Like a raging warrior. Where the waters flowed
In a bath of fire the fish shall be stifled; *(985)*
Sundered from life, their struggles over;
The monsters of the deep no more shall swim.
5 Like molten wax the water shall burn.
More marvels shall appear than mind may conceive,
When tempest and whirlwind o'erwhelm the earth,
And rocks are riven by the roaring blast.
Men shall wail, they shall weep and lament,
10 Groan aghast with grovelling fear.
The smoke-dark flame o'er the sinful shall roll,
The blaze shall consume their beakers of gold,
All the ancient heirlooms of kings.
The shrieks of the living shall shrill aloud
15 Mid the crack of doom, their cry of fear,
Their howl of despair, as they struggle to hide.
No guilty wretch shall refuge find,
Not one shall escape the scorching flame;
On all it shall seize, as it sweeps through the world.
20 It shall leap and run and ruthlessly bore
In the bowels of the earth, it shall burn aloft,
Till the ancient stains of earthly sin
By the purging billows are burnt away.

THE VISION OF THE CROSS

(Ascribed to Cynewulf)

List to the words of a wondrous vision,
25 Dream that I dreamt in the dead of night,
When stilled in sleep were the sons of men!
Methought on a sudden I saw a cross

Upreared in the sky, and radiant with light.   (5)
Brightest of trees, that beauteous beacon
Was dipped in gold, and bedight with jewels:
Four at the base, and five on the beam
5 Glistened on high; 'twas no gallows-tree,
Emblem of shame, but the souls of the blest
Were gazing upon it, God's bright angels,
The glorious creation, all kindreds of men.
'Twas a tree of triumph; but troubled was I,
10 Stained with sin, as I stood and gazed
On the Cross of glory, aglow with light.
Layers of gold, and glittering jewels
Covered its bark, and buried the wood.
Still through the gold that garnished its side,
15 I was 'ware of wounds where once it had bled,
Scars of a battle old. I was bowed with sorrow;
But the vision filled me with fear when I saw
That it changed its hue—now chased with gold,
Now stained with blood and streaming wet!
20 Long I lay thus, looking in sadness
At the Saviour's Cross, when sudden I heard it
Making melody, marked it singing;
Wondrous words the wood did utter:
"Many years ago,
          —yet I remember it all—
25 Fast by a forest-side,
          they felled me where I grew,
Severed me from my stock;
          strong foes took and shaped me
For a spectacle to men;
          made me bear their criminals,
Bore me away on their backs,
          bade me stand on a hill-top,

Band of fiends there fixed me.
  I saw the Friend of Man,
Haste with mighty hardihood
  to mount on high and clasp me.
I durst not bend nor falter,
  nor disobey my Lord;
Though I marked how all the earth
  with mighty tremblings shook.
5 The fiends I might have felled there,
  but firm I stood unshaken.
Then stripped the mighty hero,
  in sooth 'twas God Almighty.
He clomb the towering cross,
  with spirit keen and daring;
Bold in sight of the rabble,
  when our race he would deliver.
I trembled as he embraced me,
  yet bow to earth I durst not,
10 Nor prostrate fall with fear.
  'Stand fast,' my Lord commanded;
I stood, a cross uplifted!
  the King of glory I carried,
Upheld the Lord of heaven;
  my head I durst not bow.
With gruesome nails they gored me,
  the gaping wounds are open;
In bitter malice scarred me,
  strike back at the fiends I durst not.
15 They mocked us both and beat us,
  with blood my sides were running,
That flowed from the Saviour's body,
  when he bowed his head in death.

Much I endured on that mount of woe,   (50)
Throes and hate, for there I beheld
The God of hosts, hanging outstretched.
A pall of darkness dimmed his glory,
5 Shrouded his body. The shadow rushed on,
Black under clouds, all creatures wailed;
Christ was on the cross; their King was dead!

Soon a band I beheld,
    hastening swiftly forward,
Comrades seeking their Lord;
    (clearly I saw it all.)
10 Stricken with grief profound,
    forward I stooped to help them,
Eagerly bending low.
    They lifted Him down from the cross,
Released from his bitter agony;
    alone they left me there,
Standing steeped in blood,
    wounded with shafts of malice.
They folded His weary limbs,
    and watched at the head of his body;
15 Looked intent on their Lord,
    the while He took His rest,
Forspent with heavy toil.
    Then full in sight of His slayers
They hastened to hollow a grave,
    hewn from glistening marble;
Buried the Lord of Victory,
    and chanted a lay of mourning,
Sadly at eventide;
    then sorrowing took their leave;

Went from the Lord of glory.
　　There He rested alone.

Long I stood, deserted by all;　　　　　　　　(70)
At last they felled me,—fearful my fate;
They dug a ditch, and deep they buried me.
5 Erelong I was found by friends of my Lord,　　(76)
Who straightway adorned me with silver and gold.
Here mayest thou learn, my hero beloved,
What woe I endured, what work of felons,
What trials sore.　Now the time is come
10 That far and wide o'er the world I am honored.
All kindreds of men, the mighty creation,
Kneel to this sign.　For the Son of God
On me did suffer!　This makes me glory!
Sublime I am lifted aloft in the sky,
15 With might to heal all men who adore me.
Once I was set for a sign of woe,
A mark of shame, ere I showed to men,
Wandering lost, the way of life.
God who is Lord of glory, exalted me
20 High o'er the towering trees of the forest." . . . (91)

With happy heart I hailed the cross,　　　　　(122)
And fervent zeal.　No friend was near;
Alone I knelt.　I longed to depart;
My soul was eager to start on her journey.
25 Late I had lingered, my life's desire
Was to come to the cross, the conqueror's beacon:
More oft than other men, ever alone,
To worship it worthily, wanting but this:
To look on the cross whence cometh my help.

Friends have I few to defend and comfort me; (*131*)
They have left the life and delight of the world;
They have gone to greet the King of glory;
They are folded in bliss with the Father on high;
5 They live in the light of the Lord of angels;
My heart beats high for the happy day
When the cross of Christ shall come once more
To fetch me away from this fleeting life,
Bring me home to the bliss of heaven,
10 Where the saints of God sit at the feast,
Joined in raptures of joy eternal.   (*144*)

May he who suffered for the sins of men (*145-156*)
On the cross of shame, show me the way,
Guide me in grace to the goal of my hope,
15 That so I may join the saints in their joy,
And dwell forever in realms of bliss.

THE PHOENIX

(Ascribed to Cynewulf)

Lo, I have heard of a happy land
Far in the East, of a fair country,
Happier, fairer, than earth-folk know.
20 Far remote the mighty Creator
Planted this realm, where few may reach it;
Sinful mortals seek it in vain.
Blest are those fields, abloom with the fragrance
Of all sweet odors that earth exhales.
25 Peerless the island, peerless her maker,
Glorious the Lord who laid her foundations.

Her happy people hear glad singing,   (11)
Oft through Heaven's open door.
Green are her woodlands, green and ample,
Under her rainless roof outspread.
5 Winter's breath or blast of fire,
Driving hail or hoar-frost dreary,
Heat of sun or cold incessant,
Scorching noons or sleeting north-winds
Ne'er may harm this happy island.
10 Blest it lies, abloom with flowers.
Ever the same through the seasons' change.
No mountain ramparts mar those regions;
No rugged heights, as here with us;
No hill-sides steep, or hollows deep;
15 No crags or clefts, no caves or dens;
But smoothest lawns and sunny levels
Of joyful flowers face those skies.
Fathoms twelve the fair land towers
(So wise men have writ in records old)
20 O'er the loftiest peak that lifts its head,
Here among us, up to the skies.

'Tis a region calm of sunny groves
Woodlands glad, whose wondrous trees
Stand fair and fresh in unfading hues,
25 Goodly and green at God's behest.
Ever the same, summer and winter,
In living green those groves are clad,
Laden with fruit. No leaf shall waste
No branch be blackened with blast of lightning
30 Till doomsday come. When the deluge swept
With might of waters the world of men,

And the flood o'erwhelmed the whole of earth,   (43)
This isle withstood the storm of billows
Serene and steadfast 'mid raging seas
Spotless and pure by the power of God.
5 Thus blest it abides till the bale-fire come,
The day of doom when death's dark chambers,
Abodes of shade, shall be broken asunder.
No envious strife disturbs that isle;
No tears or toil or trace of woe;
10 Needy age, or narrow death;
Foe's assault, or sudden end;
No sin or sorrow, or sore distress;
No grinding want, or wealth uncertain,
No bitter care, or bed of pain;
15 No wintry weather's wild encounter
Of crashing storms, no cruel frost
Beats any man there with icy showers.
No sleet or snow assails that isle;
No pelting rains pour from the clouds,
20 Lashed by the gale; but living streams
Wondrously gush from woodland springs,
Lapping the earth with limpid ripples.
Each month of the year in the midmost grove
The winsome waters well sea-cold
25 From the mossy turf; at the time appointed
Wind through the wood in wandering streams.
For God decreed that the joy of waters
Should twelve times play through that land of plenty
Thick hangs the fruit in the forest-glades;
30 The shining clusters never decay,
The holy burden of the bending trees.
No withered blooms are wafted down;

No leaves are shed; but laden boughs   (75)
Of bounteous ever-bearing trees
Yield ever-fresh and fragrant fruit.
Green are the groves on the grassy sward
5 Decked and adorned by the deed of God,
In beauty unwasting. Through the woodlands bright
A holy fragrance floats and hovers.
Changeless through ages the isle shall remain,
Till He that uplifted the land at the first
10 Shall end his wisdom's ancient work.

A glorious bird guardeth this grove,
Noble in flight, Phœnix by name.
Alone in the land he liveth, a hermit;
Proudly dwelleth, proof against death,
15 In this wood of delight, while the world endures.
'Tis said he watches the way of the sun,
Eager to greet the candle of God,
The gleaming gem, and joyously waits
Till the day-star come at dawn from the east,
20 Shining bright o'er the billowy sea,
First of lights by the Father created,
Glorious sign of God. When the stars are gone,
Dipped in the waves of the western sea,
Or hid in the dawn, and dusky night
25 Darkling departs, then poised for flight
The strong-winged Phœnix scans the ocean,
Sky and wave, and waits the time
When the glorious light shall glide from the east
And radiant rise o'er the rounding sea.
30 This peerless bird abides by the fountain,
Haunting ever the hallowed streams.

Twelve times bathes in the bubbling spring,   (*106*)
Dipping his plumes ere day arrive,
And the twinkle of dawn; twelve times sips
The waters that well sea-cold, and wets
5 His beak at each bath in the bourne of delight.
Then after his water-play wings him triumphant
Aloft to a tree-top towering high,
Whence in the east he may easily see
The road of the sun, when rising clear,
10 The lamp of heaven shall glitter and gleam
O'er the welter of waves. The world is brightened,
In beauty glows, as the glorious gem
Flashes o'er ocean, inland afar,
Lordly day-star lighting the earth.
15 As soon as the sun o'er the salty streams,
On high doth soar, the haughty bird
Joyfully leaves his lofty perch,
Darting upward on dauntless wing,
And singing exultant, seeks the light.
20 Glorious the greeting he giveth the sun,
His spirit athrill with rapture of bliss;
Warbling melodies wondrous sweet,
With various art and voice more clear
Than ever men heard the heavens beneath,
25 Since the King of Glory, the great Creator,
Established the world. More winsome far
Than any music that men may make;
And sweeter than any earthly strain,
This trancing song. No sound of trump
30 Or horn or harp; or harmonies clear
Of organ-pipes; or purest tones
Of mortal voice, or music of the swan,

Or aught that God hath given to cheer   (*138*)
Earth's heavy toil, may touch this song.
He carols and sings in unceasing delight
Till the sun descends in the southern sky;
5 Then sinketh his song and silent falls,
The beautiful bird then bows his head
And listening alert lifteth his wings
Beating them thrice, then bideth at rest.
Ever he notes the turn of the hours
10 Twelve times by day and twelve times by night.

The lord of this grove hath leave to enjoy
At his will the wealth of this wondrous isle,
Life and delight in a land of plenty,
Until he is worn with winters a thousand
15 Of life upon earth, alone in the wood.
Then aged and wise with the weight of years
Hovers on high the hoary-plumed Phœnix,
Leaves the green island and flowering plains,
Wingeth his flight to a wide-spreading realm,
20 A lonely and uninhabited land.
There he inherits a kingdom mighty;
Bold o'er the bird-tribes beareth rule;
Lives for a season, and lords it among them,
Glorious grown, and guardeth the realm.
25 But soon he departs on swiftest pinions,
Westward winging his wondrous flight;
Thick the bird-tribes throng round their leader,
Each of them eager to aid their lord.
At length he comes to the coast of Syria,
30 With his countless horde. Then harshly thrusting
The throng away, he wheels him aside;

Seeketh a dense wood's deepest shelter   (*170*)
To hide from the crowd in the covert dark.
Tall in the grove a great tree towers,
Firmly rooted 'neath heaven's roof,
5 Named from the bird, and known as the Phœnix.
The Maker of man, the mighty Creator,
Hath granted a glorious growth to this tree.
I have heard that it passes in height by far
The tallest tree that towers on earth;
10 Its foliage fair shall flourish and thrive;
Blight shall not touch it, its branches shall wave,
Winsome and green while the world endures.

When winds are laid and weather is calm,
The lamp of heaven shines holy and pure;
15 Clouds are scattered and skies are clear;
The mighty surge of the sea is stilled;
Storms are asleep and warm in the south
Gleams the sun and gladdens the world.
Then begins the bird to build in the branches,
20 To furnish his nest for his hour of need,
When his spirit's fervor shall urge him to change
The years of his age, restoring his youth,
And renewing his life. From near and far
He gathers together the goodliest herbs;
25 Blossoms and leaves he brings from the wood;
Fills with fragrance his forest-abode;
Culls each sweet that the King of glory,
The Father, created o'er earth's wide realm,
To charm and delight the children of men.
30 So he collects the loveliest blossoms;
Treasures bright he brings to the tree.

Soon in the solitude's deep recess   *(202)*
A winsome bower the wild bird builds him,
A home in the tree-top; and houses him there,
High aloft in the leafy shade;
5 Surrounds himself with richest spices,
Herbs the rarest that earth may yield;
Makes for his body a bed of blossoms,
Fain to depart. With folded pinions
He watcheth on high and awaiteth his hour.
10　When overhead the sun in summer
Out of heaven hottest shines,
The scathing heat scorches his house;
The blossoms are warmed; the bower smokes
With incense sweet, and bursts into flame;
15 Bird and nest are burned together:
The blaze is kindled, the bale-fire wraps
In roaring flames his wretched abode,
And fiercely feeds on the Phœnix hoar,
Ancient of years. His aged body
20 Is prey to the flames: his fleeting spirit,
Hastens to its doom, when the hot blast sunders
Flesh from bone. Yet the breath of life
In the fulness of time returneth again.
Soon as the flickering flame subsides,
25 The ashes are knit and kneaded together:
When the beautiful nest is burnt to a cinder,
And body and bones of the bird are crumbled,
In the waning glow of the whitening embers
A ball is found, in the bed of ashes
30 Rolled together, round like an apple;
Out of it comes a curious creature,
Wondrous in hue, as though it were hatched,

Shining bright, from the shell of an egg.   (234)
It grows in the shade to the shape of an eaglet,
A nestling fair, then further increases,
Lustily thriving, larger still,
5 Equalling soon an eagle in size.
At length he is fledged with feathers gay,
Bright as of old with beauteous plumes,
His body renewed by the birth of fire,
Taint of evil all taken away.
10 Like as when men in the month of harvest
Gather for food the fruits of the earth;
Garner their crops 'gainst coming of winter;
Shelter and shield them from showers and storms,
Laying in stores and living in plenty,
15 While roaring winter rages amain,
And covers the fields with coat of snow;
Out of those winter-stores, wealth abounding
Shall come through the germ of life in the corn,
Cleanly sown as a seed in the spring.
20 When the sun returns, the token of life,
And his warm rays waken the wealth of the world,
Sprouteth afresh each fruit of the earth,
Each in its own kind quickened and kindled
To brighten the field. So the Phœnix old
25 After many years his youth renews;
Is girt again with a garment of flesh.
Earthly food he refuseth to touch,
Save that he drinketh drops of honey-dew
That often fall at midnight hour;
30 Tasting nought else until he revisit
His own abode and ancient home.   (264)

. . . .

THE PHOENIX A SYMBOL OF THE RESURRECTION

A man of God, with mind prophetic,   (570)
Sang of old a song inspired;
Foretold his rising to life eternal.
That we more readily might read the meaning
5 Of the fate of the Phœnix,—his fiery death:
When he brings away his body's remnant;
Gathers the ashes and embers together,
Clasped in his claws, and carries them off,
Flying sunward, when the flame subsides,
10 To the courts of the Lord, where he lives secure
Through countless years, all young again.
No foe infests that fair domain;
No hardship there can harm him further.
Thus body and soul, by the Saviour's might
15 Joined after death, shall journey together
To the land of delight, laden with savor
Of incense sweet, like the soaring Phœnix,
Where high o'er the hosts, in the house of glory,
The Sun of Righteousness radiant streams.

20 When the Saviour Christ on the souls of the blest
Shines from on high, toward heaven's gate
They mount, like beautiful birds, to meet him;
Glad is the song and glorious the shape
Of the spirits-elect in that land of joy,
25 Where envy and malice no more shall touch them:
For ever and ever from evil free,
They live in peace, apparelled in light,
Girt with glory, by God defended,
Like the Phœnix wondrous. The works of each
30 Sun-like gleam and glow in splendor,

Bright before the face of the Lord,   (600)
In clear abodes of blessed calm.
A crown of glory glittering bright,
Studded round with rarest jewels,
5 Decks the brow of each blessed saint.
The radiance floods their foreheads shining;
God's diadem adorns the righteous
With jewelled light.   They live in joy
Endless, immortal, and ever renewed,
10 In bliss secure and clothed in beauty;
At home with the Father of angels in heaven
No sorrow haunts those happy mansions;
No danger, dread, nor days of toil;
No parching thirst, nor pangs of hunger;
15 No need, nor age; the noble King
Dispenseth bounty; the spirit-host
Praise their Redeemer, the Prince of Heaven;
Honor and magnify the might of the Lord;
Shouting glad, that glorious company
20 Surround on high God's holy throne;
Saints and angels sing triumphant,
Worshipping God with one accord:
"Peace be to Thee true God!   Power and Wisdom!
Thanks to Thee evermore, throned in majesty,
25 For the gifts Thy grace doth grant us anew,
Boundless in might, dominion and glory,
High and holy!   The heavens above,
Abode of the angels, and the earth also,
Father Almighty, are full of thy majesty;
30 Thou Glory of glories, and greatest of kings!
Defend us Creator, Thou Father Almighty,
And Ruler of Heaven, who reignest on high."

Thus hymn aloud the host of the righteous,   (632)
Cleansed from guilt, in the glorious city;
Publish the praise of the Prince of Heaven;
The choir of saints keep singing on high:
5 "To Him alone belongeth all honor
Thanksgiving and worship, world without end!
Never His glory hath known a beginning,
Though He chose to be born a child upon earth,
Here among men, yet the might of His power
10 High o'er the heavens in holiness dwelt,
In glory undimmed. Though death's sharp pang
He bore on the cross, and bitter woe,
The third day after the throes of his passion
Laid low his body. He was brought to life
15 By the Father's grace. So the Phœnix stands
For a sign of the power of the Son of God,
When he wakes to the life of life from his ashes,
Girt with limbs in the glory of youth.
Thus by the sundring of soul and body,
20 To life everlasting our Lord did help us,
Even as the Phœnix, eager for flight,
Loadeth his wings with winsome herbs,
And sweetest blossoms that bloom upon earth."

Such is the burden, as scriptures tell us,
25 The songs of the saints whose souls have departed
To the joy of joys, on the journey to heaven,
And the God of grace. For a gift to the Lord
They bring a sweet-smelling savor on high
Of words and works, in that world of bliss
30 And radiant life. Render to Him
Praise and Honor, Power and Glory;

Worship and Wisdom, World without end,   (663)
In heaven above. He only is King
Of earth's wide round, and the realms of light,
With splendor girt in that glorious city.
5 Leave hath granted us *lucis auctor,*
That here we might *merueri;*
By good deeds gain *gaudia in celo;*
That so we men *maxima regna*
Might reach, and sit in *sedibus altis;*
10 Live in delight *lucis et pacis;*
Enter our home *almae letitiae;*
In bliss immortal, *blandem et mitem*
See our Saviour *sine fine;*
Prolong his praises *laude perenne,*
15 In bliss with the angels. *Alleluia.*

2. SECULAR LYRIC AND ELEGY

THE WANDERER

Many a lonely man at last comes to honor;
Merits God's mercy, though much he endured
On wintry seas, with woe in his heart,
Dragging his oar through drenching-cold brine,
20 Homeless and houseless and hunted by Wyrd.

These are the words of a wayfaring wanderer,
This is his song of the sorrow of life,
Slaughter of foemen, felling of kinsmen:

Oft in the dark, alone before dawning,
25 All to myself my sorrow I tell.

No friend have I here, to whom I may open   (11)
My heart's deep secret, my hidden spring of woe.
Well do I know 'tis the way of the high-born,
Fast in his heart to fetter his feelings,
5 Lock his unhappiness in the hold of his mind.
Spirit that sorrows withstandeth not destiny,
Heart that complaineth plucketh no help.
A haughty hero will hide his suffering,
Manfully master misery's pang.
10 Thus stricken with sorrow, stript of my heritage,
Far from kinsmen and country and friends,
Grimly I grappled my grief to my bosom,
Since long time ago, my giver of bounty
Was laid in the earth, and left me to roam
15 Watery wastes, with winter in my heart.
Forsaken I sought a shielder and protector;
Far and near I found none to greet the wanderer,
No master to make him welcome in his wine-hall;
None to cheer the cheerless, or the friendless to be-
       friend.

20 He who has lost all his loved companions
Knoweth how bitter a bedfellow is sorrow.
Loneliness his lot, not lordly gold,
Heart-chilling frost, not harvest of plenty.
Oft he remembers the mirth of the mead-hall,
25 Yearns for the days of his youth, when his dear lord
Filled him with abundance. Faded are those joys!
He shall know them no more; no more shall he listen
To the voice of his lord, his leader and counsellor.
Sometimes sleep and sorrow together
30 Gently enfold the joyless wanderer:

Bright are his dreams, he embraces his lord again,
Kisses his liege, and lays on his knee   (*42*)
Head and hands as in happy days,
When he thanked for a boon his bountiful giver.
5 Wakes with a start the wanderer homeless;
Nought he beholds but the heaving surges,
Seagulls dipping and spreading their wings,
Scurries of snow and the scudding hail.
Then his heart is all the heavier,
10 Sore after sweet dreams sorrow reviveth.
Fain would he hold the forms of his kinsmen,
Longingly leans to them, lovingly greets them;
Slowly their faces swim into distance;
No familiar greeting comes from the fleeting
15 Companies of kinsmen.   Care ever shadows
The way of the traveller, whose track is on the waters,
Whose path is on the billows of the boundless deep.

Behold I know not how I may keep
My heart from sinking, heavy with sorrow,
20 When all life's destiny deeply I ponder,—
Men that are suddenly snatched in their prime,
High-souled heroes; so the whole of this earth
Day by day droopeth and sinketh to decay. . . (*63*)
How dread is the doom of the last desolation,   (*73*)
25 When all the wealth of the world shall be waste,
He that is wise may learn, if he looks
Abroad o'er this land, where lonely and ruinous,
Wind-swept walls, waste are standing;
Tottering towers, crusted with frost,
30 Crumbling wine-halls, bare to the sky.
Dead is their revelry, dust are the revellers!

Some they have fallen on far fields of battle,   *(81)*
Some have gone down in ships on the sea;
Some were the prey of the prowling gray-wolf,
Some by their loved ones were laid in the earth.
5 The Lord of the living hath levelled their mansions,
Silenced the sound of the singing and laughter.
Empty and bare are all their habitations,
Wondrous works of the giants of old.

He that considers this scene of desolation,
10 And this dark life deeply doth ponder,—
Battle and bloodshed, burning and slaughter,
It bringeth to mind, and mournfully he asks:
Where is the warrior, where is the war-horse?
Where is the giver of bounty, where are the boon-
        companions,
15 The "dream and the gleam" that gladdened the hall?
Alas the bright ale-cup, alas the brave warrior!
Alas the pride of princes!   Their prime is no more;
Sunk under night's shadow, as though it never had
        been!
Where lusty warriors thronged, this lone wall towers,
20 Weird with dragon-shapes, wondrously carven;
Storm of ash-spears hath stricken the heroes,
Blood-thirsty weapons, Wyrd the supreme.
Wintry blasts now buffet these battlements;
Dreary snow-storms drift up the earth,
25 The terror of winter when wild and wan
Down from the north with the darkness drives
The ruinous scourge of the ruthless hail.

All this life is labor and sorrow,
Doom of destiny darkens o'er earth.

Wealth is fleeting, friends are fleeting,
Man is fleeting, maid is fleeting,
All this earth's foundations utterly shall pass. (*110*)

THE SEA-FARER

The poem translated below, has been interpreted as a dialogue
between a weather-beaten old sailor and a youth eager to go to
sea. The parts are not assigned in the original MS., and the only
warrant for our dialogue form lies in the structure of the poem
itself.

The Old Sailor:

True is the tale that I tell of my travels,
5 Sing of my sea-faring sorrows and woes;
Hunger and hardship's heaviest burdens,
Tempest and terrible toil of the deep,
Daily I've borne on the deck of my boat.
Fearful the welter of waves that encompassed me,
10 Watching at night on the narrow bow,
As she drove by the rocks, and drenched me with
spray.
Fast to the deck my feet were frozen,
Gripped by the cold, while care's hot surges
My heart o'erwhelmed, and hunger's pangs
15 Sapped the strength of my sea-weary spirit.

Little he knows whose lot is happy,
Who lives at ease in the lap of the earth,
How, sick at heart, o'er icy seas,
Wretched I ranged the winter through,
20 Bare of joys, and banished from friends,

Hung with icicles, stung by hail-stones.   (*17*)
Nought I heard but the hollow boom
Of wintry waves, or the wild swan's whoop.
For singing I had the solan's scream;
5 For peals of laughter, the yelp of the seal;
The sea-mew's cry, for the mirth of the mead-hall.
Shrill through the roar of the shrieking gale
Lashing along the sea-cliff's edge,
Pierces the ice-plumed petrel's defiance,
10 And the wet-winged eagle's answering scream.

Little he dreams that drinks life's pleasure,
By danger untouched in the shelter of towns
Insolent and wine-proud, how utterly weary
Oft I wintered on open seas.
15 Night fell black, from the north it snowed
Harvest of hail.

The Youth:

Oh wildly my heart
Beats in my bosom and bids me to try
The tumble and surge of seas tumultuous,
20 Breeze and brine and the breakers' roar.
Daily, hourly, drives me my spirit
Outward to sail, far countries to see.
Liveth no man so large in his soul,
So gracious in giving, so gay in his youth,
25 In deeds so daring, so dear to his lord,
But frets his soul for his sea-adventure,
Fain to try what fortune shall send.
Harping he heeds not, nor hoarding of treasure;
Nor woman can win him, nor joys of the world.
30 Nothing doth please but the plunging billows;

Ever he longs, who is lured by the sea.   (47)
Woods are abloom, the wide world awakens,
Gay are the mansions, the meadows most fair;
These are but warnings, that haste on his journey
5 Him whose heart is hungry to taste
The perils and pleasures of the pathless deep.

The Old Sailor:

Dost mind the cuckoo mournfully calling?
The summer's watchman sorrow forbodes.
What does the landsman that wantons in luxury,
10 What does he reck of the rough sea's woe,
The cares of the exile, whose keel has explored
The uttermost parts of the ocean-ways!

The Youth:

Sudden my soul starts from her prison-house,
Soareth afar o'er the sounding main;
15 Hovers on high, o'er the home of the whale;
Back to me darts the bird-sprite and beckons,
Winging her way o'er woodland and plain,
Hungry to roam, and bring me where glisten
Glorious tracts of glimmering foam.
20 This life on land is lingering death to me,
Give me the gladness of God's great sea.   (66)

THE HUSBAND'S MESSAGE

An exile from his country sends to his wife overseas a mes-
age, bidding her join him in his new home where he has pros-
ered. The letters are cut on a tablet of wood, and the wood
tself is supposed to speak. Compare the *Vision of the Cross,*
nd the *Riddles* for this kind of dramatic personification.

See I bring thee a secret message!
A sapling once in the woods I grew;
I was cut for a stave and covered with writing,
Skilled men cunningly carved upon me
5 Letters fair, in a faraway land.
Since have I crossed the salt-streams often,
Carried in ships to countries strange;
Sent by my lord, his speech to deliver
In many a towering mead-hall high.
o Hither I've sped, the swift keel brought me,
Trial to make of thy trust in my master;
Look thou shalt find him loyal and true.

He told me to come, that carved this letter,
And bid thee recall, in thy costly array,
5 The pledges ye plighted, the promises fair
Ye gave to each other in days of old,
When still in the land ye lived together,
Happily mated, and held in the mead-halls
Your home and abode. A bitter feud
o Banished him far. He bids me call thee,
Earnestly urge thee overseas.

When thou hast heard, from the brow of the hill,
The mournful cuckoo call in the wood,   (22
Let no man living delay thy departure,
Hinder thy going, or hold thee at home.
5 Away to the sea, where the gulls are circling!
Board me a ship that's bound from the shore;
Sail away south, to seek thy own husband;
Over the water he waits for thee.

No keener joy could come to his heart,
10 No greater happiness gladden his soul,
Than if God who wieldeth the world, should grant
That ye together should yet give rings,
Treasure of gold to trusty liegemen.
A home he hath found in a foreign land,
15 Fair abode and followers true,
Hardy heroes, though hence he was driven;
Shoved his boat from the shore in distress,
Steered for the open, sped o'er the ocean,
Weary wave-tossed wanderer he.

20 Past are his woes, he has won through his perils,
He lives in plenty, no pleasure he lacks;
Nor horses nor goods nor gold of the mead-hall;
All the wealth of earls upon earth
Belongs to my lord, he lacks but thee.

III. Charms, Riddles, and Gnomic Poetry

1. CHARMS

THE PLOUGHMAN'S CHARM

Here is the remedy how thou mayest cure thy land if it refuses to bear, or if aught untoward hath befallen it by way of witchcraft or sorcery. Strew seed on the body of the plough and repeat these words:—

> Erce, Erce, Erce, Mother of Earth,   (49)
> May the Almighty, Lord Everlasting,
> Grant thee fields, green and fertile,
> Grant thee fields, fruitful and growing,
> 5 Hosts of Spear-shafts, shining harvests,
>   Harvest of Barley the broad,
>   Harvest of Wheat the white,
> All the heaping harvests of earth!
> May the Almighty Lord Everlasting,
> 10 And his holy saints in heaven above,
> From fiend and foe defend this land,
> Keep it from blight and coming of harm,
> From spell of witches wickedly spread!
> Now I pray the Almighty who made this world,
> 15 That malice of man, or mouth of woman
> Never may weaken the words I have spoken.

Start the plough, and when the first furrow is turned, say:—

>   Hail to thee Earth, Mother of men!   (67)

Grow and be great in God's embrace,
Filled with fruit for the food of men!

Knead a loaf of bread with milk and holy water, lay
it under the first furrow and say:—

Field be full of food for men,
5   Blossom bright, for blessed thou art
In the name of the Holy who made the Heavens,
Created the earth whereon we live.
God who gavest this ground
Grant us growth and increase
10 Let each seed that is sown, sprout and be useful.

CHARM FOR A SUDDEN STITCH

Take feverfew, and plantain, and the red nettle that
grows into the house. Boil in butter. Say:—

Loud was their cry as they came o'er the hill;
Fierce was their rage as they rode o'er the land.
Take heed and be healed of the hurt they have done thee.
    Out little spear if in there thou be!
15   My shield I lifted, my linden-wood shining,
When the mighty women mustered their force,
And sent their spear-points spinning toward me.
I'll give them back the bolt they sent,
A flying arrow full in the face.
20   Out little spear if in there thou be!
    Sat a smith,
    A hard blade hammered.
    Out little spear if in there thou be!
    Six smiths sat,

Fighting spears forged they.   (16)
　　　Out spear, out!
　　　No longer stay in!
If any iron be found herein,
5　The work of witches, away it must melt.
　　　Be thou shot in the fell,
　　　Be thou shot in the flesh,
　　　Be thou shot in the blood,
　　　Be thou shot in the bone,
10　　Be thou shot in the limb,
　　　Thy life shall be shielded.
　　　Be it shot of Esa,
　　　Be it shot of Elves,
　　　Be it shot of Hags,
15　　I help thee surely.
This for cure of Esa-shot,
This for cure of Elf-shot,
This for cure of Hag-shot,
　　　I help thee surely.
20　Witch fly away to the woods and the mountains.
Healed be thy hurt! So help thee the Lord.

2. RIDDLES

THE BOOK-WORM

A moth ate a word! To me that seemed
A strange thing to happen, when I heard that
　　　wonder,—
A worm that would swallow the speech of a man,
25　Sayings of strength steal in the dark,
Thoughts of the mighty; yet the thieving sprite
Was none the wiser for the words he had eaten!

GNATS

There's a troop of tiny folk travelling swift,
Brought by the breeze o'er the brink of the hill,
Buzzing black-coated bold little people,—
Noisy musicians; well-known is their song.
5 They scour the thickets, but sometimes invade
The rooms of the town.   Now tell me their names.

THE SHIELD

Wounded I am, and weary with fighting;
Gashed by the iron, gored by the point of it,
Sick of battle-work, battered and scarred.
10 Many a fearful fight have I seen, when
Hope there was none, or help in the thick of it,
Ere I was down and fordone in the fray.
Offspring of hammers, hardest of battle-blades,
Smithied in forges, fell on me savagely,
15 Doomed to bear the brunt and the shock of it,
Fierce encounter of clashing foes.
Leech cannot heal my hurts with his simples,
Salves for my sores have I sought in vain.
Blade-cuts dolorous, deep in the side of me,
20 Daily and nightly redouble my wounds.

BARNACLE ON THE HULL OF A SAILING-VESSEL

(OR BARNACLE-GOOSE)

I'm found under water, held fast by my mouth;
Swirl of the sea-tides goes sweeping beneath me.
Fathom-deep sunk under surges, I grew,

Bending roof of billows above me,
My body adrift on a floating beam.
You'll find me alive if you lift me and free me.
Dull is my coat as I come from the deep,
5 But straight I am decked with streamers of white,
Bright when the freshening breeze brings me from
    underseas,
Heaves me up, and urges me far   *the ocean?*
O'er the seal-bath salty. Say what I'm called.

HONEY-MEAD

I'm prized by men, in the meadows I'm found,
10 Gathered on hill-sides, and hunted in groves;
From dale and from down, by day I am brought.
Airy wings carry me, cunningly store me,
Hoarding me safe. Yet soon men take me;
Drained into vats, I'm dangerous grown.
15 I tie up my victim, and trip him, and throw him;
Often I floor a foolish old churl.
Who wrestles with me, and rashly would measure
His strength against mine, will straightway find him-
    self
Flung to the ground, flat on his back,
20 Unless he leave his folly in time,
Put from his senses and power of speech,
Robbed of his might, bereft of his mind,
Of his hands and feet. Now find me my name,
Who can bind and enslave men so upon earth,
25 And bring fools low in broad daylight.

THE ANCHOR

I war with the wind, with the waves I wrestle;
I must battle with both when the bottom I seek,
My strange habitation by surges o'er-roofed.
I am strong in the strife, while still I remain;
5 As soon as I stir, they are stronger than I.
They wrench and they wrest, till I run from my foes;
What was put in my keeping they carry away.
If my back be not broken, I baffle them still;
The rocks are my helpers, when hard I am pressed;
10 Grimly I grip them. Guess what I'm called.

THE PLOUGH

My beak is below, I burrow and nose
Under the ground. I go as I'm guided
By my master the farmer, old foe of the forest;
Bent and bowed, at my back he walks,
15 Forward pushing me over the field;
Sows on my path where I've passed along.
I came from the wood, a wagon carried me;
I was fitted with skill, I am full of wonders.
As grubbing I go, there's green on one side,
20 But black on the other my path is seen.
A curious prong pierces my back;
Beneath me in front, another grows down
And forward pointing is fixed to my head.
I tear and gash the ground with my teeth,
25 If my master steer me with skill from behind.

THE SWAN

My robe is silent, when I rest on earth,
Or run by the shore, or ruffle the pools;
But oft on my pinions upward I mount,
Borne to the skies on the buoyant air,

5 High o'er the haunts and houses of men,
Faring afar with the fleeting clouds.
Then sudden my feathers are filled with music.
They sing in the wind, as I sail aloft
O'er wave and wood, a wandering sprite.

Wind?

3. GNOMIC VERSES

(From the Cotton MS.)

10 The king shall rule his kingdom; castles are seen from
    afar,   (*1*)
Reared by giants, they rise in the land,
Wondrous walls of masonry. Wind is swiftest aloft;
Far is the thunder heard. Fair are the glories of
    Christ.
Wyrd is strongest, winter is coldest,

15 Lent is hoariest, 'tis latest cold.
Harvest is merriest, to men it brings
Fruits of the year, furnished by God.
Truth is plainest. Treasure is dearest,
Gold to the children of men. Gray hairs are wisest:

20 Who longest hath lived, hath learned the most.
Troubles shall cleave. Clouds shall dissolve.
Comrades good shall encourage an ætheling
To be brave in the fight, and free of his gold.
Earls shall be daring. Iron shall ring

Against helmet in battle.   Hooded, the falcon   (17)
Shall keep his wildness.   Wolf in the forest
Shall outlaw be.   Boar in the thicket
Shall tear with his tusks.   Trusty earl
To praise shall aspire.   Spear for the hand,
5 Gold-adorned javelin.   Jewel in ring
Shall richly be set.   River with sea
Shall mingle its stream.   Mast in the ship,
Sail on the yard, sword in the breast,
10 Iron that is doughty.   Dragon in the cave,
Fierce o'er his treasure.   Fish in the water
Shall spawn its kind.   King in the hall
Shall bracelets bestow.   Bear on the heath
Surly shall roam.   Stream from the hill-side
15 Gray shall gush.   Together shall stand
Troops of comrades.   Truth in an earl,
In councillors wisdom.   The woods shall bloom
With brightest hues; hills shall stand
Green on the earth.   God is in heaven,
20 To judge our deeds.   Door for the hall,
The building's mouth.   Boss for the shield,
Fingers to fend.   Fowls in the air
Shall sport and play.   Salmon in the pool
Shall dart and shoot.   Showers from the skies
25 Windy and wet on the world shall fall.
Thief shall stalk in the dark.   Giant shall dwell on
         the fen,
Alone on the moorland.   Maid shall in secret
Go to her friend, if she fail to be bought
With gold before her folk.   The flood shall be salt,
30 Waves of the ocean that wash the land,
And break on the shores.   The beast of the field

Shall breed and bring forth. Bright in the heavens
Stars shall glitter, as God hath bid them.   (*49*)
Good against evil; youth against age;
Light against dark; life against death;
5 Host against host shall harry the land,
Foe against foe with feud shall come,
Stirring up strife. The sage shall ponder
This warring world. The "wolf" shall hang,
Pay for the wrong he wrought upon earth,
10 His guilt among men; God alone knows
The place that his soul shall seek hereafter,
Bourne of the spirits that speed to their Maker,
When the stroke of death hath sent them to God,
Where they wait for their doom. Dark is the future,
15 Dark and hidden! He alone knows,
Our Helper in need; for none comes hither,
Revisits his home to reveal to men
What manner of mansions the Almighty inhabits,
What seats of glory are God's abode.

(From the *Exeter Book*)

20 As the sea is smooth when storms are at rest, (*55-56*)
So people are quiet when peace is proclaimed.

Ship shall be nailed, shield shall be bound   (*94*)
Lindenwood decked. Dear to the Frisian wife,
And welcome the sailor that stands at the door.
25 Home is her husband, his boat's in the harbor;
She bids him in, her own provider;
She washes his weedy coat; she gets him garments
          fresh.
'Tis dear on the land where a loved one is waiting.

Wife shall be true to the man she hath wedded. (*101*)
Faithful are many, but many are froward,
They will love a stranger when their lord is away.
Long doth the seaman stay on his voyage,
5 Weary the wife that waits her dear one.
Though bitter her lot, she bideth her hour;
Safe again home she shall see her husband,
Unless he is lying, lost and sunken,
Locked in the arms of the ocean vast.   (*107*)

10 Hapless outlaws shall house with the wolves; (*147*)
The treacherous beasts oft tear their comrade.
When the gray-wolf kills, there are graves to be
     filled,
His howls are heard as hungry he roams,
Prowling for prey; no pity in his wail
15 For men he has murdered; he is greedy for more.

Prudent counsels are becoming to men.   (*166*)
To the gleeman his song, to the sage his wisdom.
As many men, so many minds:
Separate thanes have separate thoughts.
20 He longeth the least, that hath store of lays,
Or with hands of skill can strike the harp,
On whom God hath bestowed the gift of song.
Wretched who lives alone in the world,
Doomed by fate to dwell without friends;
25 'Twere better he had a brother in his house,
Both men sons of the self-same father.   (*176*)

There's sport on the ship when she runs under sail
                                        (*186*)

'Tis weary work against wind to row.
They call him a coward and craven shirk,
Whose oar is aboard with blade unwetted.

THE FATES OF MEN

(From the *Exeter Book*)

Full oft by the grace of God it happens
To man and woman in wedlock joined,
5 A child is born. They cherish it fondly,
Tend and teach it, till the time is come,
When the little one's limbs, in the lapse of years,
Have sturdy grown, and gained their strength.
So father and mother fondly rear it,
10 Nourish and guard it. But God alone knows
The gift of the years to the growing child.
Sudden death is the doom of one,
Snatched away in the spring of his youth,
By a violent end, devoured by wolves
15 That range the heath: Her unhappy child
The mother bemoans, but man may not change it.

One shall famine slay; another the flood sweep away!
One shall the battle break; another the bolt o'ertake!
One shall in darkness drear drag out his life,
20 Groping to feel where his foot may stand.
Stricken with palsy in sinew and limb,
Another shall grieve and groan at his fate.
One shall fall from a forest tree:
Fearful he wheels in wingless flight,
25 Spins through the air and swoops to the ground;
From the crown of the trunk, he crashes to earth,

Stunned and senseless, all still he lies   (25)
On the straggling roots, his soul is departing!

One shall wander, weary and foot-sore,
Far through the world, famished and needy,
5 Trudging at dawn along dewy trails,
In a land unloved and an alien soil.
Few are alive to befriend the wanderer,
Ever unwelcome are eyes of woe.
High on the gallows shall hang another,
10 Dangle and strangle, till he stiffen in death.
Bloody-beaked birds on his body shall prey;
The plundering raven shall pluck out his eyes,
Tear and claw the carcass to shreds.
Helpless he hangs,—his hands avail not
15 To ward off the scavengers that swoop through the
          air.
Hope-of-life has left that livid corpse;
Senseless and stark he suffers his Wyrd,
Drowned in the death-mist: doom of the criminal.

One shall be burnt in the weltering blaze;
20 Flames shall devour their fated victim,
Swift and sudden his sundering from life
In the lurid glow. Loud wails the mother,
As she watches the flames enfolding her darling.
One shall be slain as he sits on the mead-bench,
25 Ale-brawl ended by edge of the sword,
The drunkard's folly,—too froward his tongue! (50)

So the Lord Almighty allots unto men   (64)
Manifold fortunes o'er the face of the earth;
Dealeth their dole, their destiny holds.
30 To some he gives wealth, to some he gives woe,

Gladness of youth to some, to others glory in battle,
Strength in the war-play, with spear and with bow-
   string,   (69)
Fame and honor; to others he gives
Skill in the game of the checkered board.
5 Some become learned in lore of books.
Some have the gift of working in gold:
Of beaten metal they make bright ornaments,
And get broad lands from their lord in return,
Receive them with joy from the generous king.
10 One shall wait upon wassailing comrades,
Gladden the hearts of heroes carousing,
Large is their joy as they laugh at the revels.
One shall be found at the feet of his lord;
With his harp he shall win a harvest of wealth;
15 Quickly he tightens the twangling strings,
They ring and they swing, as his spur-shod finger
Dances across them, deftly he plays.
Another shall tame the towering falcon,
Hawk in hand, till the haughty flier
20 Grows meek and gentle; he makes him jesses,
Feeds in fetters the feather-proud bird,
With dainty morsels the dauntless soarer,
Until the wild one is weakened and humbled,
Belled and tasselled, obeys his master
25 Hooded and tamed and trained to his hand.

So marvelously God in his might bestows
Skill upon men in many lands,
Shaping their lives, and allotting their fortunes
To dwellers on earth of every kin.
30 Let each man render Him honor and praise
For the gifts His grace hath granted to mortals.

IV. Historic War Poetry

THE BATTLE OF BRUNNANBURG

(From the *Anglo-Saxon Chronicle,* 937 A.D.)

Æthelstan Lord, and leader of earls,
Gold-friend of heroes, he with his brother
5 Edmund Ætheling, agelong glory
Won in war, with weapons keen,
By Brúnnanbúrg.   They broke the shield-wall;
With offspring of hammers they hewed the linden-
    woods,
Heirs of Edward.   Oft had they driven
10 The foe from the land, and foiled the invader,
True to their blood in battle defending
Their hoard and their home.   Huge was the slaughter
They made of the boat-crews and bands of the Scots-
    men,
Doomed men fell.   The field was drenched;
15 Ran with the blood of the bravest fighters
From rise of the sun, when the radiant day-star,
Bright candle of God, came in the morning-tide
Gliding o'er earth, till the glorious creature
Sank to its setting.   The slain lay thick;
20 Maimed by the spear lay many a Northman,
Shot over shield; shattered and war-spent,
Many a Scot.   But the men of Wessex
Drove all day the Dane-folk before them;

Hung on the trail of the troop that they hated; (22)
Hewed from behind the host of the pirates,
With weapons new-whetted. Not one of the rovers
Who came with Anlaf across the water
5 Aboard his war-ship, bound for our shores,
Fated to fall, found that the Mercian
Refused him hand-play. Five young chieftains
Lay stretched on the field. Seven great earls
Of Anlaf were killed, and countless others
10 Of boatmen and Scotsmen. Barely escaped
The Northern leader. Leaving in haste,
With a handful of men, he made for his ship.
They cleared the craft, the king put out
On the fallow flood; he fled for his life.
15 Also the cunning Constantinus.
Home again stole to his haunts in the north.
Little ground had the gray old leader
To brag and to boast of the battle-encounter,
Stripped of his clansmen killed in the slaughter.
20 Alone he returned, his own son dead,
Left on the battle-field, bloody and mangled,
Brave young warrior. No bragging for him,
Grisly old traitor, of glorious sword-play;
Little for him or Anlaf to laugh about,
25 In midst of the wreck of their mighty array.
No boasting for them that they had the better
In the crashing of helmets, the heat of the conflict;
The splintering of spears, the struggle of heroes;
The grinding of weapons, the game of battle
30 They chose to play with the children of Edward.
So parted the Northmen on their nail-studded ships,
Blood-reddened wreck and remnant of lances;

Sailed o'er the deep again, Dublin to seek,　　(55)
And the shores of Ireland, shamed and defeated.

Back to their Wessex home, went the two brothers;
King and Ætheling, came to their own again,
5 Victors in triumph returned from the war;
Leaving behind the horn-billed raven
The gloomy-coated, to glut on the carcasses;
Leaving behind the white-tailed eagle
Perched on the corpses to prey on the carrion;
10 Leaving behind the haggard kite,
And the gray-wolf gaunt to gorge on the slain.

Never was made a mightier slaughter;
Never sword reaped a ruddier harvest
Of high-born heroes, here in this island,
15 Since hither of old, Angles and Saxons,
—So say the chronicles,—sailed from the eastward,
Crossed o'er the billows, to conquer the Britons;
When haughty battle-smiths hammered the Welshmen
And honor-keen earls first entered this realm.

THE BATTLE OF MALDON

(991 A.D.)

The beginning of the poem is lost. The first sixteen lines of the remaining portion describe how Byrhtnoth's men, arrived at the battle field, dismount and turn their horses loose, how one of them sends his hawk flying to the wood, and how the East Saxon alderman procceds to marshal his band on the banks of the stream. The poem continues as follows:

Byrhtnoth encouraged his comrades heartily;   (*17*)
Rode through the ranks and roused their spirits;
Marshalled his men to meet the onset;
Showed them how they should hold their shields
5 Firm in their grip, and fearless stand.
When he had briskly whetted their courage,
He leaped from his steed and stood with his people,
His hearth-band beloved and household thanes.

Then strode to the strand a stalwart Northman,
10 The viking herald. They heard him shout,
Send o'er the tide the taunt of the pirates;
Hailing the earl, he hurled this challenge:
"Bold sea-rovers bade me tell thee
Straightway thou must send them tribute,
15 Rings for ransom, royal treasure;
Better with gifts ye buy us off,
Ere we deal hard blows and death in battle.
Why spill we blood when the bargain is easy?
Give us the pay and we grant ye peace.
20 If thou dost agree, who art greatest here,
To ransom thy folk with the fee we demand,
And give to the seamen the gold they ask,
Pay with tribute for treaty of peace,
We load the booty aboard our ships,
25 Haul to sea and hold the truce."
Byrhtnoth spake, he brandished his spear,
Lifted his shield and shouted aloud,
Grim was his wrath as he gave them his answer:
"Hearest thou, pirate, my people's reply?
30 Ancient swords they will send for ransom;
Poison-tipped points they will pay for tribute;

Treasure that scarce will serve you in battle.　(48)
Go back pirate, give them my answer;
Bring them this word of bitter defiance;
Tell them here standeth, stern and intrepid,
5　The earl with his folk, to defend his country,
Æthelred's realm, the rights of my lord,
His house and his home; the heathen shall fall,
Pirates and robbers.　My people were shamed
If ye loaded our booty aboard your ships,
10　And floated them off unfought for, to sea,
Having sailed so far, to set foot on our soil.
Not all so easily earn ye our gold!
Sword-blades and spear-points we sell you first;
Battle-play grim, ere ye get our tribute!"

15　Forward he told his troop to come,
To step under shield and stand by the shore.
The breadth of the stream kept the bands asunder;
Strong came flowing the flood after ebb,
Filled the channel, and foamed between them.
20　Impatient stood by Panta stream,
East-Saxon host and horde of the pirates,
Longing to lock their lances in battle.
Neither could harass or harm the other,
Save that some fell by the flight of arrows.

25　Down went the tide, the Danes were ready;
Burned for battle the band of the Vikings;
On the bridge stood Wulfstan, and barred their way
Byrhtnoth sent him, a seasoned warrior,
Ceola's son, with his kinsmen to hold it.
30　The first of the Vikings who ventured to set

Foot on the bridge, he felled with his spear.   (78)
Two sturdy warriors stood with Wulfstan,
Maccus and Ælfhere, mighty pair,
Kept the approach where the crossing was shallow;
5 Defended the bridge, and fought with the boldest,
As long as their hands could lift a sword.
When the strangers discovered and clearly saw
What bitter fighters the bridgewards proved,
They tried a trick, the treacherous robbers,
10 Begged they might cross, and bring their crews
Over the shallows, and up to the shore.
The earl was ready, in reckless daring,
To let them land too great a number.
Byrhthelm's son, while the seamen listened,
15 Called across, o'er the cold water:
"Come ye seamen, come and fight us!
We give you ground, but God alone knows
Who to-day shall hold the field."

Strode the battle-wolves bold through the water;
20 West over Panta waded the pirates;
Carried their shields o'er the shining waves;
Safely their lindenwoods landed the sailors.
Byrhtnoth awaited them, braced for the onslaught,
Haughty and bold at the head of his band.
25 Bade them build the bristling war-hedge,
Shield against shield, to shatter the enemy.
Near was the battle, now for the glory,
Now for the death of the doomed in the field.
Swelled the war-cry, circled the ravens,
30 Screamed the eagle, eager for prey;
Sped from the hand the hard-forged spear-head,

Showers of darts, sharp from the grindstone. (*109*)
Bows were busy, bolt stuck in buckler;
Bitter the battle-rush, brave men fell,
Heroes on either hand, hurt in the fray.
5 Wounded was Wulfmær, went to his battle-rest;
Cruelly mangled, kinsman of Byrhtnoth,
Son of his sister, slain on the field.

Pay of vengeance they paid the Vikings;
I heard of the deed of the doughty Edward:
10 He struck with his sword a stroke that was mighty,
Down fell the doomed man, dead at his feet.
For this the thane got the thanks of his leader,
Praise that was due for his prowess in fight.
Grimly they held their ground in the battle,
15 Strove with each other the stout-hearted heroes,
Strove with each other, eager to strike
First with their darts the foe that was doomed.
Warriors thronged, the wounded lay thick.
Stalwart and steady they stood about Byrhtnoth.
20 Bravely he heartened them, bade them to win
Glory in battle by beating the Danes.
Raising his shield, he rushed at the enemy;
Covered by buckler, he came at a Viking;
Charged him furious, earl against churl,
25 Each for the other had evil in store.
The sailorman sent from the south a javelin,
Sorely wounding the war-band's leader;
He shoved with his shield, the shaft snapped short
The spear was splintered and sprang against him;
30 Wroth was Byrhtnoth, reached for his weapon;
Gored the Viking that gave him the wound.

Straight went the lance, strong was the leader; (*140*)
Sheer through the throat of the pirate he thrust it.
His dart meant death, so deadly his aim.
Swiftly he sent him a second javelin,
5 That crashed through the corslet and cleft his bosom,
Wounded him sore through his woven mail;
The poisonous spear-head stood in his heart.
Blithe was the leader, laughed in his breast,
Thanked his Lord for that day's work.

10 Now one of the pirates poised his weapon;
Sped from his hand a spear that wounded
Through and through the thane of Æthelred.
There stood at his side a stripling youth;
Brave was the boy; he bent o'er his lord,
15 Drew from his body the blood-dripping dart.
'Twas Wulfmær the youthful, Wulfstan's son;
Back he hurled the hard-forged spear.
In went the point, to earth fell the pirate
Who gave his master the mortal hurt.
20 A crafty seaman crept toward the earl,
Eager to rob him of armor and rings,
Bracelets and gear and graven sword.
Then Byrhtnoth drew his blade from the sheath,
Broad and blood-stained, struck at the breast-plate.
25 But one of the seamen stopped the warrior,
Beat down the arm of the earl with his lance.
Fell to the ground the gray-hilted sword;
No more he might grasp his goodly blade,
Wield his weapon; yet words he could utter;
30 The hoar-headed warrior heartened his men;
Bade them forward to fare and be brave.

When the stricken leader no longer could stand,
He looked to heaven and lifted his voice: (*172*)
"I render Thee thanks O Ruler of men,
For the joys Thou hast given, that gladdened my life.
5 Merciful Maker, now most I need,
Thy goodness to grant me a gracious end,
That my soul may swiftly speed to Thee,
Come to Thy keeping, O King of angels,
Depart in peace. I pray Thee Lord
10 That the fiends of hell may not harm my spirit."
The heathen pirates then hewed him to pieces,
And both the brave men that by him stood;
Ælfnoth and Wulfmær, wounded to death,
Gave their lives for their lord in the fight.

15 Then quitted the field the cowards and faint-hearts;
The son of Odda started the flight.
Godric abandoned his good lord in battle,
Who many a steed had bestowed on his thane.
Leaped on the horse that belonged to his leader,
20 Not *his* were the trappings, *he* had no right to them.
Both of his brothers basely fled with him,
Godwin and Godwy, forgetful of honor,
Turned from the fight, and fled to the woods,
Seeking the cover, and saving their lives.
25 Those were with them, who would have remained,
Had they remembered how many favors
Their lord had done them in days of old.
Offa foretold it, what time he arose
To speak where they met to muster their forces.
30 Many, he said, were mighty in words
Whose courage would fail when it came to fighting.

There lay on the field the lord of the people,   (*202*)
Æthelred's earl; all of them saw him,
His hearth-companions beheld him dead.
Forward went fighting the fearless warriors,
5 Their courage was kindled, no cowards were they;
Their will was fixed on one or the other:
To lose their life, or avenge their leader
Ælfwiné spoke to them, son of Ælfric,
Youthful in years, but unyielding in battle;
10 Roused their courage, and called them to honor:
"Remember the time when we talked in the mead-hall,
When bold on our benches we boasted our valor,
Deeds of daring we'd do in the battle!
Now we may prove whose prowess is true.
15 My birth and my breeding I boldly proclaim:
I am sprung from a mighty Mercian line.
Aldhelm the alderman, honored and prosperous,
He was my grandsire, great was his fame:
My people who know me shall never reproach me,
20 Say I was ready to run from the battle,
Back to my home, and abandon my leader,
Slain on the field.   My sorrow is double,
Both kinsman and lord I've lost in the fight."
Forward he threw himself, thirsting for vengeance;
25 Sent his javelin straight at a pirate.
Fell with a crash his foe to the earth,
His life-days ended.   Then onward he strode,
Urging his comrades to keep in the thick of it.

Up spake Offa, with ashen spear lifted:
30 "Well hast thou counselled us, well hast encouraged;
Noble Ælfwiné, needs must we follow thee.

Now that our leader lies low on the field,   (*233*)
Needs must we steadfastly stand by each other,
Close in the conflict keeping together,
As long as our hands can hold a weapon,
5 Good blade wield. Godric the coward,
Son of Odda, deceived us all.
Too many believed 'twas our lord himself,
When they saw him astride the war-steed proud.
His run-away ride our ranks hath broken,
10 Shattered the shield-wall. Shame on the dastard,
Who caused his comrades like cowards to fly!"
Up spake Leofsunu, lifted his linden-wood,
Answered his comrades from under his shield:
"Here I stand, and here shall I stay!
15 Not a foot will I flinch, but forward I'll go!
Vengeance I've vowed for my valiant leader.
Now that my friend is fallen in battle,
My people shall never reproach me, in Stourmere;
Call me deserter, and say I returned,
20 Leaderless, lordless, alone from the fight.
Better is battle-death; boldly I welcome
The edge and the iron." Full angry he charged,
Daring all danger, disdaining to fly.

Up spake Dunheré, old and faithful,
25 Shook his lance and shouted aloud,
Bade them avenge the valiant Byrhtnoth:
"Wreak on the Danes the death of our lord!
Unfit is for vengeance who values his life."
Fell on the foe the faithful body-guard,
30 Battle-wroth spearmen, beseeching God
That they might avenge the thane of Æthelred,

Pay the heathen with havoc and slaughter.   (*264*)
The son of Ecglaf, Æscferth by name,
Sprung from a hardy North-humbrian race,
—He was their hostage,—helped them manfully.
5 Never he faltered or flinched in the war-play;
Lances a plenty he launched at the pirates,
Shot them on shield, or sheer through the breast-plate;
Rarely he missed them, many he wounded,
While he could wield his weapon in battle.
10 Still Edward the long held out at the front;
Brave and defiant, he boasted aloud
That he would not yield a hair's breadth of ground,
Nor turn his back where his better lay dead.
He broke through the shield-wall, breasted the foe,
15 Worthily paid the pirate warriors
For the life of his lord ere he laid him down.
Near him Æthelric, noble comrade,
Brother of Sibryht, brave and untiring,
Mightily fought, and many another;
20 Hacked the hollow shields, holding their own.
Bucklers were broken the breast-plate sang
Its gruesome song. The sword of Offa
Went home to the hilt in the heart of a Viking.
But Offa himself soon had to pay for it,
25 The kinsman of Gadd succumbed in the fight.
Yet ere he fell, he fulfilled his pledge,
The promise he gave to his gracious lord,
That both should ride to their burg together,
Home to their friends, or fall in the battle,
30 Killed in conflict and covered with wounds;
He lay by his lord, a loyal thane.

Mid clash of shields the shipmen came on,   (*295*)
Maddened by battle. Full many a lance
Home was thrust to the heart of the doomed.
Then sallied forth Wistan, Wigelin's son;
5 Three of the pirates he pierced in the throng,
Ere he fell, by his friends, on the field of slaughter.
Bitter the battle-rush, bravely struggled
Heroes in armor, while all around them
The wounded dropped and the dead lay thick.
10 Oswold and Eadwold all the while
Their kinsmen and comrades encouraged bravely,
Both of the brothers bade their friends
Never to weaken or weary in battle,
But keep up their sword-play, keen to the end.
15 Up spake Byrhtwold, brandished his ash-spear,
—He was a tried and true old hero,—
Lifted his shield and loudly called to them:
"Heart must be keener, courage the hardier,
Bolder our mood as our band diminisheth.
20 Here lies in his blood our leader and comrade,
The brave on the beach. Bitter shall rue it
Who turns his back on the battle-field now.
Here I stay; I am stricken and old;
My life is done; I shall lay me down
25 Close by my lord and comrade dear."

[Six more lines and the MS. breaks off. There cannot have
been much left. The battle is over. The words of old Byrhtwold
make a fitting close for these renderings of Old English verse.]

NOTES

AIDS TO THE STUDY OF OLD ENGLISH POETRY

What the study of classic antiquity is to the later and greater periods of English literature, the study of Germanic antiquity is to the period of its earliest beginnings. This study has been unduly neglected in our schools and colleges, because of the inaccessibility and highly technical character of most of the literature connected with the subject. The following brief book-list is confined to works accessible in English, and not too technical for the student and general reader. It is in no sense a "bibliography," and the strict limitation to books in English has compelled the omission of even so excellent a little volume as Axel Olrik's *Nordisches Geistesleben*, or such noble essays as Uhland's on the *Thor* and the *Odin Myth*, or so thoroughly readable a book as Golther's *Germanische Mythologie*, all of which deserve to be translated into English. *Starred books are especially recommended.

MYTHOLOGY. J. S. Stallybrass, *Teutonic Mythology*, translated from the 4th ed. of Jacob Grimm's *Deutsche Mythologie*. A standard work of reference.—M. S. Smith, *Northern Mythology* (Temple Primers), translated from the German of Professor D. F. Kaufmann. The best brief sketch of Germanic mythology.—Anderson, *The Prose Edda*.—Vigfusson and Powell, *Corpus Poeticum Boreale*. Gives the poetic Edda, in the original, with a prose translation at the foot of the page.—*The Mythologic Poems of the Edda*, edited and translated with Introduction and Notes by Olive Bray, Viking Club Series.

HEROIC LEGEND AND SAGA. M. B. Smith, *Northern Hero Legends* (Temple Primers), from the German of O. Jiriczek. Axel Olrik, *Heroic Legends of Denmark*, translated by Lee Hollander and published by the American-Scandinavian Foundation as the fourth volume in its series of Scandinavian monographs. Especially important for the study of the Saga-material in Beowulf. H. M. Chadwick, *The Heroic Age,* Cambridge University Press, 1912. *Origin of the English Nation,* 1907. Miss M. G. Clark, *Sidelights on Teutonic History During the Migration Period.* W. P. KER, *The Dark Ages.* R. W. CHAMBERS, *Beowulf, An Introduction to the Study of the Poem,* 1921.

NORSE SAGAS. *The Volsunga Saga,* translated by Magnusson and Morris (Camelot Series).—*The Grettis Saga,* by the same.—*The Njals Saga.* (Abridged from original ed. of Sir G. W. Dasent, Grant Richards, Everyman Library 1900.)—*Saxo Grammaticus,* translated by Oliver Elton. The Danish History of Saxo is a mine of legendary lore. W. S. Collingwood and Jón Stefansson, *A Pilgrimage to the Saga-steads of Ireland* 1899. Illustrated. By the same, *The Life and Death of Cormac the Skald, being the Icelandic Kormaks Saga rendered into English.* 1902. Illustrated. E. Magnusson and W. Morris, *Three Northern Love Stories and Other Tales, Translated from the Icelandic.* Longmans Green & Co., London 1901. The American-Scandinavian Foundation (25 W. 45th St., New York. Henry Goddard Leach, secretary) publishes a series of Scandinavian sagas and monographs.

GERMANIC INSTITUTIONS. F. B. Gummere, *Germanic Origins.* The best survey of the subject in English. Knut Stjerna, *Essays on Beowulf* (trns. J. R. Clark Hall) Viking Club Extra Series Vol. III. Illustrated. Paul du Chaillu, *The Viking Age.* Every student of Old English literature should be familiar with the *Germania* of Tacitus, at least in translation.

HISTORIES OF OLD ENGLISH LITERATURE. The best general history of this period is Bernhard Ten Brink's *Early English Literature,* translated by H. M. Kennedy (Henry Holt and Co.). The best aesthetic criticism of Old English Literature is found in the books of Stopford Brooke, *The History of Early English Literature* and *English Literature from the Beginning to the Norman Conquest;* the first is a detailed study of Old English Poetry; the second is a briefer recast of the first, with added chapters on King Alfred and West Saxon prose. Stopford Brooke writes with a fine appreciation of the poetic values of Old English verse. His translations are spirited, though their diction tends to be too archaic, and they often miss the rhythms of the original. See also the chapter on the Old English Period in Vol. I of the Cambridge History of English Literature. W. P. Ker, *Epic and Romance*, a stimulating study of Germanic epic. The same author's **History of English Literature* (Medieval) in the Home Library Series, Henry Holt & Co. W. M. Hart, *Ballad and Epic* (Vol. XI of Harvard Studies and Notes, Ginn and Co., 1907). A valuable study in early literary forms.

OLD ENGLISH POETRY. The introductions to the volumes of the Belles Lettres (D. C. Heath and Co.) and the Albion (Ginn and Co.) series of Anglo-Saxon poetry contain much of interest to the general student of Old English Literature. Professor Gummere's *Oldest English Epic* translates into English alliterative verse *Widsith, Deor's Lament, The Finnsburg Fragment, The Waldere Fragments,* and the whole of *Beowulf:* the best complete verse translation of *Beowulf,* remarkably close to the rhythm and language of the original. The same poems, "Done in Common English after the old manner," by C. E. Scott-Moncrieff, Dutton, 1921. For other references to Beowulf literature and translations, see notes on Beowulf, p. 197. Cook and Tinker, *Translations from Old English Poetry,* and Faust and Thompson, *Old English Poems* (Scott, Foresman & Co., 1918), contain selections of Old English Poetry exclusive of Beowulf, the latter in the original metres. For the Christian Poetry see A. J. Barnouw, *Anglo-Saxon Christian Poetry,* translated by Louise Dudley. The best survey of Caedmon and Cynewulf criticism will be found in the excellent introductions to Professor Kennedy's prose translations of the *Poems of Cynewulf* and of the *Caedmon Poems* (E. P. Dutton, 1910 and 1916). For Gnomic Poetry see the introduction to Miss B. C. Williams' *Gnomic Poetry in Anglo-Saxon* (Columbia University Press, 1914).

THE OLD ENGLISH ALLITERATIVE METRE

Anglo-Saxon poetry from its earliest beginnings to the Norman Conquest was composed in the ancient alliterative measure common to all the people of Germanic stock. Though this measure continued to be used in England after the Conquest (see *Layamon's Brut, Sir Gawayne, Piers*

Ploughman), even as late as the sixteenth century, it grad-ually declined during the Middle English period, and was either supplanted or fundamentally modified by measures of foreign origin. For a brief discussion of Old English metre, see Professor Gummere's *Handbook of Poetics,* Chap. VII (Ginn and Co.), and Professor R. M. Alden's *English Verse* (Henry Holt and Co.). For a differing but stimulat-ing discussion of Old English rhythms by a scholar who is himself a poet, see William Ellery Leonard, University of Wisconsin Studies in Literature and Philology No. 2.

1. THE FOUR-STRESS ALLITERATIVE LINE. Old English rhythms are based on the Germanic law of accentuation, ac-cording to which the most important words or parts of words were emphasized by a strong stress of the voice. This involved the subordination of *quantitative* accent based on the length of syllables, to *stress accent* based on their significance. When such stressed accents or beats of the voice recur at regular intervals, we perceive *rhythm;* and even though the intervals between the individual beats may vary, our sense of rhythm will be awakened if we can note a *regular recurrence of groups of beats,* in twos or threes or fours. Now the chief characteristic of Old English verse is that its words were so arranged that there was a constant recurrence of two pairs of heavy beats, and that the most important of these heavy beats began with the same sound (alliteration). This gives us as the unit of Old English verse *a line of four beats, divided into two halves by a pause, but linked together by alliteration.*

> *Hy*ge sceal þe *heard*ra, *heor*te þe cenre;
> *Mod* sceal þe *ma*ra, þe ure *mæg*en lytlaþ.
> —*Battle of Maldon.*
> (Heart must be keener, courage the hardier;
> Bolder our mood, as our band diminisheth.)

2. ALLITERATION. When words or syllables begin with the same sound, they are said to alliterate. Alliteration is still used in English verse, but it is largely ornamental and casual, as *e.g.* in Shelley's *Cloud:*

That orbed *m*aiden, with white fire laden
  Whom *m*ortals call the *m*oon
*Gl*ides *gl*immering o'er my *fl*eece-like *fl*oor
  By the *m*idnight breezes strewn.

In Old English poetry, on the other hand, alliteration was
structural and *regular*. As it was much older than writing,
it was and is concerned with sounds, not letters. *King* and
cook keep good company in alliteration, though they begin
with different letters. *King* and *knight* do not, though they
begin with the same letter.[1] Furthermore, as alliteration
was addressed to the ear and not to the eye, it always fell
on stressed syllables. Thus *forsaken* and *feeble* do not alliterate, even though they begin with the same sounds; while
forsake and *beseech* do alliterate, though they begin with
different sounds. In the latter case *for* and *be* are merely
prefixes, and stress and alliteration alike fall on the significant syllables. As in the great majority of Old English
words the first syllable was the significant syllable, both
stress and alliteration generally fall on first syllables. Take
these lines:

  The *f*olk of the *f*en in *f*ormer days (p. 42, l. 27)
  *N*amed him Grendel: un*kn*own his father,
  Or what his *d*escent from *d*emons obscure.

In "named" and "unknown," the alliteration, though not
apparent, is real. In "descent" and "demons," on the other
hand, the alliteration, though apparent, is not real, because
it does not fall on the stressed syllable in "descent."

As the function of alliteration in Germanic verse is to link
together the two halves of the four-stress line, the first
stressed syllable of the second half-verse must always be a
member of the alliterative group. We may therefore call
this syllable the *alliterative dominant*. In the majority of
cases *both* stressed syllables of the first half-verse alliterate
with the dominant. When only one of them alliterates, it
is preferably *the first,* but it may be the second. Examples
of the three resulting types of alliteration in the order of
their frequency follow:

[1] In Old and Middle English when the *k* of knight was still pro-
nounced, they of course alliterated.

1 : 2 : 3 : Ge*wat* þa ofer *wæg*holm *wind*e gefysed
        *Flot*a *fam*igheals, *fug*le gelicost. (*Beowulf,* l. 217.)
      (*Went* then o'er the *wave*-sea, by the *wind* favored
      The *floater foamy*-necked, to a *fowl* likest.)

1 : 3 : On *flod*es æht *feor* gewitan (l. 42).
      (In the *flood*'s power *far* to wander.)

2 : 3 : Geseah he in *rec*ede *rinc*a manige (l. 728).
      (Saw he in the *win*e-hall of *war*riors a many.)

The fourth stress never alliterates with the third, or dominant in Old English verse of the classic period, but it may
alliterate with the second and rarely with the first, when
these are not in alliteration with the dominant. This gives
us two additional types of alliteration.

1 : 3 : 2 : 4 (alternating alliteration) :

      *Hild*e-*wæp*num and *heap*o-*wæd*um (l. 39).
      (With *brav*e *weap*ons and *bat*tle-weeds.)

1 : 4 : 2 : 3 : *Wit* þæt ge*cwæd*on *cniht*-*wes*ende (l. 535).

      (*We* that *boast*ed when *boys* we *were.*)

All vowels alliterate :

      *Is*ig and *ut*fus *æþ*elinges fær (l. 33).
      (*Ic*y and *out*bound, *eth*eling's barge.)
      *Inn*an and *ut*an *ir*enbendum (l. 774).
      (*In*side and *out*side with *ir*on bands.)

3. THE PAUSE OR CÆSURA. The Old English alliterative
line is regularly divided into two half-verses by a pause between the second and third stress. This *cæsura* is sometimes merely rhythmic, sometimes it is a sense pause. Compare these two lines :

      Ofer hronrade hyran scolde, (l. 10)
      Gomban gyldan : þæt wæs god cyning!

or these :

      Willing comrades may crowd around him (l. 23)
      Eager and true. In every tribe, etc.

Though the cæsura always comes between the second and
third stress, it does not always come in the middle of the
line, as the half-verses may be of unequal length. Compare

Grette Geata leod,||gode þancode
Wisfæst wordum,||þæs þe hire se willa gelamp

(1. 625).

Monotony is avoided by this inequality in the length of half-verses (see next section, *unstressed syllables*), and by run-on lines, where the meaning "runs on" from the end of one line into the next (*enjambment*). Compare

Egsode eorl, syþþan ærest wearþ (6)
Feasceaft funden; he þæs frofre gebad.

Or

          Then climbed aboard
The chosen troop; the tide was churning
Sea against sand; they stowed away
In the hold of the ship their shining armor, etc.

In spite of such devices, the fixed cæsura is responsible for a certain monotony in the movement of Old English epic verse, in striking contrast to the rich modulations of Greek epic verse or the epic verse of Milton and Tennyson, with its free treatment of the cæsura.

4. UNSTRESSED SYLLABLES. While the number of stressed syllables in Old English verse is constant,[1] the number of unstressed syllables varies freely. Compare the following lines:

Gód mid Geátum, Gréndles dǽda (1. 195).
Gewát þa ofer wǽgholm winde gefýsed (1. 217).
Gewát him þa to wároþe wícge rídan (1. 234).
Se þe his wórdes gewéald wíde hǽfde (1. 79).
Mánna ǽngum, þara þe hit mid múndum bewánd
(1. 1461).

Unstressed syllables are added most freely at the beginning of the second half-verse. The varieties of half-verses have been reduced by Professor Sievers to five fundamental types, but a discussion of them is beyond the scope of this note. (For a brief statement of Sievers' types see Alden, p. 152.) The most important result of the Old English

---

[1] In the expanded or "long line" that is sometimes found, (see *Fall of Man* and *Vision of the Cross*), there are *three* stressed syllables in each half-verse or bar.

freedom with regard to unaccented syllables is *variation in the rapidity of the verse,* or *tempo.*

> Gewát þa ofer wægholm, wínde gefýsed

is a rapid line, and admirably suggests the buoyant movement of the boat.

> Gómban gýldan: þæt wæs gód cýning
> (Gave him gold, 'twas a good king)

is a slow line, and suggests weight and dignity. The importance of the proportion of stressed to unstressed syllables in the tempo of verse-rhythm may be illustrated by a comparison between Old English and blank verse. Blank verse belongs to the "syllable-counting" variety of English verse, *i.e.* there are normally ten syllables in every line, five unaccented syllables alternating with five accented. This is the metrical scheme of the iambic pentameter. (We need not here touch on the moot question of the relation of quantity to stress. While the length of syllables is by no means a negligible factor, either in old or modern English verse, the fact remains that English rhythms, old or modern, are based on the Germanic stress accent, to which quantity has been made subordinate.) The following line from *Paradise Lost* is a "normal" iambic pentameter so far as number of syllables and accents are concerned:

> And swims or sinks or wades or creeps or flies.

It has however an abnormal number of pauses. If we subject a number of consecutive lines of *Paradise Lost* to the test of reading aloud, we shall note that Milton not only constantly departs from the scheme of regular alternation of unaccented with accented syllables, but that even the number of *main stresses* in each line varies considerably. Thus in the first sixteen lines of *Paradise Lost,* there are ten lines with four main stresses, two with three, and only four lines with the "normal" number of five. Moreover, the line

> For Hot, Cold, Moist, and Dry, four champions fierce

has seven accents; and the line

> Rocks, Caves, Lakes, Fens, Bogs, Dens and Shades of Death

has even eight. In all these lines the number of syllables remains practically constant. Now, when the number of main stresses is reduced, the tempo of the line is accelerated; when the number of accents is increased the tempo of the line is retarded.

Compare

>In the begínning how the héavens and eárth

with

>O'er bóg, o'er stéep, through stráit, róugh, dénse, or ráre.

In iambic pentameter, therefore, the tempo is modified by varying the number of main stresses, while the number of syllables remains constant. In Old English verse, on the other hand, *the tempo is modified by varying the number of syllables, while the main stresses remain constant.* Fundamentally different as is the rhythm of blank verse from that of the Old English alliterative line, it is interesting to note that owing to this variability of tempo, individual lines with identical rhythm may be found:

>Rose out of Chaos: or if Sion hill (*Paradise Lost*).
>Hynþu and hrafyl. Ic þæs Hrothgar mæg (*Beowulf*).
>Strongly to suffer and support our pains (*Paradise Lost*).
>Swæse gesiþas, swa he selfa bad (*Beowulf*).

5. RISING AND FALLING RHYTHMS. The rhythm of Old English verse is predominatingly falling, *i.e.* the rhythmic units are composed of stressed followed by unstressed syllables:

>Gúþmod grúmmon, gúman onétton

is a typical line. Examples of falling rhythms in modern English are

>Tell me not in mournful numbers (*trochaic*)

and

>Solemnly, mournfully, dealing its dole (*dactylic*).

Of rising rhythms

>To strive, to seek, to find and not to yield (*iambic*)

and

>I saw from the beach when the morning was shining
>A bark o'er the waters move gloriously on (*anapæstic*).

The reason for the prevalence of falling rhythms ("dactylic" and "trochaic") is inherent in the structure of Old English, which was rich in light formative syllables, *added* to the root. In modern English these formative syllables have dropped off, often being replaced by particles *preceding* the root. In every such case a naturally falling rhythm has been changed into a naturally rising rhythm. Cf. Old English *síngan* (falling), with *to sing* (rising); *Gódes lúfu* with *the lóve of Gód; Wélandes gewéorc* with *the wórk of Wáyland*. Accordingly, rising rhythm (iambic, anapæstic) seems to be more natural to the genius of modern English than to that of Old English, whose falling rhythms fit it so well for describing the crash of combat, and the blows of sword and battle-axe, falling on helmet and shield.

6. COINCIDENCE OF RHYTHMIC AND EMPHATIC STRESS. One of the most important differences between Old English epic verse and modern English epic verse, as found, *e.g.*, in Milton and Tennyson, remains to be stated. In Old English verse there is never any conflict between rhythmic and emphatic stress, *i.e.* between the stress required by the metric scheme and the stress required by the meaning of the line. In reading Old English verse, if the words important to the sense are strongly emphasized, and the unimportant words are hurried over, the rhythm will invariably be brought out. On the other hand, if the opening passage of *Paradise Lost* is accented according to the sense alone, something very like prose will result. While if we accent according to the metric scheme alone, and without any regard to the sense, something very like sing-song will result. The music of Milton's blank verse, and of all great English blank verse, is due to the free interplay and balanced conflict between sense and rhythm. You must read with the rhythm in your ear, and the sense in your mind. There is consequently a double focus for the attention, a *rhythmic* and a *logical*. *In Old English poetry rhythmic and logical focus coincide*. The rhythmic structure of Old English verse may be compared to the old Germanic hall, whose four solid corner posts squarely support the burden of the roof. While English blank verse may be compared to a Gothic cathedral, whose groined ceiling seems to hover overhead upheld by the interplay of complicated thrusts taken up by arch and buttress and clustered column.

THE RENDERING OF THE OLD ALLITERATIVE LINE IN MODERN FORM

Any attempt to reproduce exactly and accurately the Old English alliterative line must necessarily fail, first because the language has changed, and second because our ear has changed with it. The "gait" of English verse has become smoother and more regular; and the rider accustomed to the pace of a well broken saddle-horse is apt to be unseated by the gait of a Pegasus that bucks. It is especially the second half-verses with their initial rush of unaccented syllables that are trying to the modern ear. In a line like the following:

> Mánna ǽngum þara þe hit mid múndum bewánd,

where the second half-verse starts with a mad career of unstressed syllables and then brings up suddenly on two heavy stresses, the incautious rider is apt to come a cropper at the close.

Again, the juxtaposition of stressed syllables is much more common in Old English than in modern English verse, and offers another difficulty to the modern ear. Cf. such a line as

> Ongán céallian þa, ofer céald wáter.
> (Began calling then o'er the cold water).

The only way to get accurately the movement of Old English verse is to learn to read it in Old English. But it is not impossible to reproduce for a wider circle of readers the spirit of the old rhythm, by preserving its essential features in a form adapted to the requirements of modern English speech. These essential features, which any translation professing to reproduce the old alliterative line must preserve, are the following:

1. THE FOUR-STRESS LINE.

> Glory great was given to Beowulf.

2. THE MEDIAL CÆSURA.

> Done were his days; the Danes were glad.

Unless a passage like the following clearly strikes the ear as exceptional, the translation fails to reproduce one of the most important features of Old English metre:

Spray-frosted trees o'erspread it, and hang
O'er the water, with roots hard-wedged in the rocks.

3. THE ALLITERATIVE SCHEME, based on the first stressed syllable of the second half-verse, the "alliterative dominant." Nearly all the verses in our translation will be found to conform to one of the five alliterative types given above. In the few instances where there is no alliteration, or where two stresses in the second half-verse alliterate (see especially the lyrics), metrical considerations have been waived in the interest of poetry. The proportion of 1 : 2 : 3 alliterations, however, is much less, and of alternating alliterations 1 : 3 : 2 : 4, and 1 : 4 : 2 : 3 is much greater than in Old English.

4. THE PREVALENCE OF FALLING RHYTHM. The preponderance of falling rhythms, with their heavy stresses on the beginnings of words or word groups, must be maintained at all hazards. Though it is undoubtedly true that the prevalent "natural" rhythm, for narrative verse at any rate, in Modern English has become rising (iambic), it is too much to say with Swinburne that "dactylic forms of verse are unnatural and abhorrent to the English language," unless we use the word dactylic strictly in the classic sense as a *quantitative* foot. On the other hand, the loss of inflectional syllables, which has changed hundreds of dissyllabic words (*singan, sing; Godes, God's* or *of God; scipu: ships,* etc.) into monosyllables, seriously affects the proportion of masculine to feminine endings of half-verses, upon which so much of the total effect of the verse-rhythm depends. In the first 100 lines of *Beowulf,* 81 of the first half-verses, and 71 of the second half-verses have feminine endings, *i.e.* end with an unstressed syllable. If we compare the first selection in our translation, we find that in 52 lines 43 first half-verses and 37 second half-verses have feminine endings in the original, while only 17 first half-verses, and 25 second half-verses have feminine endings in the translation.

5. VARIATION OF SPEED OR TEMPO, due to irregular number of unstressed syllables. Modern English does not permit the same freedom as Old English in the use of un-

stressed syllables, especially at the beginning of the half-verses (anakrusis). But the translator must avoid going to the other extreme of awaking the sense for the regular tempo of iambic or trochaic four-stress rhythm (octosyllabic verse). A succession of lines such as this:

> Of little use that life he deemed

or:

> Do thy best now, dearest Beowulf
> Shield thy life and show thy valor

would utterly fail to reproduce the variety of movement, and the often breathless haste of Old English verse, though reproducing faithfully enough the four beats, the medial cæsura, and the alliteration on the significant syllables. On the other hand, a prevailingly dactylic or anapæstic movement, the "tumbling measure" of later verse, would be too light and rapid. Compare *e.g.* the tempo of *Piers Ploughman* with that of the *Beowulf* selections. The elimination of many of the "hypermetric" syllables of the anakrusis, and their more even distribution between stresses, together with the unavoidable neglect of the quantity of stressed syllables in Old English, has probably given to our translation a somewhat lighter and more rapid movement, in its total effect, than the hammer-blow style of the Old English verse.

6. COINCIDENCE OF RHYTHMIC AND EMPHATIC STRESS. This is one of the most essential features to be preserved. Significant words must receive the rhythmic stress. No words of minor significance (particles, prepositions, etc.) must require the rhythmic stress.

> Í stand bý thee tó the end.

This line breaks the rule by the emphasis it places on *by* and *to*. The irregularity here is intentional, and was introduced for a certain dramatic effect, which the Old English poet could obtain by other means.

Though we are accustomed to think and write of the Germanic alliterative measure as obsolete, or having only an antiquarian and philological interest, it would be easy to show that English poetry, especially blank verse, from Marlowe's

"Black is the beauty of the brightest day"

to Arnold's

"Mixed with the murmur of the moving Nile"

is thick-sprinkled with lines that remember the movement, still stirring in our pulses, of our ancestral four-stress alliterative measure.

THE MANUSCRIPT SOURCES OF OLD ENGLISH POETRY

Nearly the entire body of surviving Old English poetry is found in four unique manuscripts; all of them written about the eleventh century, toward the close of the Old English period.

1. THE BEOWULF Ms., containing the *Beowulf* and an incomplete poem on *Judith and Holofernes*. This Ms. was written about 1000 A.D. and is now kept in the British Museum. Our first knowledge of it dates from 1705, when the librarian Wanley, cataloging the Anglo-Saxon Mss. in the library of Sir Robert Cotton, described it as "telling of the wars which a Dane Beowulf waged against the king of Sweden." In 1736 the Ms. was badly injured by fire. The first printed edition of *Beowulf* was made in 1815 by the Scandinavian scholar Thorkelin, who had copied the Ms. in England. Thorkelin's translation and notes were destroyed by the British bombardment of Copenhagen in 1807, and his valuable Ms. copy of the poem which preserves many words that can now no longer be read, narrowly escaped destruction. All editions of the Beowulf text are ultimately based on this Cotton Ms. in the British Museum and on Thorkelin's transcripts.

2. THE JUNIAN Ms. This Ms. was discovered about 1630 by Archbishop Usher and by him presented to Francis Dujon of Leyden, who called himself Junius, and printed its contents under the title *Caedmon's Paraphrase*, in 1655. (For the relation of the poems in the Junian Ms. to Caedmon see note on *The Fall of Man*). The Junian Ms. contains narrative poems on Biblical subjects in the epic style of alliterative verse: three Old Testament narratives, *Genesis, Exodus, Daniel*, and one New Testament narrative

known as *Christ and Satan.* The Ms. is illustrated (see the facsimiles in Professor Kennedy's *The Caedmon Poems*), and is now kept in the Bodleian library at Oxford. The poems of the Junian Ms. were the earliest to become generally known and their study marks the beginning of the modern revival of interest in Old English poetry.

3. THE EXETER BOOK. This Ms. book formed part of the library which Leofric the first bishop of Exeter collected and left to his church. Leofric died in 1071 and the Ms. has been in the cathedral library of Exeter ever since, 850 years. It contains a varied collection of O. E. poems, chiefly Saints' Legends in the narrative style of epic verse, and gnomic poetry. Among the most important poems in the Exeter book are the *Juliana* and *Guthlac* (Saints' Legends) Cynewulf's *Crist,* partly lyrical, and partly narrative and dramatic, the *Phoenix,* an allegorical Christian narrative wih a lyrical ending, the elegies of *The Wanderer* and *The Seafarer,* and collections of *Riddles* and *Proverbs* in alliterative verse.

4. THE VERCELLI BOOK. This Ms. was discovered in 1832 by a German scholar in the cathedral library at Vercelli near Milan, where it is still kept. It contains chiefly prose homilies, but among these are interspersed six poems, among them Cynewulf's *Elene,* a version of the legend of the Finding of the Cross by St. Helena, *The Fates of the Apostles* and *Andreas,* Saints' Legends in the Epic style, and the *Dream of the Rood,* a lyric-dramatic poem on the subject of the Cross of Christ. How this Ms. book came to Vercelli is not known, but it has been plausibly conjectured that there was at Vercelli, near the southern outlet of the main Alpine passes into Italy, a hospice for Anglo-Saxon pilgrims to Rome, and that some pious English traveller may have left this Ms. to the library of the hospice, from which it later found its way into the cathedral.

I. EPIC POETRY

1. Heroic Epic

Old English Heroic Epic constitutes that body of earliest English narrative poetry which grew out of the traditional stories brought by the Germanic settlers of England from their continental home. Its chief characteristics are: 1. It is Germanic and Northern.[1] 2. It is pagan and uninfluenced by the Christian tradition of the Latin Church.[2]

In discussing Germanic Epic it is important to distinguish between *Heroic Tradition, Legend, or Story* (Heldensage) and *Heroic Poetry* (Heldendichtung). The Heroic tradition, orally handed down, is the stuff out of which the singer (Scop, gleeman) made his "lays," short poems to be sung or recited at the feast in hall, and out of which later poets, perhaps on the basis of "lays," wove long epic poems. Thus out of the traditional story of a hero Beowulf, brought by Angles and Saxons from the continent, *lays* were made and sung in the halls, and out of these and the *epic tradition* he remembered, the Beowulf poet made his epic poem. Thus the Nibelungen Legend or Story, the greatest Epic tale of the old Germanic time, gave rise to a great body of prose and poetry of which the poems in the Edda, (10th cent.?) the Volsunga Saga (13th cent.) and the Middle High German Nibelungenlied (close of 12th cent.) are the chief literary monuments.

[1] The word *Nordic* is used to suggest the *racial* origin of the peoples of Northern and Northwestern Europe. The word *Germanic* denotes their *linguistic* and *cultural* unity. The main divisions of Germanic are: 1. East Germanic, including the Goths, both Ostrogoths and Visigoths. 2. North Germanic, including the Scandinavians, Danes, Icelanders, Swedes, "Norsemen." 3. West Germanic. The Old English (Anglo-Saxons) belong to this division, of which the continental representatives are the Teutonic peoples, High and Low Franks and Saxons, Alemanni, etc. English and German are both West Germanic languages. Care should be taken not to confuse *Germanic* and *German*. *German* (Deutsch) is the literary language of the *High German* division of the Teutonic dialects. *Germanic* (Germanisch) is a generic term covering all that is included in East, North and West Germanic.

[2] Professor Bugge, a great authority on Germanic antiquities, believes that the specific Norse mythology of the Eddas has been profoundly influenced by Christianity, that Baldr is the White Christ, and Loki Lucifer, etc.

THE HEROIC AGE. The Epic tradition of the Germanic peoples was developed in the time of the great folk-wandering or migration of nations that began in South Eastern Europe with the incursion of Huns and Goths into the Roman Empire, and ended with the Anglo-Saxon conquest of Roman Brittania. The battles of Franks and Moors in France and Spain, out of which grew the Charlemagne Legend and the Song of Roland, and the great expeditions of the Northmen of the Viking age, represent a transition to another time, and the blending of the old Germanic heroic tradition with other elements. The heroes and events of the genuine Germanic epic tradition, then, belong to this older Heroic Age. They have a *historic* foundation. Ermanric, Attila, Theodoric, Offa, even Beowulf, are *historic* figures. The close of the Nibelungenlied is a reminiscence of an actual historic occurrence, the destruction of the Burgundians by the Huns in the fifth century. Beowulf, the hero of the Old English epic, fought with his chief Hygelac, the Chochilaicus of the chronicles in an actual raid against Franks and Frisians about 520 A.D.

But back of the *historic memories* of the heroic age, stretches the tradition of a *common life,* common customs, common institutions, a tradition so tenaciously preserved that passage after passage in epic poems of the 8th century and later can be corroborated and illustrated by the *Germania* of Tacitus. And back again of this body of common custom and life that enters into the tradition of the Germanic heroic age, there hovers, vague and indistinct, the shadow of a common belief in supernatural powers, wrought by later poets, more or less consciously into something like a definite mythology. Through the mists of our earliest epic loom the figures of Sceaf, Beowa, Ing (the Freyr of the Norse poems) and much more distinctly, Weland, the smith. Thus *historic reminiscence, a heroic way of life,* and *myth* are the strands out of which Epic tradition is woven in Germania as well as in Greece.

Old English epic tradition developed no body of mythologic poems such as the Scandinavian skalds have left us in the poems of the Elder Edda. Woden, the Odin of the Norse poems, is scarcely mentioned in O. E. poetry and the only figure of the older mythology that seems to have been thoroughly acclimated in England was Weland the smith, the Vulcan of northern mythology. Famous weapons in the epic poems are known as "Weland's work." *Deor* a scop who has fallen on evil days, comforts himself by recalling to mind an incident in the Weland myth that is illustrated on a curious casket of whale-bone (The "Franks' casket) now in the British Museum, and corroborated by one of the finest songs of the Edda. Alfred translates the Fabricius of Boethius by "Weland." Almost down to our own time the tradition of the magic smith survived in Berkshire, and Scott in *Kenilworth,* and more recently Kipling in *Puck of Pook's Hill* have kept alive the memory of Wayland, the mythical Germanic Hephaistos.

Just as the early conversion of the English to Christianity prevented the elaboration of old heathen myth into literary forms, so the early separation of the Anglo-Saxons from the main body of their Germanic kinsfolk darkened the memory of the historic tradition of the Heroic Age, and made easier the substitution of Biblical for Germanic tradition, as stuff for epic composition. Yet here too there survives evidence of the fact that the English shared in the common epic tradition. The oldest of the historic cycles was the Gothic, with Ermanric and Theodoric as its chief heroes. Ermanric, his followers and his foes are remembered in *Widsith* and *Beowulf* (see notes on Ermanric, Hama, Brisingamen. For his story see M. B. Smith *Northern Hero Legends*).

The greatest hero of the older epic tradition was Sigfried (Norse, Sigurd), the hero of the Nibelungen Legend. In this legend the streams of Frankish, Burgundian, and Gothic epic tradition unite; East, North, and West Germanic peoples contributed to the legend. Sigfried is a Frank, Gunther (O. E. Guthere) and Hagen (O. E. Hagena) are Burgundians. In the hall of Attila where the final fight occurs, Theodoric the Ostrogoth is the chief hero. Many of the names of this epic cycle were familiar to the English as is evidenced by the reference to them in *Widsith*. One of the episodes in Beowulf alludes to incidents in the life of Sigmund the father of Sigfried, that are more fully related in the *Volsunga Saga* (see note on Fitela, *Beowulf* l. 872), though strangely enough the *Beowulf* poet makes Sigmund instead of Sigfried the slayer of the dragon. In the *Waldere Fragments* we have the remnants of a longer epic based on characters and incidents that belong to the Nibelungen Legend. (See M. B. Smith, *Northern Hero Legends,* Walharius).

The surviving body of Old English poetry that represents this Germanic tradition is not large if we except *Beowulf. Widsith, the Waldere Fragments, Deor's Complaint* and the *Finnsburg Fragment* represent all the salvage. (See Prof. Gummere's *Oldest English Epic* and Chadwick's *The Heroic Age.*) But we cannot conclude that the Old English made no other poems but the ones that have come down to us, out of this epic material. As Professor Ker says: "We can speak about what we know, but not as though we knew everything about Anglo-Saxon poetry."

The longest and most important Old English heroic poem, *Beowulf,* in many ways stands curiously apart from the common Germanic epic tradition. The only adventures of the hero that are fully narrated are romantic rather than epic, *i.e.* purely imaginary events made to appear real, rather than real events heightened and colored by the imagination. Romance is *imaginary* reality. Epic is *imagined* reality. While there is in the Odyssey the same interweaving of romantic and epic material (see Ker, *Epic and Romance*), the romantic elements are in the Greek poem introduced by way of *episode* (Odysseus himself narrates them at the Phaiakian banquet), while in *Beowulf* the main strand of the narrative is purely imaginary (fights with monsters and a dragon) and the historic tradition is episodically and loosely introduced and confusedly handled. It is not the action in Beowulf that gives it its epic dignity, but the *manner of life* portrayed and the *character* of the hero unfolded from youth to age. The *Nibelungenlied* is infinitely richer in human and dramatic interest, and its close rises to heights of great epic poetry. In *Beowulf* there is none of the tragic conflict that makes the *Nibelungenlied* so moving. The *Beowulf* is much more *moralized,* deliberately and consciously didactic in aim, than the *Nibelungenlied.* Beowulf is the type of hero that every man in arms should wish to be in the England of the 8th century. He is a proto-Wordsworthian "Happy Warrior," and Wordsworth's Northumbrian predecessor of the 8th century already shows some of the qualities which differentiate English from continental European poetry.

But though *Beowulf* cannot be compared with the *Nibelungenlied* for dramatic and imaginative handling of epic tradition, the spirit of the old Germanic heroic age lives in the English poem as it does not in the German, where ideals of medieval chivalry and Christian sentiment have wrought a land-change into something rich and strange,—and alien to the Germanic past. So, in spite of the fact that we must guard against praising *Beowulf* for what it is *not*, it remains the greatest single poetic monument, both in spirit and form, of the heroic age of Germanic antiquity.

BEOWULF

Historic Interest of the Poem.—Among Old English poems whose subject-matter belongs to the old heathen time by far the most important is *Beowulf*. There were similar hero-poems in vogue, not only among the Old English, but also among their kinsfolk, the Goths, the Franks, and the Northmen; but with the exception of a few fragments, all of these have been lost or transformed by the spirit of a later age; so that the poem of Beowulf, belonging to England, as it does, has a still wider interest as being the earliest, and the only complete epic of the heroic age of the Northern peoples preserved in the ancient verse form.

Date.—*Beowulf* is preserved in a single Ms. now kept in the British Museum. It is written in the dialect spoken in Wessex in the eleventh century. This West Saxon version is possibly directly due to the interest which King Alfred (†901) took in the older poetry of his people, as a result of which copies were made in his time and after, of poems written in the North of England in the seventh and eighth centuries. The original Ms. was probably written in Northumbria toward the end of the seventh century, after the introduction of Christianity in the north (637), and before the Danish invasions put an end to Northumbrian culture (end of eighth century). *Authorship.*—No author is known; we cannot even apply the word "author" in the modern sense,—in the sense in which we speak of Milton as the author of *Paradise Lost*. There are numerous theories of authorship. These may be divided into two classes. (1) *The ballad theory,* which conceives the poem to be the result of piecing together various lays or early ballads sung by minstrels in the hall. According to this theory, the making of the Epic out of earlier lays was a more or less mechanical business, and the scholars who have developed it have emphasized the inconsistencies and incongruities of style and structure with much ingenuity in the interest of their theory. Some of the greatest *Beowulf* scholars, like Muellenhoff and Ten Brink, have held this theory, and at one time it had wide acceptance. For a survey of the ballad theory of *Beowulf* see J. E. Routh, Jr., *Two Studies on the Ballad Theory of the Beowulf,* Johns Hopkins dissertation, 1905. (2) *The theory of a single poet.*—Those who hold that *Beowulf* is the work of a single poet do not deny that the poem is based on oral lays sung in the hall to the accompaniment of the harp, but they insist that the Epic poet did more than piece these lays together. He took the theme of the lays, and much of their old traditional phrasing, but broadened the treatment by description, characterization, more subtle motivation through the introduction of long speeches, etc., so that now the story became matter for reading rather than for song or chanted recital in hall. Those who hold this theory explain the inconsistencies and incongruities of the poem as we have it, as being due to the peculiarities of Old English poetic style, and lay stress on the many evidences of unity of plan and structure, as, for instance, the consistently developed character of the hero himself. There has been in recent years a reaction against the extremes of the ballad theory as worked out by Muellenhoff, Ten Brink, and their followers, and the weight of scholarship is inclining to some form of the single authorship theory. See the first chapter of *Northern Hero Legends,* where the distinction between the ancient choric hymns, the later Epic lays, and the still more recent literary Epic is clearly and succinctly drawn. Assuming, then, a single author for *Beowulf,* he must have been a Northumbrian poet of the late seventh or early eighth century, who used ancient lays of Beowulf's fight against monsters, but softened and civilized the character of Beowulf after the model of the converted kings of Northumbria, thus making him in every respect the contemporary ideal of English heroism. No one who is familiar with the writings of King Alfred can fail to be struck by the similarity of tone between his sentiments and many of Beowulf's speeches. So the landscape, the manners and customs, and in general the setting, must be ascribed to this unknown Anglian poet. Also, of course, the superficial Christian coloring, and the scattered biblical allusions.

Sources.—The sources of *Beowulf* were oral lays, brought over by the Angles in the sixth century from their old homes on the continent, where they were the neighbors of Jutes and of Danish folk. This explains how it comes that while the scenery and characterization point to seventh-century North-England, the scenes and characters are all continental Germanic, Danish, Swedish, Jutish, etc. Hrothgar is a Dane. The poem opens with a genealogy of Danish kings. The hall Heorot was in Denmark. Beowulf belonged to the Geats, according to some, a tribe of southern Sweden, according to others, the Jutes, inhabitants of Jutland. *Historic Elements.*—Though historic memories do not constitute the main strand of the *Beowulf* narrative, as they do of the *Nibelungenlied,* there are recollections of actual occurrence imbedded in the folk-lore and semi-mythical adventures which are in the centre of interest. Thus the raid which Chocilaicus (Latinized Frankish form of the Old English Hygelac) made about 520 A.D. against Franks and Frisians, according to Gregory of Tours, and in which the invader lost his life, is several times alluded to in *Beowulf.* The hero was a nephew of Hygelac, and probably accompanied his uncle on this raid. Soon after this he succeeded his kinsman as king of the Jutes. Beowulf is therefore a historic figure who ruled over the Geats or Jutes during the middle of the sixth century,—the very time when the Angles, their neighbors, began to migrate to England. *Myth and Folklore.*—In Old English genealogies occurs the name of Beowa as one of the mythical founders of the royal line. It has been supposed that Angles and Saxons, before their migration to England, celebrated him in song, and that the adventures of Beowulf in the poem belonged originally to this mythical Beowa. When the fame of the historic Beowulf was at its height, towards the close of the sixth century, the deeds of the older shadowy Beowa, of like-sounding name, were transferred to Beowulf, and thus out of mingling of myth and historic tradition the lays on which the poem was founded are supposed to have arisen. According to this "mythologic theory" of the origin of Beowulf,[1] he was originally a kind of Sun-god, like Freyr of the Norse mythology, and Grendel is variously interpreted as an embodiment of the terrors of the misty moors, the stormy sea, the pestilence of the morass, etc. Owing to changing conceptions as to the origin of nature myths, recent scholars reject many of the conclusions of the mythological interpreters, and refuse to see in Beowulf and his fights against the monsters any profound supernatural significance. No doubt in the stories of Beowulf's encounter with the nicors, with Grendel and his dam, there are reminiscences of actual fights with bears, walrus, whales, etc.; and in so far as these have been "monstrified" by popular imagination, we are dealing with mere folklore. But in the story of the Sheaf-child (see note on myth of the Sheaf-child), and of Beowulf's last fight with the fire-dragon, it is difficult not to recognize some of the deeper significance that the "mythologic interpretation" finds in them. See Stopford Brooke's *History of Early English Literature,* Chap. V. For parallels to the Beowulf story in Norse Literature see *Grettis Saga* (translated by Magnusson and Morris), and the *Saga of Hrolf Kraki.* (The relations of the latter to Beowulf are discussed by W. W. Lawrence, *Modern Language Publications,* June, 1909, p. 220. Professor Lawrence sharply criticizes the mythologic interpretation of Beowulf.)

[1] At the present day the generally accepted theory as to Beowa follows Olrik in making him a vegetation divinity ("corn spirit") rather than a sun-god. My friend Dr. Kemp Malone reminds me that Freyr "was undoubtedly an agricultural divinity." Cf. for an interesting modern instance of the mythopoetic imagination, the "Spirit of the Wheat" in Frank Norris' *Octopus.*

Saga Material in Beowulf.—For recent discussions of the saga material in Beowulf see Axel Olrik, *Heroic Legends of Denmark,* H. M. Chadwick, *Origin of the English Nation; The Heroic Age;* Miss M. G. Clarke, *Sidelights on Teutonic History during the Migration Period.* R. W. Chambers, *Introduction to the study of Beowulf.*

Translations.—For a complete list of earlier Beowulf translations see C. B. Tinker. The most useful prose versions for the student are the following: (1) C. G. Child, Riverside Literature Series, No. 159, Houghton Mifflin Co. (2) C. B. Tinker, New York, Newson and Co., 1902. (3) J. R. Clark Hall, London, 1911. (Valuable introduction.) Professor Gummere's translation (*Oldest English Epic,* Macmillan, 1909), gives a close reproduction of the original metre. (Good notes.) Prof. W. E. Leonard in *Beowulf and the Niebelungen Couplet,* U. of Wisconsin, 1918, gives specimens of his spirited translation into rimed ballad couplets. (Complete translation forthcoming.)

THE MYTH OF THE SHEAF-CHILD

The Epic of *Beowulf* opens with a partly mythic genealogy of the Danish King Hrothgar, about whose hall, Heorot, the adventures of the first part centre. Scyld, the mythic founder of the line, is called "Scefing," "ing" being the regular patronymic ending in Old English, this formula, Scyld Scefing, = Scyld the Sheaf-Child, came to be interpreted as equivalent to Scyld the son of Sceaf, and this imagined father of Scyld is actually mentioned in Old English genealogies. Of him early chroniclers tell the same story here related of Scyld Scefing. Thus Ethelward, a chronicler of the tenth century, relates how Sceaf as a little child drifted ashore on an island called Skaney, in a boat loaded with arms, and how he later became king of that people. William of Malmesbury, telling the same story after Ethelward, adds that the child was asleep, his head resting on a *sheaf of wheat.* "The region where he ruled is called Old Anglia, whence the English came into Britain, and it is situated between the Saxons and the Jutes." If William has here preserved an ancient feature of the story it would seem that the myth of the sheaf-child was originally Anglian, and was imported into the Danish genealogy. Some scholars think that Scyld was the common ancestor of Danish and English tribes. According to the mythologic interpretation, we have here an ancient culture myth. Ship and sheaf symbolize navigation and agriculture; the weapons and treasure symbolize war and kingship. The four together would symbolize the civilization of the low-German tribes of the North Sea coast, and Scyld Scefing would represent the founder of this civilization.

1.—1. LIST TO AN OLD-TIME LAY. A free rendering of the opening lines:

> Hwæt, we Gar-Dena in gear-dagum,
> þeod-cyninga þrym gefrunon.

> What! we of the Spear-Danes in days of yore
> Of the people-kings the prowess have heard.

Ge-frignan (pret. gefrægn, gefrunon; German fragen) is the verb used in the regular epic formula "I have heard," or "we have heard," lit. "have learned by asking" which suggests the manner of handing down epic tradition before the days of literature.

1.—18. BEOWULF'S FAME, etc. This Danish Beowulf, heir of Scyld Scefing, is not to be confused with the hero of the poem, who was a Geät or Jute. He is probably identical with the Beowa of the Old English genealogies, who is there mentioned as a son of Scyld.

2.—10. OUT IN THE BAY A BOAT WAS WAITING. This mode of burial was common among the old Northmen. When Sigmund in the *Volsunga Saga* carries his dead son *Sinfjotli* (Fitela in *Beowulf*) to the shores of a fjord, he meets a man in a boat, who ferries the body across the water. This is Odin conveying the dead to his kingdom. Sometimes fire was set to the burial ship. In the *Ynglinga Saga*, Haki, mortally wounded, has one of his ships loaded with armor and bodies of the slain; tarred wood is stacked over all, and when the wind draws from the land, the sails are hoisted, the pyre kindled, and the burning ship is sent to sea. The prose *Edda* tells how the body of Balder the good was laid on the ship *Ring-horn*. On the funeral pyre were placed Balder's ring, and his horse with its costly trappings. Then, in the presence of all the gods, the burial ship was lighted and sent seaward. At a later time it was customary to place both ship and body in a barrow or burial

vault. In 1880 a well-preserved Viking boat with human
remains was unearthed near Gokstad in Norway. For
northern burial customs see Knut Stjerna, *Essays on Beowulf*, (pp. 97 ff.) and article on Oseberg Ship, Am. & Scand.
Rev., July 1921. With the story of Scyld Scefing compare
Tennyson's *Coming and Passing of Arthur*.

3.—1. The numbered sections of the Beowulf Ms. have
been kept for convenience of reference and comparison with
the original and with other translations, although they by
no means consistently represent natural divisions of the
poem and were probably not intended to do so. Chambers
in his revision of Wyatt's edition (1914) has relegated the
section numbers to the margin. The sub-heads under the
Roman numerals are of course the translator's. Though
Mr. Bradley is probably right in his hypothesis that these
section numbers in the O. E. Mss. were connected with the
method of transcription of the text (see article *Beowulf* in
the *Encyclopaedia Brittanica* by Henry Bradley and *Pro-
ceedings of the British Academy,* Vol. VII, 1915), the fact
that all Beowulf editions and translations use them gives
them a practical reference value. 1. BEOWULF WAS KING.
This is again the Danish Beowulf. Cf. Chadwick, *Origin
of the English Nation* 273, 291.—4. HEALFDENE, known
in Scandinavian sources as Halfdan or Haldanus. The
name Half-Dane means that his mother was foreign-born.
—8. HEOROGAR. Eldest son of Healfdene. Beowulf the
hero, on his return from Denmark, gives to his lord the
armor he had received from Hrothgar saying: Heorogar
had it first but did not give it to *his* son Heoroward, so it
came into his brother's hand, who gave it to Beowulf.
HROTHGAR, the king of the Danes at the time of Beowulf
the hero's visit, and the builder of Heorot. The *Saga of
Rolf Kraki* and Saxo know him. HALGA, the youngest
brother of Hrothgar, and the father of Hrothulf mentioned
l. 1017; the Helgi of the *Rolf Kraki Saga.*—9. SIGENEOW.
The Ms. is defective at this point, all that is left of a possible name being elan. I have followed Kluge who using
the *Rolf Kraki Saga* reads:

> hyrde ic þæt [Sigeneow[1] wæs Sæw]elan cwen

[1] Olrik however considers Sigeneow no proper name for a
daughter of Healfdene, since all the names of the royal family alliterate on H.

The Scylfings were a Swedish dynasty descended from Scylf. The name is extended to the Swedish people just as that of the Scyldings is to the Danes. On the interest shown by the Old English poet in these Scandinavian royal lines, cf. Ker: "The history in it (*Beowulf*) is not English history . . . . Everywhere and in every possible way the old heroic poets seem to escape from the particular nation to which they belong, and to look for their subjects in some other parts of the Teutonic system. In some cases, doubtless this might be due to the same kind of romantic taste as led later authors to place their stories in Greece or Babylon, or anywhere far from home. But it can scarcely have been so with *Beowulf;* for the author of *Beowulf* does not try to get away from reality; on the contrary, he buttresses his story all round with historical tradition and references to historical fact; he will not let it go forth as pure romance." (*English Literature, Medieval.* Home University Library, p. 35.)—25. HEOROT HE NAMED IT. "Stag hall" (Old English *heorot,* hart, stag), probably derived its name from the antlers that adorned the gable-ends. In the Finnsburg lay there is an allusion to the "horned gables of the hall." For a description of the Scandinavian hall, see Clark Hall's *Beowulf,* p. 174. The building was rectangular, with rows of pillars running down each side. The space between wall and pillars was raised in two tiers above the main floor, and served for seats. In front of these were ranged the tables,—boards laid on trestles, and removed at night, when the retainers slept in the hall. The hearth was in the centre, and the smoke found its way out through openings in the roof. Halfway down the tier of seats, generally on the south side, was the "high-seat," occupied by the lord of the hall. For a description of the customs of a Germanic hall, see note on *Widsith.*

The site of Heorot can almost certainly be identified with Leire in Seeland, Denmark, which, according to Scandinavian tradition, was the capital of the kings whose names correspond to Hrothgar and Hrothulf.

4.—4. SUNDER SONS FROM FATHERS. The O. E. *apumswerian* means "son-in-law and father-in-law." Hrothgar's daughter Freawaru married Ingeld. *Widsith* relates how Ingeld later attacked Hrothgar "at Heorot." Cf. Clark, *Sidelights,* 103 ff. 5. DEMONSPRITE *i.e.,* Grendel, whose name is mentioned later. Grendel's connection with the "powers of darkness" in the Christian sense is emphasized by his taking special offence at the gleeman's song of praise to the Creator. The old conflict between day and night, darkness and light, winter and summer, which the northern myths made so much of, is here given a Christian coloring. Grendel who dwells in the dark, hates God, who has made sun and moon triumphant over darkness.—11. HOW THE ALMIGHTY. Although the Danes were pagans, as the poet himself insists a little farther on, he here introduces a minstrel who sings of the creation in the vein of Caedmon. Professor Klaeber has shown that the Beowulf poet knew the Old English *Genesis,* and quoted from it. This is the first of numerous instances of a superficial Christian coloring given the story by the poet.—21. GRENDEL, the monster that ravages Hrothgar's hall, is a strange combination of man and beast. In appearance manlike, but "huger in bulk than human kind," he is compared to an outlaw banished from the habitations of men. His name helps to humanize him. The other monsters have no names. He is his mother's only son. His father is unknown, though by a curious allusion to a Jewish legend, his descent from Cain is suggested. He has hands and arms and fingers, and human feelings surge in his breast. He laughs, he wails. He is filled with hatred and envy at the sound of human revelry. Yet with all these human traits, he is at bottom more beast than man. His "hands" and "fingers" are armed with huge claws. He tears his victims like a wild beast, gulps their blood, and devours their bodies. His lair is among "wolf-cliffs wild." Though he has the power of human feeling, he lacks the power of human utterance. His gruesome song, that the Danes hear from the wall, is a mere poetic figure for the howl of the wounded beast. There is a touch of the supernatural about him, too. His body is spelled against sword-stroke. Iron cannot hurt him. His mother's den, in which he dies, is beneath the surface of a haunted mere. Mysterious gleams flash from its depths at night. He is descended from demons. There is something diabolical about him, and when Beowulf kills him, he departs to the "fiends' domain." An interesting comparison might be drawn between Grendel and Shakespeare's Caliban.—26. OFFSPRING OF CAIN. This connection of Grendel with Cain is again referred to line 1261. The tradition that Cain was the ancestor of evil monsters comes from the apocryphal book of Enoch and was also known to the author of the O. E. Genesis.

5.—2. JOTUNS. O. E. eoten, Norse jotun, the giants of Norse mythology. "The giants that warred against God" (O. E. gigantas) come from Genesis VI. 4. Their war against God is again alluded to l. 1688. 7. ASLEEP AFTER REVEL. The warriors slept in the hall after the feast when the tables were removed. Hrothgar and his queen slept in the "bowers," buildings within the main enclosure but separate from the hall. After Grendel's ravages of Heorot, they all slept in the bowers.

6.—15. REFUSING TO END THE FEUD. In the *Battle of Maldon* the heathen pirates "Danes," offer to desist from their raids if the English will pay ransom, but Byrhtnoth refuses to buy indemnity by enforced tribute. Here the *Danes* are represented as willing to pay Grendel to let them alone. But Grendel would neither make and keep a treaty nor pay indemnity (wergild) for the damage he had done.— 24. HELL-RUNES. Runes were the letters used by the Germanic peoples before writing became general. They were probably modifications of the Latin letters for the sake of more easily carving them on wood, curved lines being straightened, and lines running with the grain being made diagonal so as to prevent the splitting of the wood, *e.g.* F = ᚠ. "Write" means to carve or cut; Beowulf in his last fight "writes" the dragon in two, a sword-writing mightier than the pen's. The runes were used for inscriptions on swords, drinking-horns, etc. and inspired the sense of magic and mystery that letters always have for the unlettered, so that "rune" came to mean "mystery." This sense was emphasized by the use of rune-staves (Germ. buch-stabe) in reading omens. Hence the transition to magic witchcraft was easy. Hel-rune for "witch" occurs in O. E. glosses, and Jordanes tells that Filimer king of the Goths, found witches among his people, *quas Haliu-runnas cognominat.* See the examples of runes given in the note on Cynewulf, p. 233.—31. THAT HE MIGHT NOT VISIT HIS GOODLY THRONE. A difficult passage. The "he" is generally understood to refer to Grendel who was prevented from touching the seat of Hrothgar—no he þone gift-stol gretan moste. I follow Holtzmann in making "he" refer to Hrothgar.

7.—5. AT HEATHEN ALTARS. The poet probably knew more about the old pagan cult than he cared to reveal, but he crosses himself and delivers an earnest exhortation to worship the true God.—9. THE HOPE OF THE HEATHEN ON HELL WAS FIXED. So Milton in *Paradise Lost* makes the old Semitic divinities and even the gods of Greece, inhabitants of hell and vassals of Satan. To the Northumbrian poet of the 8th century the Danes as he knew them were heathen. But the character of Hrothgar is his own creation and therefore much nearer the ideal of a Christian Anglian king of the 8th cent.—24. HYGELAC'S THANE. Beowulf, the hero. His name is not mentioned until he himself proclaims it at Hrothgar's court 149 lines farther on! To introduce the hero's name attached to another, and to introduce the hero himself without a name is certainly a defect of workmanship. The character of Beowulf is admirably conceived and so consistent throughout, that this in itself is the most convincing refutation of the "accretionary" theory of the origin of the poem. About the facts of Beowulf's life the poem gives us the following information: He is the son of Ecgtheow of the Swedish line of the Scylfings. His mother, whose name is not mentioned, was a daughter of Hrethel king of the Geatas (see note on Jutes below), and a sister of Hygelac who succeeded Hrethel as king. In his boyhood he came to the court of Hrethel and was reared by his uncle Hygelac as a "sister's son", a relationship held in special regard by Germanic peoples (*sororum filiis idem apud avunculum qui apud patrem honor,* to sisters' sons the same regard is paid by uncle as by father, Tacitus, *Germania* XX). Like many other legendary heroes (cf. Saxo's Hamlet) he was in youth despised as slothful (he was called "a slacker" wendon þæt he sleac waere), but when he grew up he had the strength of thirty men in his grip and became a famous fighter against sea-monsters. His greatest youthful exploit was his swimming match with Brecca. This and the three main adventures of the poem, the fight with Grendel and Grendel's mother in Hrothgar's land, and the fight with the dragon in his own land in old age, belong to folklore or myth. But there is genuine historic reminiscence in the statement that he accompanied Hygelac on his fatal raid against Franks and Frisians. (See note on Hygelac below.) According to the poem Beowulf saved his life on that occasion by another great swimming feat, returning home alone "laden with thirty coats of mail" (l. 2361). He refused the throne offered him by Hygelac's widow, acted as guardian to Hygelac's son Heardred, and on the death of the latter became king of the Geatas and had ruled over them fifty years when his last fight took place. In the description of his funeral ceremonies a mourning "woman" is mentioned. Bugge, who has restored the passage, suggests that Beowulf in finally accepting the offer of Hygelac's throne "took his widow into the bargain as was usual." But Beowulf expressly mentions the fact that he has no heir to whom to leave his armor.

Though epic tradition had probably combined the feats of a mythical hero Beowa and the deeds of a historic Beowulf who lived in the middle of the 6th century, the *character* of Beowulf is as much the creation of the Old English poet, as Hamlet's *character* is Shakespeare's creation. That character reflects the ideals of a ruler prevailing at the Christian courts of Northumbria in the 8th century. Beowulf's feats are primitive and naïve, but though we are told again and again that his strength lay in the grip of his hand, it is something else that grips us as we read of his exploits: his gentleness in union with strength, his dignity, his nobility, his contempt for meanness and pettiness (see especially his retort to Unferth), his entire freedom from guile, his loyalty, his love of adventure and daring combined with prudence, (like Whitman's soldier *"bold, cautious, true"*), his ambition for fame coupled with forgetfulness of self, his honest pride in his achievements free from contemptuous arrogance. No wonder Hrothgar says:

> "Me þin mod-sefa
> licaþ leng swa wel, leofa Beowulf."

(Thy "mod-sefa" dear Beowulf I love better the longer I know thee.) The Anglo-Saxons were too unsophisticated to have a word for character, though they knew the thing without the word, and it is the *character* of Beowulf that grips Hrothgar and us. Two names, one of fiction one of history, *Beowulf* and *Alfred* ought to be sufficient to refute the widely-spread notion that the Old English were not *civilized* until they were Prussianized by the Normans. The "polish" of civilization came later, but the grain that took the polish can best be studied in the character of Beowulf and the writings of Alfred.—24. HYGELAC. The king of the Geatas. Identical with the Chochilaicus who according to Gregory of Tours made a raid into the territory of Frisians and Merovingian Franks between 512 and 520. Hygelac had already loaded his booty aboard his ships, when he was surprised by Theudebert, son of the Merovingian Theoderic, and slain in battle. (*Historia Francorum* III, 3 written in the 6th century). This event is four times referred to in the poem 1202, 2201, 2354, 2912 ff.—25. THE DAUNTLESS JUTE. O. E. god mid Geatum, good (brave) among the Geatas. Beowulf is called a Geat in the poem, and most Beowulf critics identify the Geatas with the inhabitants of what is now Southern Sweden, south of the great lakes (The Swedish *Götar*, Old Norse *Gautar*). I have followed Bugge and Gering in identifying the Geatas with the Jutes a tribe of northern Jutland and neighbors of the Angles and Saxons in their old homes, and have consistently translated so. This is not the place to give the arguments pro and con (see Chambers *Introduction*, p. 8 ff., where a strong case is made out for the Götar as against the Jutes). Even if we accept the theory that Beowulf came from southern Sweden, "Jutes" is a better English word than "Geats."

8.—12. HE WAS WISE IN SEAMANSHIP. I take the "lagucraeftig (Sea-crafty) man" to refer to Beowulf himself. Sigfrid, the hero of the Nibelungenlied is also described as knowing the right ways across the waters, "Die rehten wazzerstraze sint mir wol bekant." Seamanship was a necessary accomplishment of the ideal northern hero.

9.—24. NO HOUSE-CARL HE. Beowulf's armor and appearance prove that he is no mere retainer in the hall of a king, but himself a leader of noble lineage.

10.—6. ECGTHEOW, the father of Beowulf, married the only daughter of Hrethel, king of the Geatas, and father of Hygelac. Having slain Heatholaf the Wylfing, Ecgtheow seeks protection at the court of Hrothgar in the early days of Hrothgar's rule. Hrothgar accepts his fealty and settles the feud by money-payment. (Wyatt's note).

11.—15. SHONE THE BOAR-HEADS. The images of the boar on the crests of the helmets, frequently mentioned in the poem. The boar was sacred to Freyr, the favorite god of the Germanic tribes about the North Sea and the Baltic. See Clark Hall's *Beowulf* for pictures of helmets showing the boar-crest. Tacitus noted these boar-helmets as characteristic of the Aestii: Insigne superstitionis, formas aprorum gestant, (marks of their superstition, they wear boar-images.) York is a contraction of eofor-wic (German eber) boar-town, and in the name of New York the philological bones of this beast that played so important a rôle in old Germanic life and tradition, lie buried.

12.—1. THE STREET WAS STONE-PAVED. O. E. straet, from the Latin strata via, paved road, one of the early West Germanic borrowings from Latin. The Germanic peoples built neither houses nor roads of stone, and the stone-paved street is a memory of the Roman roads known to the Northumbrian poet.—24. I AM BEOWULF CALLED. The first mention of the hero by name.

15.—2. BYRNIE. O. E. byrne, the corslet. The most common kenning for it is "ring-net." The corslet of ring-mail was composed of small fine iron rings which were so arranged that every ring was interlocked with four others. A complete corslet of this kind, found at Vimoor (Funen), was made up of about 20,000 rings, and it is estimated that it must have taken a man something like a year to make it. Like the sword, the corslet was a valued heirloom, and Beowulf leaves his own to Wiglaf at his death. (See fig. 6 in Clark Hall's *Beowulf*.)—19. WITH NICORS I WRESTLED. Sea-monsters, variously interpreted; here probably the walrus (whale-horse). Vigfusson's Icelandic dictionary defines them as "fabulous water goblins, mostly appearing in the shape of a gray water-horse." The word is common Germanic. In modern English Old Nick has become a landlubber and got mixed up with Nicholas. From the German feminine form, we get "nixy." Matthew Arnold's *Neckan* is from the Swedish "næcken." See *Cent. Dict.* "Nick" and "nicker."—21. CRUSHED IN MY GRIP. Beowulf's strength is in his grip. He prefers his hands to weapons in a fight, and like many heroes of Northern Saga finds swords of little use.

16.—6. HIS FAITH MUST PUT IN THE JUDGMENT OF GOD. *i.e.* the battle will decide who is right, but the judgment of God decides the battle. It is the ancient (and modern) faith in trial by combat. 20. THE WORK OF WELAND, the famous smith of Germanic epic tradition. See introductory note on Heroic Epic. So WYRD WILL BE DONE. "Wyrd" (Norse Urd, one of the three Norns) is the Old English goddess of fate, whom even Christianity could not entirely displace. "Fair are the glories of Christ; Wyrd is strongest," says an Old English proverb. (See *Gnomic Verses,* p. 75, l. 4.) The weird sisters, *i.e.* the "fate sisters," in *Macbeth* are survivals in Scottish tradition of the Germanic Wyrd. For a striking picture of the Norse "weavers of Fate," see the *Icelandic Njals Saga,* Chap. 157 (Dasent's translation, *The Story of Burnt Njal,* republished, London, Grant Richards, 1900; and Gray's *Fatal Sisters.*) It is difficult to determine how far Wyrd was still thought of in a personal way by the Old English poets. Wyrd and God hold a balance of power in all the older poetry. Our word "doom" has gone over to the realm of fate, whereas for the Anglo-Saxons after the conversion it was used of the Judgment of God, as still in our "dooms-day."—23. For the gist of Hrothgar's reference to Ecgtheow see note 10—7.

17.—7. THEY BOASTED. O. E. beot, boast has not the unfavorable modern connotation, "nor was it Dutch courage that inspired the utterance. As in the Indian war-dance so at the Germanic feast in hall or camp before battle, the warrior was expected to make his 'beot,' or promise of prowess,—and to keep it." Gummere. 23. WHILE THE MINSTREL SANG. Cf. *Widsith,* p. 76, l. 25.

18.—6. BRECCA. Beowulf's adventure with Brecca is paralleled by his feat of swimming off with the thirty suits of armor (see note on Beowulf 7—24). Swimming and diving were accomplishments expected of northern heroes. The sagas often mention the fact that their heroes were expert swimmers, *e.g.* the *Kristni Saga* of Olaf Tryggvason who fought the English at the battle of Maldon. The Njals' Saga says of one of its heroes "he could swim like a seal."

16. SEVEN DAYS AND NIGHTS. O. E. seofon niht "a sennight." The Germanic peoples reckoned by nights instead of days (cf. fort-night) Tacitus noted this custom (*Germania* XI) *Nec dierum numerum ut nos, sed noctium computant.*

21—2. YOU MURDERED YOUR BROTHERS, YOUR CLOSEST OF KIN.—To turn against one's kin was considered the basest of all crimes among the Northern peoples, just as defense of kinsfolk was the first duty. In the Scandinavian sources Gothmund hurls the same charge at Sinfjotli (Fitela). "Nought can stifle call of kin" says the poet when Wiglaf comes to the aid of Beowulf his kinsman in his last fight.

26.—30. ALE-SPILLING FRAY. Literally "ale-bereavement,"—reminiscent of the wild oversetting of tankards and spilling of ale when the hall was suddenly attacked. For famous Germanic hall-fights see the close of the *Nibelungenlied* (Needler's translation), the Old English *Finnsburg Fragment* (Gummere's *Oldest English Epic*), and the fine Eddic lay of *Hamthir,* where there is a vivid picture of an "ealu-scerwen," an ale-spilling:

"There was tumult in the hall, the tankards were upset
 The men lay in blood that mingled with beer."

28.—6. POINT WOULD NOT PIERCE, etc. "Spells" which protected those who knew them, against injury, were familiar to our Germanic ancestors. See *Charm against a Sudden Stitch,* and note. Later, Beowulf's sword refuses to bite on the body of Grendel's mother. She was spelled against all swords but her own, and it is with this that Beowulf finally kills her. In the *Njals Saga* (Chap. 30), Hallgrim has a sword "which he had made by seething spells; and this is what the spells say, that no weapon shall give him his deathblow save that sword. When a man is to be slain by that sword, something sings in it so loudly that it may be heard a long way off." This belief in "spells" and charmed weapons lasted a long time. Macbeth smiles at swords and laughs weapons to scorn, because he thinks he has been spelled against them by the witches, and when he meets Macduff, he says:

> "Let fall thy blade on vulnerable crests;
> *I bear a charmed life.*"

For charmed weapons, cf. *Faerie Queene,* Bk. I, Canto IV, stanza 50.

29.—5. THIS TOKEN THEY SAW. Beowulf probably hung his battle-trophy on some projection above the door on the outside of the hall; for later we are told that Hrothgar sees it as he is standing on the steps outside. For an interesting Norse parallel see the Icelandic *Saga of Grettir the Strong,* Chaps. 35 and 36. (Translated by Magnusson and Morris.) In this story the hero fights a cat-monster. "The men of Bard-dale say that day dawned on her while they wrestled, and that she burst when he cut the arm from her." The parallels are probably due to a modification and domestication of the Grendel story in Iceland. Cf. also the Icelandic saga of *Bodvar Bjarki* (Lawrence, *Mod. Lang. Publ.,* June, 1909, pp. 220 sq.).

29.—6. THE HAND OF GRENDEL. The O. E. speaks of hand, arm, and shoulders and combines the whole into "grap" Grendel's gripe or clutch. Though described in human terms he uses his "grap" like a wild beast. It is later described as having steel-like spurs. Perhaps there are reminiscences of fights with "the bear that walks like a man." Human beings that had changed into the forms of wild animals were considered especially dangerous. See note on wer-wolf. 13. NOT ONE OF THEM FELT REGRET, *i.e.* they exulted in Grendel's defeat. One of the numerous examples of *litotes,* emphasis by understatement, characteristic of O. E. poetry and especially the *Beowulf* poet. So Beowulf deems the life of Grendel, on whom all epithets of wanton destructiveness have been heaped, as "of little use to mankind." So after Grendel's attack on Heorot, when the hall stood empty at night, "it was easy to find men that slept elsewhere." So when Unferth the boaster sees Grendel's clutch placed by Beowulf over the entrance of the hall, he is "more sparing of brags" *i.e.* he is utterly silenced, Beowulf has "shut him up."

30.—872. The episodes have been omitted in the translation as most of them deal obscurely with battles and feuds the elucidation of which, even when possible, lies beyond the scope of this book. But it should not be forgotten, as Professor Ker points out, that this episodic material gives a reality and solidity to the poem which is lost by their entire omission. The most *vivid* portions of the poem are the least *real,* and the most *real* are the least *vivid,* and this is one of the chief defects of Beowulf as an epic poem. The episode of Sigmund has a special interest, because it shows that the Nibelungen Legend was known in England, and because this allusion to it antedates by centuries the *Volsunga Saga,* the *Nibelungenlied,* and even the Eddic poems. Sigmund is called wreccena wide maerost, "most widely known of heroes." As noted before, the dragon slaying is here attributed to Sigmund instead of Sigfrid. The *Volsunga Saga* preserves the story of Sigmund and Sinfjotli (Fitela). The O. E. poet rightly calls Sigmund Waelse's eafera, son of Waels (Vols) and Waelsing, -ing or -ung being the patronymic, whereas the *Volsunga Saga* erroneously calls Sigmund's father Volsung.

31.—6. STOOD ON THE STEP. O. E. stod on stapole. A much-discussed passage. "Stapol" generally means column, but Beowulf had placed Grendel's claw *outside* the hall. I have followed Miller's interpretation (Anglia XII, 398 adopted by Chambers) of stapol as the *stone step* leading up to the entrance of the hall over the door of which, under the gable-end, hung the trophy. 24. ANCIENT OF DAYS. O. E. eald metod "old creator." "Old" here suggests dignity and the affectionate loyalty due to age, and what is venerable with age. It is steeped in Germanic feeling and there is a touch of naive simplicity that is absent from the Hebrew "Ancient of Days." Professor Gummere translates "That the God of ages was good to her." 33.—24. NOT EASY IT IS. Litotes for impossible, *i.e.* escape from death. 34.—12. HROTHGAR AND HROTHULF. Hrothulf, Hrothgar's nephew is the Hrolf Kraki of Danish Saga. The queen later on expresses the hope that Hrothulf, should he by the death of Hrothgar become guardian of her young sons, will prove a faithful protector to them. This hope was not to be realized. Hrethric, Hrothgar's son was deposed and slain by Hrothulf, and Hrothulf himself was killed by Heoroward, son of Heorogar, Hrothgar's elder brother, and his hall burned over his head. These details, obscurely alluded to in the poem, we learn from later Scandinavian sources. 28. OFFSPRING OF FILES. O. E. fela laf, "leavings of files," kenning for sword. In B. 2829, and the Shield Riddle the sword is called hamera laf, leavings of hammers.

35.—8. The heir of Ing. O. E. eodor Ingwina, ruler of the Ingwins, "friends of Ing," a name given to the Danes as worshippers of Freyr who bore the surname Ing.

36.—6. THE SUDDEN ASSAULT ON THE SONS OF FINN. For the relation of this episode to the *Finnsburg Fragment* see *Oldest English Epic*, p. 70, and Chambers' *Introduction*, Part III, pp. 245-289, where the relation of the Beowulf Episode to the *Finnsburg Fragment* is fully discussed.

37.—14. HRETHRIC. See note on Hrothulf, 34—12. 16. Beowulf is of course the special hero of the haeleþa bearn "the children of the warriors," and the picture of him sitting among the youngsters (giogoth) with Wealhtheow's two boys nestling close to him adds a human touch to a character very little "sentimentalized" in the modern sense. The "riotous band" is not in the text but everything else is.

37.—22. HAMA . . . GEM OF THE BRISINGS. The collar the queen gives to Beowulf is compared to the Brisinga men, a famous necklace which in the Eddic poems adorns the goddess Freyja. For *Hama* see note on *Life of the Gleeman*, WUDGA AND HAMA 77—10.

40.—24. NOR WAS BEOWULF THERE. After the killing of Grendel, the retainers again sleep in the hall, but Beowulf, like the king, sleeps in the bowers near by.

41.—2. BAD WAS THE BARGAIN, *i.e.* The Jutes had lost a man the first night in the hall of the Danes, and now the Danes had paid the loss with loss of their own man, but it was a futile exchange.

45.—8. THEY SAW IN THE WATER SEA-SNAKES, etc. Cf. the fine assortment of sea-monsters in the *Faerie Queene*, Bk. II, Canto XII, 22-25:

"Spring-headed Hydras and sea-shouldering whales
Great whirlpooles which all fishes make to flee;
Bright Scolopendræs arm'd with silver scales;
Mighty Monoceroses with immeasured tayles.
The dreadful Fish that hath deserved the name
Of Death, and like him lookes in dreadfull hew;
The griesly Wasserman, that makes his game
The flying ships with swiftness to pursew;
The horrible Sea-Satyre, that doth shew
His fearfull face in time of greatest storme;
Huge Ziffius, whom Mariners eschew
No less then rockes, (as travellers informe)
And greedy Rosmarines with visages deforme."

45.—13. SUDDEN THEY FLED. So, in the *Faerie Queene,* when the palmer smote the sea with his staff,

"all that dreadful armie fast gan fly
Into great Tethys bosome, where they hidden lye."

46.—22. SWIFTLY HE SANK, etc. In the story of Grettir, the hero fights a giant in a cave under a waterfall. It is clearly a reminiscence of Beowulf's adventure. "Then Grettir dived under the force (waterfall), and hard work it was, because the whirlpool was strong, and he had to dive down to the bottom before he might come up under the force, and the river fell over it from the sheer rocks. He went up into the cave, and there was a great fire flaming from amidst of brands; and there he saw a giant sitting withal, marvellously great, and dreadful to look on. . . . And the giant was fain to reach for a sword that hung up there in the cave; but therewithal Grettir smote him afore into the breast, and smote off well-nigh all the breast, bone and belly, so that the bowels tumbled out of him and fell into the river, and were driven down along the stream; and as the priest (who has been holding a rope for Grettir to pull himself up by) sat by the rope, he saw certain fibres all covered with blood swept down the swirls of the stream; then . . . he thought for sure that Grettir was dead, and got him home. But Grettir went up the cave, after he had killed the giant, and kindled a light, and espied the cave.

The story tells not how much he got therein, but it must have been something great."

47.—9. THOUGH EAGER TO SMITE HER, HIS ARM WAS HELPLESS. So in the story of Grettir: "She held him to her so hard that he might turn his hands to no account save to keep fast hold on the middle of the witch."—18. Now FIRST HE DISCERNED. It may well be that the *Grettis Saga* preserves the original form of the story in which the hero first meets his adversary within the cave as Chambers suggests (*Beowulf* ed. p. 76). But there is no real difficulty in supposing that Beowulf could not *recognize* (ongietan) his foe *under water*, and that in her grip *under water*, he could not well wield his weapon. By the light in the cave he saw who she was (ongeat) and in the free air of the cave the swinging blow was possible even though, as Chambers holds against Gummere there is nothing said of his "having extricated himself from the coil."—21. SANG ON HER HEAD THE HARD-FORGED BLADE. The sword in Germanic Epic has a well-marked personality. It has its proper name, its pedigree and history, its runic inscription on the hilt, with the name of the maker. It was faithful to its owner, or on occasion it failed him like a traitor, as here. Often it encouraged him, and spurred him on to do his best. It drank the blood from the wound in battle-gulps, and sang its war-song wild on the head of the foe. Oaths were sworn on the sword, and if a sword-oath is broken, the blade will not bite but on the owner's head. Swords were among the most precious heirlooms handed down from father to son. "They were not inanimate tools of war, but seemed alive, endowed with supernatural powers, witnesses and symbols of the most important transactions of life, intimate comrades in the hour of need." (Uhland.)—Moreover, every sword had its own peculiar ring, by which it could be recognized, like the sound of the human voice. In the story of Offa (see Uhland's ballad, *Der Blinde Kœnig*, and *Saxo*, V, 4, p. 96), the blind old king, Wermund, listening to a dual combat between his son and a Viking chief, recognizes the triumphant voice of his old sword, and knows that his son is victorious.—23. BATTLE-FLASHER. A fine kenning for the sword. As Uhland points out (*Deutsche Heldensage*), swords were often named for their light-giving power. Valhalla was lighted by swords. In the *Finnsburg Fragment,* during a night-attack upon the hall, the "sword-light flashed as though all Finnsburg were on fire."

48.—6. THE MURDEROUS HAG BY THE HAIR HE CAUGHT. The Ms. reads *eaxle* = shoulder, emended by Sweet to *feaxe* = hair, which improves both the sense and the alliteration.—18. ALL HAD BEEN OVER WITH ECGTHEOW'S SON. A desperate attempt on the part of the Christian poet to hold the balance between the providence of God and the prowess of the hero. Yet the passage is quite in keeping with the sentiment of line 572: "Wyrd will often deliver an undoomed earl, if his courage is good."

49.—24. THE LIFELESS BODY SPRANG FROM THE BLOWS, etc. Not an act of wanton revenge, but probably in order to prevent Grendel's double or ghost from haunting the hall.

53.—16. RUNES WERE WRIT. Literally: Through rune-staves it was rightly marked, set and said, for whom the sword, etc. "Read" is the regular word that denotes deciphering of runes. (Cf. German "rathen," and see note on Hell-rune, 6-24)—31. NOT HEREMOD THUS, etc. Like Ermanric among the Goths, Heremod became for the Danes the stock example of a bad and cruel king. He is here introduced as the anti-type of the good king, just as for readers of the poem Beowulf himself was the type of the noble king and hero. See Chadwick, *Origins,* 148 ff.

55.—9. THE HARDY ONE, i.e. Beowulf. The syntax offers difficulties, but the main point is clear: Hrunting had failed Beowulf in the fight. But he does not taunt Unferth who lent him the sword. So Beowulf's courtesy is put in strong relief and the parting from Unferth is contrasted with the meeting (Gummere).

57.—13. KISSED THE KING, ll. 13 and 15 are Professor Gummere's. Literally: Kissed the king of noble lineage, the lord of Scyldings, the best of thanes, took him by the neck, the tears fell, etc. The language of the recognition scene between Joseph and Benjamin (Gen. 45:14) naturally suggests itself to any translator at this point: "And he fell upon his brother Benjamin's neck and wept. . . . Moreover he kissed his brethren, etc."

58.—7. Said the Weder folk would welcome the sight of them. Professor Gummere renders:

> but "Welcome!" he called to that Weder clan

O. E.

> cwæþ þæt wilcuman Wedera leodum
> scaþan scirhame, to scipe foron.

"Quoth that welcome to the Wederfolk the shining-mailed warriors to their ship fared." The Weder folk are of course Beowulf's people, but Gummere's rendering does violence to the syntax both of wilcuman and faran. The coast-guard says: You are faring to your ship, welcome to the Wederfolk, *i.e.* to the Weder-folk at home your return is welcome.

58.—18. Its sea-suit. O. E. þa wæs be mæste mere-hrægla sum. "There was by the mast a sea-garment." Our modern "suit of sails" keeps the same figure.—26. Stood on the shore. They seem to have driven right upon the beach before the wind. This sudden and somewhat unseamanlike landing may be due to the ecclesiastical poet's unfamiliarity with boats, or it may represent actual practice. Boats are described as grating on the shingle, driving upon the sand, and also as riding at anchor. Probably they were beached for loading and unloading where tide and bottom permitted, and then floated and anchored or moored. The coast guard sees Beowulf's men on their arrival bearing their shields "over bolcan," (gunwale?), but Beowulf finds his boat riding at anchor on his return. Cf. the sea-voyages in *Elene, Andreas, Guthlac.*

60.—Beowulf's fight with the Fire Dragon. The story of the dragon and treasure are common motives of Germanic Epic. See the tale of Sigurd and Fafnir, in the *Volsunga Saga,* on which Wagner has based his Sigfrid-drama.—27. Uprose with his shield. Probably an old Epic formula. So in the Latin Waltharius (see Scheffel's *Ekkehard*), the hero "in clipeum surgit."

61.—24. As the worm coiled back. "Worm" is the native Germanic word for dragon.—27. The shield of iron, etc. A difficult passage, which none of the translators has made clear. I take the verb "wealdan" to refer to the shield, and by supplying the pronoun "his" or "him" (*i.e.*

the shield) as object of "wealdan," to wield, we get the following sense: Beowulf, having a brand-new iron shield, had a right to expect that it would last longer than it did, seeing that he wielded (it) for the first time (*forman dogore*), on that occasion (*by fyrste*).

62.—25. FLED TO THE WOOD. For a parallel situation, and reproach of the cowards, see the *Battle of Maldon*, p. 171, l. 186. The speech of Ælfwine (*Maldon*, ll. 195 sq.) closely echoes that of Wiglaf, and illustrates the Germanic trait of loyalty to the leader which Tacitus had noted long ago (*Germania*, Chap. 14): "Base it is for the followers (*comitatus*) not to equal the courage of the leader; but infamous and disgraced for the rest of his life is he who returns from the battle surviving his lord."

63.—2. WIGLAF WAS CALLED. Wiglaf was a kinsman of Beowulf (see Beowulf's last speech), and therefore doubly bound to stand by his lord.

65.—10. BROKEN WAS NÆGLING. The name of Beowulf's sword. Other famous sword-names were Hrunting (thruster), the sword Unferth gave to Beowulf; Miming, the sword Wayland the smith made for Sigurd according to the *Thidrekssaga;* Balmung, Sigfried's sword in the *Nibelungenlied.* See note on p. 47-21.—13. HIS HAND WAS TOO HEAVY. Saxo tells the same thing of Offa. No sword was of such stiffness that he did not shiver it at the first stroke into many pieces, "crebra partium fractione dissolveret!" See also *Volsunga Saga*, Chap. XV, Sigurd's sword-test.

66.—2. THRUST FROM BELOW, etc. The dragons of Germanic folklore have scaly backs that no sword may pierce, and can only be killed from below. In the *Volsunga Saga*, Sigurd kills the dragon Fafnir by digging a pit in his path and stabbing him from below.—20. WORK OF THE GIANTS. Tacitus says that the Teutons abhorred stone walls. To the Angles and Saxons who invaded England in the fifth and sixth centuries, accustomed as they were to wooden halls of the Heorot type, the remnants of Roman architecture were "Giants' work." "Castles are seen from afar, reared by giants they rise in the land, wondrous walls of masonry," say the *Gnomic Verses*. The word translated "castles" is the Roman *castra*.—22. UPHELD THAT HILL-VAULT, etc.

Literally "earth-house." This name is said to be still applied in Scotland to the underground structures known as Picts' houses. See "earth-houses," *Cent. Dict.*

68.—2. MANY A SUN-BRIGHT JEWEL HE SAW. Dragon-guarded treasure played a great rôle in Germanic folklore. The best known is the famous Nibelungen hoard won by Sigfried when he kills the dragon. The towering banner, with gold inwoven, may be a reminiscence of a legionary standard left behind in the hurried withdrawal of the Roman garrisons under Honorius, 410 A.D. The military standard of the Roman emperors consisted of a staff or lance carrying a purple banner on a cross-bar. The banner usually bore the effigy of the emperor. But Constantine, who, it will be remembered, was proclaimed at York, after his conversion to Christianity placed upon it, woven in gold, the mystic monogram consisting of the Greek letter X(= Ch) and P(=R), standing for "Christ." (For a detailed description of the Labarum, see Eusebius' *Life of Constantine,* quoted in note on *Elene.*) It is far from improbable that some such standard, hidden away with other Roman treasure, was discovered by Anglian invaders of the North of England.

69.—21. BEOWULF'S BARROW. So Achilles had his tomb "high on a jutting headland over wide Hellespont, that it might be seen from afar off the sea by men that now are and by those that shall be hereafter." (*Odyssey,* Book 24, Butcher and Lang's translation.)

70.—2. TO FIND THE REWARD OF THE FAITHFUL. A Christian touch out of keeping with what Beowulf has just said about Wyrd sweeping away the last of his line to the land of doom. For a similar mingling of the Christian and the old Germanic mood in contemplating the hereafter, see the close of the Gnomic verse from the Cotton Ms., p. 157, 14-19.

74.—22. JOINED IN THE WAIL. See note on *Beowulf* for the theory that he had a wife. Cf. the lament of Andromache over Hector (*Iliad* 24, 725 ff.), which has the same governing motive, the fear that now the tribal hero is dead nothing but captivity awaits the defenceless folk (Chambers).

75.—14. THE BATTLE-BRAVE RODE. So Jordanes describing Attila's funeral tells how mounted horsemen rode round his body chanting his famous deeds. Cf. also the burial of Achilles (*Odyssey* 24, 68-70). "And many heroes of the Acheans moved mail-clad around the pyre,—both footmen and horse, and great was the noise that arose."

THE LIFE OF THE GLEEMAN
FROM THE WIDSITH

In the *Widsith* we have an interesting example of the distinction made above, between *Epic tradition,* and *Epic poetry.* Widsith is not an epic poem; there is only a slight strand of narrative in it, and that is personal rather than narrative, but it is made up of allusions and references to a very ancient form of that *epic tradition,* out of which the earliest *heroic lays* of the Germanic peoples were made. Around the names of the leaders of Goths and Vandals, Lombards, Franks, Burgundians, and Huns, who collided with each other and with the waning power of Rome from the fourth to the sixth centuries, the great cycles of Germanic Epic tradition arose.

The earliest home of this tradition was the hall of the king, where among heroes and nobles the gleeman chanted his lay. It is not a poetry of the people in the true sense, but a poetry of the fighting class. Though "popular" as opposed to "literary" in its origins, we get in it no reflection of the life and interests of the people as a whole. (See note on *Riddles and Gnomic Poetry*).

The *form* of the epic lay, in continuous verse chanted or recited to the accompaniment of the harp, as distinguished from earlier choric songs in strophic form mentioned by Tacitus, seems to have been first developed among the Goths, and to have spread from them to the Franks and other West-Germanic tribes. Cassiodorus, a historian of the sixth century, tells how Chlodwig, the founder of the Frankish kingdom, asked Theodoric the Ostrogoth to send him a gleeman practised in the art of chanting lays to the accompaniment of the harp, and the Old English *Widsith* is a striking testimony to the large contribution made by the vanished Goths to Old Germanic Epic.

The Epic Lay, at first a recital of actual occurrence, became in time overlaid with legendary and mythical material. Names and events were confused; where memory failed, imagination supplied color and detail, until often there was little left that was historic but the names of the heroes themselves looming dim through the centuries. Out of such historic and legendary lays of the great halls, poets of a later generation wove long and stately epics, to be read and recited, but no longer sung as of old. The Byzantine historian Priscus gives an interesting picture of a Germanic hall of the fifth century, and of the gleeman's song. Sent as an emissary to the hall of Attila, whose court was patterned after the Germanic fashion, Priscus describes how he and his companions, before entering, were offered the drinking cup and heard the ancient Germanic greeting "wæs hæl" (wassail). Then they passed to the seats ranged along opposite sides of the hall. In the centre raised above the others was Attila's seat, and on his right was the seat of honor. The guests were greeted in order by the king, who drank the health of each, and was greeted standing by each in return. When evening came, torches were lighted, and two gleemen standing opposite to Attila, recited lays in which they praised his victories and his prowess in war. "All the guests gazed upon the gleemen; some were pleased by their lays, others were reminded of their own battles and were filled with enthusiasm, but some wept, the strength of whose bodies had been sapped by time and whose fiery spirits age had subdued."

The poem of *Widsith* owes its preservation to the fact that it was copied into the Exeter Book (see introductory note: Exeter Book). *Widsith* comprises 143 lines. Our selection gives 1-9, 88-111, 127-143. Widsith is the name of a typical and imaginary gleeman or minstrel, who has visited many lands and sung in the halls of many kings. (Old English *wīd,* far, wide; *sīþ,* journey.) In Old English the singer was called "scop," from Old English *scieppan,* to shape, to create (cf. derivation of *poeta*). The catalogue of tribes and rulers that forms the core of the poem points to the period before the English left their continental homes on the Elbe and Weser. It is customary to refer to these lists as having merely an antiquarian value. But in the days when Attila, Ermanric, Theodoric, Offa, Hrothgar, Gunther, Wudga, Hama, and the rest of them were heroes of well-known lays, the mere mention of their names must have had an imaginative and emotional value entirely lost to us. "Bare lists of words," says Emerson, "are found suggestive to an imaginative and excited mind." These memories of the heroes of Germanic Epic preserved in a long tradition of oral lays, running back to continental times, and variously modified in transit, were finally written down by a monkish scribe who could not resist the temptation of extending the itinerary of Widsith by including the Israelites and the Assyrians, the Medes and the Persians, the Saracens, and the Moabites, and sundry other impossible bookish tribes and countries. In spite of these incongruities and interpolations, *Widsith* remains one of the most interesting records, as it certainly is the oldest, in the literature of the Old English, dealing with the Epic memories common to all the Germanic races. (Cf. R. W. Chambers *Widsith: A study in Old English Heroic Legend,* Cambridge, 1912. A mine of information on the Germanic tribes and heroes mentioned in the poem. Also Professor Gummere's *Oldest English Epic,* where the whole of *Widsith* is translated and commented on, and W. W. Lawrence, *Modern Philology,* 1906, Vol. IV, p. 329.)

76.—1-9. The first nine lines form an introduction written in England, probably in the eighth or ninth century, and consequently much more recent than the core of the poem, which antedates the Anglo-Saxon settlement. "Widsith," the far-wanderer, is described as belonging to the Myrgings, a Low-German tribe dwelling near the mouth of the Elbe, the old home of the Angles. He undertakes a journey to the court of the Ostro-Gothic King Ermanric, in the company of his queen Alhild. The object of this journey seems to have been the marriage of Alhild to Ermanric; hence she is called weaver-of-peace. She leaves her home to become the bride of the Ostrogoth, just as in the *Nibelungenlied,* Kriemhild leaves her brothers to marry Attila the Hun. Ermanric, king of the Ostrogoths, is a historic figure. He died by his own hand in 375 A.D., on account of the destruction of his kingdom by the Huns. In early Gothic tradition he was remembered as a great and famous king, whose tragic death, so unlike that of the typical Germanic hero, made a profound impression on his people, and naturally lent itself to the transforming touch of the imagination. Jordanes, a Gothic historian writing nearly two hundred years after the death of Ermanric, still calls him the noblest of the Amalungs. In later West-Germanic and Norse epic tradition his character was entirely changed, and he became a type of the tyrant and traitor, cruel and faithless. According to *Deor's Complaint,* he had a wolfish heart, and the writer of the *Widsith* prologue calls him ruthless traitor and treaty-breaker. This later tradition represents him as having killed his own son, and having his innocent wife Swanhild torn to pieces by wild horses. For the story of him see *Northern Hero Legends,* pp. 29 ff.

76.—10. I WAS WITH ERMANRIC, etc. Lines 9-87, omitted in the translation, comprise lists of tribes and rulers supposed to have been visited by Widsith. Line 88 returns to the subject of Ermanric, and this makes so close a connection with the prologue that one wonders whether the intervening portions were not interpolated. Dr. Lawrence, in his exhaustive study of the structure and interpretation of *Widsith,* says: "This is perhaps the most important division of the poem." It is noticeable that the character which Widsith himself gives to Ermanric differs from that ascribed to him by later tradition, for the "ruthless traitor" of the prologue is here pictured as a noble and generous king. This in itself is an evidence that the core of the poem is older than the prologue.—12. GAVE ME A RING. One of the commonest kennings or descriptive epithets applied to the king in Old English poetry is ring-giver, bracelet-bestower. Professor Gummere notes that the heavy gold ring is marked with its value, and that spirals of gold twisted about the arm were broken off by the king, each round having a definite value. Hence the king is also called the ring-breaker.—19. EDWIN'S DAUGHTER. Edwin, a Langobard or Lombard king, known to history as Audoin. The original home of the Lombards was on the Elbe, near the Angles or Myrgings. Edwin's son, Alboin, invaded Italy in 568. In a passage omitted in the translation, Widsith says, "I was with Ealfwine [Old English for Alboin] in Italy." Paul the Deacon, a Lombard historian, tells how Alboin forced his wife, Rosamond, to drink from a cup made of the skull of her own father, whom he had killed. (See Swinburne's tragedy, *Rosamund, Queen of the Lombards*.) Historically it is of course impossible that Alhild, Edwin's daughter, hence sister of Ealfwine or Alboin, who invaded Italy in the sixth century, should have been a contemporary of Ermanric, who died in the fourth, and that Widsith, who says he was with Alboin in Italy, should have been with Ermanric "all that while"; but Epic tradition has no sense of historic perspective. The heroes of the past are contemporary in the great Epic cycles,— they are seen on the same plane, just as the distant mountain ranges, fold on fold, merge into one sky-line for the eye. So in the *Nibelungenlied*, Theodoric, the great Ostrogoth, is present at the court of Attila the Hun, who died two years before Theodoric was born.

77.—10. WUDGA AND HAMA. According to Jordanes, Widigoia (Old English Wudga, Widga) was a Gothic hero who fell in the wars against the Sarmatians before the time of Ermanric. There were lays about him, and he was soon drawn into the cycle of Ermanric's heroes, and together with Hama became champion of the Gothic king in his wars against the Huns. The battle near Wistlawudu, *i.e.* Vistula-wood, here alluded to (the place is mentioned in l. 121 of the original), seems to be a reminiscence of the ancient homes of the Goths on the Vistula, before they wandered south to the Danube. If this be so, it is the most ancient historic reminiscence in Germanic Epic. Hama is the Heime of Middle High German Epic. He is mentioned in *Beowulf* as the captor of a famous necklace, "Brisingamene." As champions of Ermanric, this pair underwent the same process of moral deterioration as their leader, and in later tradition become the types of brave but cruel and ruthless slayers. In this capacity they figure in the fine Middle High German poem of Alphart's Death. (See *Northern Hero Legends*, p. 122.)

77.—16. THUS FATED TO WANDER. The poem closes on

the minor chord that rings through so much of Old English poetry. So Beowulf says:

> "To each of us here the end must come
> Of life upon earth: let him who may
> Win glory ere death. I deem that best,
> The lot of the brave, when life is over."

"Vitae summa brevis spem nos vetat inchoare longam." But the Germanic conclusion is not Horace's or Omar's "Let us drink and be merry, for to-morrow we die," but rather "Let us fight and win fame, for to-morrow we fall." See also the closing lines of the *Battle of Maldon* (p. 174), and the fine stanza in the Norse *Lay of Hamthir*:

> "We have fought a good fight, on fallen Goths we stand;
>   Like eagles on treetops high, on the heap of the slain we
>   perch.
> Glory great is ours, whether we die to-day or to-morrow,
> For none shall live till evening, when the Norns have
>   spoken the word."

It is the same note that Tennyson strikes in the *Ballad of the Revenge;* and the brave speech of Sir Richard Grenville seems to echo the very words of the old Germanic hero:

> "We have fought such a fight, for a day and a night
> As may never be fought again.
> We have won great glory, my men,
> And a day less or more
> At sea or ashore,
> We die,—does it matter when?"

2. BIBLICAL EPIC

Most of Old English narrative poetry on biblical subjects is found in the *Junian Ms.* (see introductory note) and belongs to a school of poetry that is known as *Caedmonian,* from the early ascription of these poems to Caedmon. The conversion of the Old English to Christianity brought them for the first time into the stream of the *Latin* as contrasted with the *Germanic* cultural inheritance, and resulted in the substitution of Bible Story (literary) for the older Epic tradition (oral). But the change was very gradual and there are various overlappings. Thus the *Beowulf* poet knew the O. E. *Genesis,* and the author of *Exodus,* knew the *Beowulf.* But more important than questions of exact date, is the fact that both in form and spirit, these biblical epics continue the older epic tradition. There is a change of *characters,* but not of *character.* The old motives, and ways of life persist under alien names. (For illustrations see notes on *The Fall of Man.*)

FALL OF MAN

The selection given in the text comprises the greater part of the so-called *Younger Genesis (Genesis B),* a fragment of some 600 lines in ninth or tenth century West Saxon. This fragment is found imbedded in the West Saxon version of an older Northumbrian poem on the same subject, and was probably inserted to fill a gap in the Ms. of the older poem, *Genesis A.* Owing to certain peculiarities of diction and structure, Professor Sievers in 1875 argued that this interpolation, which he called *Genesis B,* was translated into the West Saxon from a continental Old Saxon original. The subsequent discovery (1894) of fragments of this Old Saxon original in the Vatican Library at Rome brilliantly verified the hypothesis of Professor Sievers. My colleague, Professor G. H. Gerould, suggests *M. L. N.* May 1911, that a copy of the Old Saxon poem was brought to England by a certain Saxon clerk who came from Liege, and was in the service of Archbishop Dunstan and his successor, and who wrote the first biography of Dunstan, signing himself B. If this hypothesis be correct, we must assign to the *Younger Genesis* a date somewhat after 970, which is considerably later than that usually given.

In the same Ms. with the *Genesis (A* and *B)* are found poems and poetic paraphrases of other portions of the Biblical narrative, *Exodus, Daniel, The Temptation of Christ.* Its contents were first published in 1655 as *Cædmon's Paraphrase* by the Dutch scholar Junius, (See introductory note *Junian Ms.*) who was under the impression that he had discovered the poems attributed by Bede to Cædmon. (See Bede's *Ecclesiastical History,* Bk. IV, Chap. 24, Temple

Classics ed.) Modern scholarship has proved this assumption unwarranted, and none of the poems of the Junian Ms. are now ascribed to Cædmon.

As Junius was a friend of Milton's it is not at all unlikely that he acquainted the author of *Paradise Lost* with the Old English poem on the *Fall of Man.* On this question see Masson's *Life of Milton,* 6, 557 note. Stopford Brooke, *E. E. L.,* Chap. XV, p. 281, and Chaps. XVI and XVII, for parallels between Milton and the Old English *Genesis.* Also A. S. Cook, "Milton and Cædmon," *Academy,* 34, 420. Prof. C. W. Kennedy gives an excellent summary of the contents of the Junian Ms. and of Caedmon criticism in the introduction to his prose translation of *The Cædmon Poems.* E. P. Dutton & Co., 1916.

The Old English *Fall of Man,* with all its crudities and wearying repetitions, is full of dramatic vigor, and shows considerable skill in characterization and handling of motive.

78.—1. THE RULER OF HOSTS, etc. Note how the conception of the Germanic *comitatus* underlies this portrayal. God is pictured as leader and overlord rather than as creator; he bestows power and is the giver of treasure; his bounty is the source of endowments physical and mental.—7. HE DOWERED THEM ALL, etc. The Old Saxon poet is characterized by his fondness for lines of redundant beats, the "Schwellvers," as Professor Sievers calls it. I have tried to give the effect of this by the use of five and six beat lines with medial pause.—11. HIS LORD HE WAS BOUND TO SERVE. As the chief virtue of the lord is generosity, the chief duty of the thane is loyalty. By emphasizing these Germanic motives, the Saxon poet puts Satan in the wrong at the very outset, whereas Milton's first portrait of the rebel angel tempts us to sympathy if not admiration. No Germanic audience would have felt anything but unmixed disapproval of a disloyal thane no matter how fine his spirit.

79.—16. IN THE NORTH AND WEST. In Talmudic tradition the North was the region of the demons, the East of God, the South of the Angels, and the West of Man. In *Gen. A,* Satan strives with God to possess a home and highseat in the North. In l. 339 Eve says: "I can see where He sits himself,— 'tis South and East—the world's creator." In Cynewulf's *Crist* (see p. 121-8) the Saviour appears on

Judgment Day in the South and East. Cf. Milton's "Home-ward with flying march, where we possess *the quarters of the North*," *Paradise Lost*, V, 688. In *Henry VI*, Pt. I, V, Sc. 3, Satan is called "Monarch of the North." For a fine poetical rendering of this tradition, see Stephen Hawker's *Quest of the Sangrail*, pp. 178-180. (*Poetical Works* of R. S. Hawker. John Lane, London and New York, 1899.)

80.—21. EVER FIRE OR FROST. So Milton:

> "the parching air
> Burns frore, and cold performs the effect of fire."

(See the whole passage, *Paradise Lost*, II, 594-603.)

81.—8. THIS NARROW PLACE IS NOTHING LIKE, etc.

> "Is this the region, this the soil, the clime,
> Said then the lost archangel, this the seat
> That we must change for heaven," etc.
>
> —*Paradise Lost*, I, 243.

—23. BUT IRON BONDS ARE ALL ABOUT ME. The illu-strated Ms. shows Satan held fast in the mouth of hell, which is pictured as a dragon. Compare with Satan's speech the argument of Beelzebub in *Paradise Lost*, II.

83.—7. IF ANY THERE BE WHOM ERST I FAVORED. Again the Germanic stress on the duty of the thane to repay in time of need the generosity of his lord. Cf. Wiglaf's speech, *Beowulf*, 63-18, and *Battle of Maldon*, 202-11. The concep-tion of sending a substitute for Satan because he himself is unable to go, seems original with the Old Saxon poet. Milton makes Satan undertake the journey himself.—14. ON FEATHERY PINIONS FLY THROUGH THE AIR. The feather-robe or suit of wings is familiar to Germanic my-thology. When Smith Wayland, the Germanic Vulcan, was hamstrung by his foe to prevent his escape, he donned his feather-robe and flew out through the smoke-hole of his smithy. Avitus, a Latin poet of the fourth century who wrote a poem on the Fall of Man, and whose work the Old Saxon poet may have known, ascribes to Satan the power of changing into beast or bird:

> "Alitis interdum subito mentita volantis
> Fit species."

84.—6. SET HELMET ON HEAD. The West-Saxon has

hæleþ-helm, i.e. hero-helmet, but Koegel suggests that the Old Saxon read *heliþ-helm, i.e.* helmet of concealment, the "tarn-kappe," or cap of invisibility of Germanic folklore. In the *Heliand,* an Old Saxon alliterative poem on the life of Christ, the Devil wears his "heliþ-helm" to deceive men. —8. HE MOUNTED ALOFT, etc. Cf. *Paradise Lost,* II, 927:

> "At last his sail-broad vans
> He spreads for flight, and in the surging smoke
> Uplifted, spurns the ground; thence many a league
> As in a cloudy chair ascending rides,"

and contrast the music of Milton's interlinked alliterations with the hammer-blow style of the Anglo-Saxon.

85.—18. IN THE SHAPE OF A SERPENT. The Old English word is "worm," the same used for the dragon in *Beowulf.* The "worm" of Germanic folklore is a dragon or serpent monster.

87.—8. FAR FROM THE EAST. See note on 79-15.

90.—29. YET DID SHE IT ALL IN DUTY AND LOVE. The old poet saves the character of Eve and enlists our pity for her. How different from Milton's Eve, compact of vanity and shallow deceitfulness! (*Paradise Lost,* IX, 816 ff.) In the Old English poem Adam yields from utter weariness, a very human touch. Milton makes him eat

> "Against his better knowledge, not deceived
> But fondly overcome with female charm."

91.—12. HE LAUGHED ALOUD AND LEAPED FOR JOY. Contrast with this exultant note, Milton's "Back to the thicket slunk the guilty serpent."

THE DROWNING OF THE EGYPTIANS

The *Exodus* is one of the poems found in the Junian Ms. Its date is unknown, but it is certainly much older than the *Younger Genesis,* and was probably composed in Northumbria. It contains 589 lines, and the translated passage fairly illustrates the descriptive vigor of the poem, its imaginative intensity and vividness of phrase, and also the variation and repetition so characteristic of Old English verse. While long stretches of verse in the Junian Ms. are mere alliterative paraphrase of the Bible story, the *Exodus* stands out as an independent poem, created by the imagination of the unknown author out of the Old Testament narrative. For a literary appreciation, see Stopford Brooke, *E. E. L.,* pp. 315-324. For a brief, critical discussion of the problems involved see Professor F. A. Blackburn's introduction to his edition of *Exodus and Daniel* in the Belles Lettres Series (D. C. Heath and Co., 1907). The *Exodus* presents unusual difficulties to the translator. This is not the place to justify the renderings adopted. Students of Old English should compare Professor Blackburn's notes on the passage.

94.—20. WHEN THE DARK UPHEAVAL O'ERWHELMED THEM ALL. This rendering is based on Professor Blackburn's emendation of a corrupt passage in the text. Professor Blackburn translates: "Then on them fell the hugest of wild waves, dark with its towering mass."

3. SAINTS' LEGENDS

A considerable part of Old English narrative poetry deals with Saints' Legends, and reflects the early popularity of this type of medieval literature among the Anglo-Saxons. A special interest attaches to the Old English poems of this genre, because the name of the foremost Old English poet is intimately associated with them. In two long poems, *Elene* and *Juliana,* and the fragment of a third *The Fates of the Apostles,* we find the name *Cynewulf* woven into the text. Others, like *Andreas* and at least the second part of *Guthlac,* are by many scholars ascribed to Cynewulf although we do not find his name signed to these poems.

The older Epic was northern, pagan, and Germanic in origin, and though in its literary form it shows the Christian influence and no doubt owed its preservation to the monastery, its ideals were those of the pre-Christian heroic age of the Germanic peoples. With the introduction of Christianity, the Biblical narrative gradually displaced the older epic tradition, and we find the events and characters of the Old and New Testaments and the apocrypha, kindling the imagination of the epic poet, though the spirit of the narrative poems in the Junian Ms. and of *Judith and Holofernes* is still that of the pagan epic, with its delight in warfare and its emphasis upon the old Germanic virtues: generosity in the king, loyalty in his followers, bravery in battle, and love of fame. In the legendary narratives of which *Elene* and *Guthlac* are examples, there is a distinct change of atmosphere. Not only do these poems derive their subject-matter and inspiration from the legendary literature of the Latin church, but the monastery and the saint have definitely taken the place of the hall and the warrior as the centre of outlook upon life. The gleeman is gone and fidelity to the faith supplants loyalty to the leader in battle; heavenly joy and rewards take the place of the revelry and ring-giving in the mead-hall. The tone has become ecclesiastical, and the temper more inward and spiritual. The battle is now with the powers of evil. In the place of Beowulf's wrestlings against monsters of fen and mere, we have wrestlings against principalities and powers, the spirits of evil and against their chief, Satan himself. And yet the ecclesiastical poet, like the monks in Arnold's *Grande Chartreuse* ofttimes hears the old martial music beating upon the walls of his quiet retreat and his imagination kindles to the appeal of the old call to action, battle, and adventure. For the finest sea-piece in Old English poetry we must go, not to *Beowulf,* but to the *Elene,* and whenever the war-trumpets sound, the poet forgets his Latin legend, and watches the raven circling over the host, or listens to the eagle and the wolf holding converse over the bodies of the slain.

In form, the poetry of Saints' Legends carries on the epic tradition,—the old formulas, the conventionalized figures, the kennings for ship and sea and sword and spear recur again and again; there is the same parallelism of structure, and the goal of the narrative is finally reached by the same circuitous route, along the same "by-paths and indirect crook'd ways" as in *Beowulf.* Poems like *Elene* and *Andreas* lie nearer the old epic highways; their action is mainly outward, there is abundance of adventure, journeys by land and sea, the crashing of lance against shield. In others again as in *Juliana* and *Guthlac,* the conflict is mainly an inner one,—materialized to be sure and projected into the outer world of demons and angels—but still in essence inward and spiritual, with the ideals of sainthood dominating the whole. We have chosen *Elene* as a type of the former, and *Guthlac* as a type of the latter, in these selections. (For Saints' Legends as a literary type see G. H. Gerould, *Saints' Legends,* Houghton Mifflin Co., 1916.)

THE LEGEND OF THE CROSS

The Legend of the Cross. The story of the emperor Constantine's conversion to Christianity through the apparition of the cross on the battlefield, and of the subsequent discovery of the true cross by his mother Helena (O. E. *Elene*), gave rise to a vast body of medieval legendary lore. The story of the quest and discovery of the Grail, the cup used by the Saviour at the last supper, and of the lance with which his side was pierced, belong to the same legendary complex. While the Cross legend remained almost entirely ecclesiastical, the Grail and lance legend, through blending with Celtic folk-lore, and association with the Arthurian cycle, early entered the secular literature of the Middle Ages. Tennyson's *Holy Grail* and Stephen Hawker's fine *Quest of the Sangrail,* are modern versions of this grail quest. In Wagner's *Parsifal,* based on Wolfram's medieval poem, the quest of the sacred lance has become the leading motif. Tennyson's Galahad may be compared with Guthlac as early and late treatments of the saintly ideal in English poetry. On the Cross legend among the Anglo-Saxons, see note, p. 241 ff, W. O. Stevens, *The Cross in the Life and Literature of the Anglo-Saxons* (Yale Studies XXIII, Henry Holt & Co.) and A. S. Cook, *The Old English Elene, Phoenix and Physiologus,* Yale University Press, 1919.

The Sources of the Elene. The *Elene* is a poem of 1320 lines found in the Vercelli Book. (See note on Vercelli book, p. 189.) The narrative proper ends with line 1235. Lines 1236-1320 constitute an autobiographic epilog in which the poet Cynewulf introduces his name in runic characters. Cynewulf may have used as his source the *Acta Sanctorum,* where St. Helena's journey to Jerusalem and her discovery of the cross and nails is described. A later and completer form of the story is found in the *Golden Legend. Historic data.* Eusebius in his *Life of Constantine* (Book I, Chap.

28) tells the following story: "About midday, when the
sun was beginning to decline, he saw with his own eye the
trophy of a cross of light, in the heavens, and above the
sun, and bearing the inscription: Conquer by this." (The
whole passage will be found translated in Cook's edition of
the *Elene,* p. XXII.) Helena's journey to Jerusalem
is related in the ecclesiastical histories of Socrates and So-
zomen. The latter tells how Helena obtained her knowledge
of the place where the cross was buried from one of the
Hebrews, who had it by tradition from his forefathers. This
is the original source of the Judas incident in Cynewulf's
poem. The later history of the cross is variously told. According to general tradition part of it was left by Helena
in Jerusalem, in the church built on the site of the discovery.
This portion was said to have been carried off in 614 but
recovered by the emperor Heraclitus in 628. Its restoration
to the church at Jerusalem was later commemorated on
"Holy Rood Day" (Sept. 14). A fragment said to have
been brought by Helena to Constantinople was supposed to
have been later removed to the Sainte Chapelle in Paris.

The Authorship of the Elene. At the close of the poem
the name "Cynewulf" is woven into the verse in runic characters. The same name, similarly signed, is found in three
other poems, *Crist, Juliana,* and the *Fates of the Apostles.*
(See note on Cynewulf's *Crist,* p. 239). Immediately preceding the runic insertion there is a passage in which the
poet gives some account of himself. As this autobiographic
epilog, though not a part of the narrative proper, is attached to *Elene,* and as it is our chief source of information concerning Cynewulf himself, we give it here in translation, reproducing the combination of rime and alliteration
in which it is written. (The so-called *Rime-poem,* see p.
246, uses the same device, which is frequent in Scandinavian
alliterative verse.)

> Thus weary of the strife of this woful life, (1236)
> I spun my song, and studied it long.
> Deeply I pondered, darkly I wondered,
> When the night-watches fell; nor knew I well
> The rood's strange story, till a radiant glory
> Unlocked by the might of its marvellous light

The gates of my mind. Guilty I pined,
By woe enchained, by wickedness stained,
Sorrow-driven, my sins unshriven,
Till I learned the way of weaving a lay,
In age to uphold my heart consoled.
God through his power gave me the dower
Of story and song. His spirit was strong
My words to unwind, to awaken my mind,
Loosen the lays that I lift in his praise
With love and delight, while I live among men.[1]
Not once, but often within me I pondered
The cross of glory, ere I came to unfold
The marvel rare of the radiant tree
As I found it in books in the fulness of time
Writ to reveal the victory-token.[2]

After this come the lines in which Cynewulf has inscribed his name. In reading the runes in this passage it
must be remembered that instead of being called by their
sounds as in the English (Latin) alphabet, the runes are
named after familiar words that begin with their respective
sounds, just as in our rimed children's alphabets. Thus
"th," indicated by the runic symbol þ which became a regu·
lar letter in the Anglo-Saxon alphabet, was called "thorn."
In the signed passage in *Elene*, the runes play a double rôle.
As *letters* they spell out the name *Cynewulf;* as *words* they
fill out the sense of the lines. In an Old English poem that
gives the key to rune-words,—a rimed rune alphabet—the
rune letters occurring in CYNEWULF are given the following
names: ᚻ-C cen, fire, torch; ᚤ-Y yr, bow; ᚾ-N nyd,
need; ᛗ-E eoh, horse; ᚹ-W wyn, joy (cf. winsome);
ᚢ-U ur-(ox) (German aur-ochs); ᛚ-L lagu, water; ᚠ-F
feoh, wealth (fee); C, Y, and U cannot well have the
meaning in Cynewulf's lines that they have in the rune-
poem, but he might easily after the manner of the rebus
have used them for other words of the same sound (cf. eye,
I; hour, our; you, yew). Thus cen, besides meaning "fire"
or "torch" might stand for the adjective "cene," keen-
hearted; "yr" for the first syllable of "yrmþu," woe;

<hr />

[1] At this point the rimed portion ends.
[2] See note on *The Vision of the Cross*, p. 241.

and "ur" for the pronoun "ur" our. Thus interpreted the passage would read as follows, inserting for the letters of Cynewulf's name the meaning they bear in the margin:

C cene
keen-hearted
Y yrmþu, *woe*

N nyd, *need*
E eoh, *horse*

W wyn, *joy*

U ur, *ours*

L lagu, *water*
F feoh, (fee)
wealth

Beaten by care-billows, the **C** droops
Though often treasures and appled gold
He had gained in the mead-hall, he mourns his **Y**.
By **N** companioned he now endures
A narrow fortune, though aforetime his **E**
Measured the mile-paths, merrily pranced
With jewelled bridle-rein. **W** is fled,
Gone with the years. Youth is departed,
The old-time pride. **U** was once
The gleam of youth, but the years have gone;
The prime of life is passed forever,
Rushed away, like running **L**,
Like a flowing stream. So fleeting is **F**
To all under heaven. So earth's bright hues
Wane 'neath the welkin like a wind that riseth
Roaring aloud, o'er the land it rages,
Sweeps the skies and scours the main,
Then suddenly ceasing, silent falls
Narrowly penned in its prison cell.

The rune-passage is appended in the original for comparison:

> A wæs sæc oþ þæt
> cnyssed cearwelmum, **ᚻ** drusende
> þeah he medohealle maþmas þege,
> æplede gold. **ᚱ** gnornode
> **ᚾ** gefera nearusorge dreah
> enge rune, þær him **ᛗ** fore
> milpaþas mæt, modig þrægde,
> wirum gewlenced. **ᚹ** is geswiþrad
> gomen æfter gearum. geogoþ is gecyrred
> ald onmedla. **ᚢ** wæs geara
> geogoþhades glæm. nu synt geardagas
> æfter fyrstmearce forþ gewitene,
> lifwynne geliden, swa **ᛚ** toglideþ
> flodas gefysde. **ᚠ** ægwham biþ
> læne under lyfte.

For a fuller discussion of the rune-passage see Cook's *Crist* Albion ed.: 151 ff., C. W. Kennedy, *Poems of Cynewulf* 7 ff. C. F. Brown, Englische Studien 38, 196, and Cook's *Elene*, p. 98 ff. Earlier scholars tried to construct a biography of Cynewulf out of the allusions in the rune-passage to the "appled gold" in the mead hall, and the "prancing steed," suggesting that he was a wandering minstrel, and like the author of Deor's complaint suffered misfortunes in later life. But Professor Brown has shown that the rune signatures themselves are not autobiographical, and all that remains is the testimony to a profound religious experience, a "conversion," the genuineness and depth of which is borne out by the character of the poems to which Cynewulf has signed his name.

95.—5. IN THE CIRCLE OF YEARS. The first two lines are from Professor Kennedy's prose rendering. The date of the battle was 312, and it was actually fought against the generals of Maxentius. Constantine had been proclaimed emperor by the army, at York in 306. The date of Helena's discovery is given as 326. But it was not until the end of the 4th century and in the West that the legend of St. Helena appeared.

97.—20. TO CAESAR HIMSELF AS IN SLUMBER HE LAY. The source of Constantine's vision is in the *Life of Constantine* by Eusebius Bk. 1, chaps. 28-31. The whole passage is translated in Cook's *Crist,* p. 190. According to Eusebius the vision of the cross in battle came first and the dream after. In Cynewulf's poem nothing is said of the vision on the battle-field.

98.—22. GAVE ORDERS TO MAKE. See the description of Eusebius: "At dawn of day he arose and . . . calling together the workers in gold and precious stones, he sat in the midst of them, and described to them the figure of the sign he had seen, bidding them represent it in gold and precious stones. And this representation I have myself had an opportunity of seeing. Now it was made in the following manner: A long spear, overlaid with gold, formed the figure of the cross, by means of a piece laid transversely over it. On the top of the whole was fixed a crown, formed by the intertexture of gold and precious stones; and on this, two letters indicating the name of Christ symbolized the Saviour's title by means of its first characters—the letter P (the Greek R) being intersected by X (Gr. Ch) exactly in its centre; and these letters the emperor was in the habit of wearing on his helmet. From the transverse piece which crossed the spear was suspended a kind of streamer of purple cloth covered with a profuse embroidery of most brilliant precious stones." See note 68-13.

101.—11. THEY DROVE O'ER THE FLOOD. Compare the description of the storm in Andreas l. 369 ff.

> The sea grew stormy, stirred was the deep,
> The home of the whale; the horned fish played,
> Gambolled in the waves, and the gray sea-mew
> Circled greedy; the sky was darkened,
> The gale waxed stronger, the surges roared,
> The billows rose, the rigging moaned,
> They were drenched in brine by the breaking seas,
> And terror of ocean entered their hearts.

Wedercandel swearc is exactly "the lift grew dark" and *onhrered hwælmere* is "and gurly grew the sea" of the ballad of *Sir Patrick Spens* and with *waedo gewaette* compare:

> O laith, laith were our gude Scots lords
> To wet their cork-heeled shoon

107.—15. THERE SINCE THAT DAY. Our selection closes with line 1032. Section XIII of the Ms. describes the discovery of the nails used at the crucifixion, and then follows the personal passage discussed in the introductory note to Elene.

THE LIFE OF GUTHLAC

In the Exeter book are found two poems, formerly considered as one, on the life of St. Guthlac. The first (A) runs to line 790 and is known as *Guthlac the Hermit;* the second (B) from 791 to 1353 and is known as *Guthlac's Death.* Our selection is from the latter, which has far higher poetic merit, and may well have been written by Cynewulf, though there is no convincing evidence as to his authorship.

The Source.—Guthlac was an English saint, of the eastern fens. His life was written about the middle of the 8th century by Felix of Croyland, a monk attached to the abbey that rose on the site of Guthlac's retreat. "Wilder even than the western woodland was the desolate fen-country on the eastern border of Mercia stretching from the 'Holland,' the sunk, hollow land of Lincolnshire, to the channel of the Ouse, a wilderness of shallow waters 'and reedy islets wrapped in its own dark mist-veil, and tenanted only by flocks of screaming wild-fowl. . . . Here Guthlac, a youth of the royal race of Mercia, sought a refuge from the world in the solitudes of Crowland, and so great was the reverence he won, that only two years had passed since his death when the stately abbey of Crowland rose over his tomb. Earth was brought in boats to form a site; the buildings rested on oaken piles driven into the marsh; a great stone church replaced the hermit's cell, and the toil of the new brotherhood changed the pools around them into fertile meadowland." (J. R. Green, *A Short History of the English People,* p. 67.)

The date of Guthlac's death is given by Felix as 714. In the Latin life (*Acta Sanctorum* vol. II for April, 37 ff.) we are told that Guthlac was accompanied to the island of Croyland (Crowland) in the fens by two companions from his monastery. One of them, Beccel by name, became jealous of the saint and tried to poison him. But Guthlac divined his intention, and Beccel repented and became Guthlac's devoted servant until his death. The name of Guthlac's sister is given as Pega.

Guthlac B follows the Latin life more closely than A. The author of the first Guthlac poem imagines the saint's retreat in a mountainous country (O. E. beorg cf. lines 73, 119, 146, 163, 234, 300, 354, 410, 705). There is no reference at all to mountains in the second Guthlac, but the poet correctly places the saint's retreat on an island (line 1299 *beofade þaet ealond*), and in true Cynewulfian manner describes in detail the journey by water made by Beccel after Guthlac's death. The hounding of Guthlac by evil demons, the apparition of the heavenly messenger, (St. Bartholomew in the Latin life), the radiance above the death-bed are all regular features of the Saint legend, but the warmth of the friendship between the saint and his young disciple, the dramatic touches, and the tender human quality are the poet's own, and are not unworthy of Cynewulf. For an excellent summary of Guthlac criticism see C. W. Kennedy, *The Poems of Cynewulf*, pp. 51-56.

II. LYRIC POETRY

The term "Lyric Poetry" is here loosely used to designate poems in which the note of personal emotion predominates. Lyric poetry in the more specific sense, the Old English had none. All the poems classed as "lyric" are in the Germanic alliterative verse, but both in the poems classed as religious lyrics and in those classed as secular lyrics, especially in those of the Cynewulfian school, there is something of the "lyric cry," and the *Wanderer* and the *Seafarer* come near to being true lyrics.

1. RELIGIOUS LYRIC
CÆDMON
NORTHUMBRIAN HYMN

The familiar story of Cædmon, the shepherd poet of Whitby, is told by Bede in his *Ecclesiastical History* (Bk. 4, Chap. 24, Temple Classics). Cædmon began to compose poetry about 670, and the Northumbrian hymn in all probability represents his first attempt at sacred song. A peculiar interest therefore attaches to this hymn, because it is the first passage of English poetry whose date and authorship are definitely known. The original Northumbrian version of the hymn is preserved in an old Ms. of Bede's history, and was copied there about 737. We give the original Northumbrian verses below, as a specimen of the oldest form of English verse,—older than the West Saxon version of the *Beowulf*.

> "Nu scylun hergan hefænricas uard,
>   metudæs mæcti end his modgidanc,
>   uerc uuldur-fadur, swe he uundra gihuæs
>   eci dryctin or astelidæ.

He aerist scop ælda barnum
heben til hrofe haleg scepen;
tha middungeard moncynnes uard,
eci dryctin æfter tiadæ
firum foldan, frea allmectig.
Primo cantauit Cædmon istud carmen."

(See Professor Kennedy's *The Caedmon Poems*.)

CYNEWULF

HYMN OF PRAISE

The *Hymn of Praise* is taken from Cynewulf's *Crist*, Part I, ll. 347-377. The *Crist* is a poem of three parts in which are celebrated the Advent, the Ascension, and the Second Coming of Christ (Doomsday). There is in the Old Saxon dialect a poem called the *Heliand*, Saviour (German, *Heiland*), probably by the same writer who composed the *Younger Genesis*, which presents the life of Christ in narrative form on the background of Germanic manners and customs, in the style of the old Germanic Epic. The *Crist*, on the other hand, is a series of essentially lyric poems, based on the antiphones, hymns, and homilies of the Latin Church. "We must conceive of Cynewulf as so thrilled by the sweet and solemn chanting of the greater Antiphones of Advent . . . that he gladly yielded to the impulse to reproduce them in English under the form of variations. . . . He abridged, expanded, suppressed, or transferred, as his genius suggested, freely interpolated matter from other sources, and welded the whole together by closing with a magnificent doxology." (A. S. Cook, *Introduction to Crist*, p. XLII. Albion Series, Ginn and Co.) The personal, lyric note predominates in Cynewulf's *Crist*, and the rough music of the old alliterative verse is softened to express the new emotions of a personal religion. The passages from the *Crist* are especially notable as affording an early instance of that liturgic genius of the English language which finds its fullest expression in the Book of Common Prayer.

Near the close of the second part of *Crist*, the name "Cynewulf" is woven into the verse in runic characters. The same name, similarly signed, is found in three other

poems, *Elene, Juliana,* and *The Fates of the Apostles,* all
of them based on Latin saints' legends. For a translation
of all these signed passages, see Professor Cook's introduction to the *Dream of the Rood* (Clarendon Press, Oxford,
1905). In the passage of the *Elene* (ll. 1237-1257) immediately preceding the runic insertion, the poet gives some
account of himself from which we gather that he was at
the time an old man, and that he had undergone a deep religious experience, as a result of which his spirit, previously fettered by sin, found peace, and was inspired to
sacred song. He was probably a Northumbrian, and lived
at the end of the eighth century. Many other poems besides the ones above mentioned have been ascribed to Cynewulf, among them the *Phœnix* and the *Dream of the Rood,*
or *Vision of the Cross,* both of which are represented in the
translations. Though neither of these poems is signed,
there is good reason for thinking they are by Cynewulf.
For a survey of Cynewulf criticism, and a summary of its
results, see Cook's introduction to his edition, quoted above,
and Kennedy's introduction to *Cynewulf's Poems translated into English Prose.*

THE VOYAGE OF LIFE

These lines are based on the following passage of Gregory's homily on the Ascension: "But let hope, as an anchor
of the soul fixed within the heavenly country whither Jesus
our forerunner is entered, hold us steadfast amid the fluc-
tuations of this mortal life." Our selection is typical of
the way in which Cynewulf expands and makes poetry out
of his Latin originals.

DOOMSDAY

This passage is from *Crist,* Part III, ll. 867-874; 878-909;
972-1006. Many of the hymns and homilies of the Latin
Church dealt with the Last Judgment, and the subject was
a favorite one with the Old English writers. Compare the
well-known hymn *Dies irae, dies illa.* Cynewulf was probably familiar with an alphabetic hymn quoted by Bede, beginning thus:

"Apparebit repentina, dies magna domini
  fur obscura velut nocte improvisos occupans."

(Suddenly shall appear the great day of the Lord, like a
thief in the night falling on the unsuspecting.)

"Clangor tubae per quaternas terrae plagas concinens
  vivos una mortuosque Christo ciet obviam."

(The blast of the trumpet, sounding through the four quarters of the earth, shall call before Christ the living and the
dead.)   Professor Cook prints the whole hymn in his introduction to the *Crist,* p. 171, and quotes Stopford Brooke:
"This trumpet voice of the heart belongs to the English nature, and the lofty music of Milton's praise came down to
him in legitimate descent from the earliest exultations of
English psalm."

122.—8. FROM SOUTH AND EAST, etc.   See note on the
Fall of Man, 79-15.

THE VISION OF THE CROSS

The Vision of the Cross, generally called the *Dream of
the Rood,* is found in the Vercelli Book.   The authorship
of the *Vision* is unknown, but there are strong reasons for
believing that Cynewulf wrote it.   The *Elene,* one of Cynewulf's signed poems, is inspired by the story of Constantine's famous vision of the cross; and the discovery of the
true cross by Consantine's mother Helena (Elene) forms
the main subject of that poem.   In the personal passage referred to above (see note on *Elene*), Cynewulf says:

"Not once but often within me I pondered
  The Cross of Glory, ere I came to unfold
  The marvel rare of the radiant tree
  As I found it in books in the fulness of time,
  Writ to reveal the victory-token" (ll. 1253-1257).

Even if we do not interpret these words as a direct reference to the *Vision,* as some critics have done, the personal
note in the *Vision of the Cross* is so close to that revealed
in the personal passages of the *Crist* and the *Elene,* that it is
difficult to believe that Cynewulf did not write this tender-
est and most deeply felt of Old English religious poems.

For a convenient review of the authorship problem, see Cook's edition (*Dream of the Rood*, Clarendon Press, 1905), and Kennedy's introduction to the *Poems of Cynewulf*, pp. 62-68. The dramatic personification of inanimate objects is a common device in Old English poetry. Cf. *The Riddles* and *The Husband's Message*.

Apart from its literary value, a peculiar interest attaches to the *Vision of the Cross* because some lines of the poem are inscribed in runic characters on the Ruthwell Cross, an ancient monumental stone, still preserved at Ruthwell in Annandale, near the Scottish border.

123.—24. LIST TO THE WORDS OF A WONDROUS VISION. Compare the vision of Constantine: "About midday, when the sun was beginning to decline, he saw with his own eyes the trophy of a cross of light, in the heavens, above the sun, and bearing the inscription: Conquer by this." (Eusebius, *Life of Constantine*, Bk. I, Chap. 28. Cynewulf describes this vision of Constantine in *Elene*, ll. 68-85. There is a similar Cross vision at the close of the *Crist*, ll. 1083 sq.)

124.—5. 'TWAS NO GALLOWS-TREE. In the Old English, as in the other Germanic dialects, the word "gallows" was also used to signify the cross. See *Cent. Dict.*, "Gallows." In form the T-shaped St. Anthony's cross closely resembled a gallows.—24. MANY YEARS AGO, etc. A portion of the *Vision* is in the longer alliterative line also appearing in the *Younger Genesis*. As the expanded lines predominate in the narrative portions, and the shorter lines in the lyric portions, I have used the lines of different length to mark this distinction throughout.

125.—6. THEN STRIPPED THE MIGHTY HERO. The heroic note comes out strong here. The voluntary character of the sacrifice of Christ, emphasized by the Latin Church writers, appealed to the Germanic mind. Yet, curiously enough, in the *Heliand* it is not found,—we have mere paraphrase at this point. See also Milton's

"Most perfect hero tried in heaviest plight
Of labours huge and hard, too hard for human wight."
—*The Passion*, 13, 14.

On the Ruthwell Cross are found the words in runic characters "[Un]clothed Himself God Almighty, when He

would mount the cross, courageous in the sight of all men."
For a description of the Ruthwell Cross, and a literal rendering of three other passages from the *Vision,* inscribed
thereon, see Cook and Tinker, *Translations from Old English Poetry* (Ginn and Co., 1903), pp. 100-102.—11. I
STOOD, A CROSS UPLIFTED. Literally, "A Rood was I upreared." Professor Cook quotes from a Middle English
poem of the thirteenth century to show how this alliterative
formula persisted:

> "High upon a down
> there all folk it see may
> A mile from the town
> about the midday
> *The rood is up areared*
>
> His friends are afeared
> and clingeth to the clay.
> The rood stands in stone
> Mary stands alone
> and saith 'Welaway.' "

—12. THE KING OF GLORY I CARRIED. A cross preserved
in the Cathedral of Brussels, and said to contain fragments
of the true cross, has an Old English inscription of two
lines apparently taken from the *Vision:*

> "Cross am I called, the King long since
> Trembling I bore, with blood besprent."

126.—18. CHANTED A LAY OF MOURNING. The same
phrase is used in the description of Beowulf's burial, where
the comrades of the hero circle about his barrow in solemn
procession and say that

> "He was mildest of men and most beloved
> Kindest of kings, and keenest for honor."

All but the last phrase might have been used in the chant
of mourning at Christ's grave, but the necessary elimination
of that last epithet, "keenest for honor," shows the difference between the old Germanic and the Christian ideal.
According to the latter, "fame" is "the last infirmity of
noble mind," whereas the virtues of Beowulf culminate in
his eagerness for fame.

127.—2. LONG I STOOD, etc. The Ms. is defective at this point, and the translation compresses several lines into one. In the original it is "we" stood, "we" were felled, "we" were buried, etc. The crosses of the malefactors are meant, which according to the legend were found by the side of the cross of Christ by Helena.—87. At this point ll. 91-121 of the original are omitted. They are far inferior to the rest of the poem, and read like a homiletic interpolation.

128.—12. MAY HE WHO SUFFERED, etc. The last five lines of our version represent, but are hardly a translation of, ll. 144-156 of the original. The conditions under which Old English poetry was transmitted make it only too probable that interpolations and additions by inferior hands often mar the original. The translator whose aim it is to be faithful to the spirit of the original has a right to exercise a freedom not permissible were he editing the original text. He is certainly under no obligation to perpetuate in modern verse the maunderings of pious but prosy scribes. Of the lines in question the Clarendon Press editor of the *Dream of the Rood* says: "The conclusion . . . is in quite a different manner, and seems alien to the prevailing sentiment of the poem. It is cool and objective in tone, and has no necessary vital relation to what has preceded. Pending further elucidation, we can only conclude that it has either come here by accident, or that the poet's judgment was at fault. The poem should have ended with 148 *a*, or perhaps better with 146."

THE PHŒNIX

The *Phœnix* is a poem of 677 lines, preserved in the Exeter Book. The translation gives ll. 1-264, and ll. 570-677. The poem is unsigned, but has many of the characteristics of Cynewulf's style. For a summary of critical opinion on the question of authorship, see Cook's introduction to Cynewulf's *Crist*, p. LXIII, Kennedy's introduction to the Cynewulf poems, pp. 56-62, and Cook's *Elene, Phœnix*, etc. The *Phœnix* is based on a Latin poem by Lactantius, (ca. 300 A.D.). (The Latin poem is printed in Bright's *Anglo-Saxon Reader*, Appendix I, and an English translation in Cook, p. 124.) It is known that the works of Lactantius were in the library at York, and Cynewulf may have read the Latin poem there. The story of the Phœnix, which rises again from its own ashes, was a favorite theme of the early Christian writers, and was interpreted by them as a symbol of the resurrection of the body and the life everlasting. "This allegorical treatment of the life of beasts and birds, and also of the great tales of the world; the taking up of the whole of natural history into the realm of the spiritual —human thoughts and emotions being imputed to animals— is of great antiquity, and especially among the Semitic peoples; through the Old Testament, through the Talmud, through the parables of Christ, it descended to the early Christian writers. . . . Ambrose, for example, uses the phœnix as the symbol of the resurrection." Stopford Brooke, *E. E. L.* In a collection of a hundred Latin riddles, ascribed to Symphosius, there is the following on the Phœnix:

> "Vita mihi mors est, si coepero nasci
> Sed prius est fatum leti quam lucis origo;
> Sic solus manes ipsos mihi dico parentes."

(Death is life to me, if I begin to be born. But first comes the fate of dissolution, before the beginning of life. Thus I am alone in giving the name of parents to my ancestral shades.) The first part of the poem relates the fable of the Phœnix, after Lactantius, but the 170 lines of the original are expanded into 380 in the Old English version. The second part, containing the Christian interpretation and application of the fable, is the English poet's own addition. Though inspired by his Latin original, the vividness and beauty of the landscape belong largely to the Old English poet, and the fervors of Christian joy and hope are entirely his. The *Phœnix* is interesting as one of the earliest examples in English literature of ideal landscape. Contrast in this respect the landscape in *Beowulf,* and compare with the landscape in the *Pearl.*

129.—14. NO HILL-SIDES STEEP NOR HOLLOWS DEEP. Examples of this sort of rime combined with alliteration are not uncommon in Old English verse. Lines 15-16 of the *Phœnix* read:

> "Ne forstes fnæst, ne fyres blæst
> Ne hægles hryre, ne hrimes dryre."

This complicated form was common in Old Norse poetry. There is in the Exeter Book an Old English poem of 87 lines, the so-called rime-poem, (see p. 232) composed in this fashion. See also the personal passage in *Elene*, p. 232.

132.—30. HARMONIES CLEAR OF ORGAN-PIPES. Organs were introduced into church-worship in England by Theodore of Tarsus, Archbishop of Canterbury, toward the close of the seventh century.—32. MUSIC OF THE SWAN. Literally "the feathers of the swan." The Anglo-Saxons believed that the music of the swan was made, not with its voice, but with its feathers, as the wind swept through them. See the Swan riddle, p. 155. The words describing the sound of the singing feathers, are the same in the *Phœnix* passage, and in the riddle. The Latin poem has "olor moriens," in allusion to the fabled song of the dying swan.

133.—14. WORN WITH WINTERS A THOUSAND. The Germanic peoples counted years by winters, and days by nights. The phrase is therefore equivalent to "a thousand years old." Cf. *Beowulf*.

136.—9. TAINT OF SIN ALL TAKEN AWAY. Literally "sundered from sin." This ornitheological observation anticipates the Christian application of the second part of the poem.—10. LIKE AS WHEN MEN, etc. This is one of the few elaborate similes found in Anglo-Saxon literature.

137.—1. A MAN OF GOD, etc. An allusion to Job xix: 26, "And though after my skin, worms destroy this body, yet in my flesh shall I see God." In l. 549 of the original, express mention is made of the "sayings of Job" (the word is *giedding*, a proverbial saying in alliterative speech, something to be quoted and handed down). Then follows, ll. 552-569, a free paraphrase of the Vulgate version of Job xix: 25-27.—16. TO THE LAND OF DELIGHT. "The popular consciousness of the Anglo-Saxons assimilated the idea of the kingdom of heaven under the old epic figure of the tribal family-seat, the ancestral homestead, *eþel, eard*. Neither of the chief Old German religious poems *Otfrid* and *Heliand* nationalized the conception of the life hereafter. To the poet of the *Heliand* it is a world of light which he is unable to picture in detail. (See also the emphasis on light as a characteristic of heaven in the *Younger Gene-*

sis of Old Saxon origin, *J. D. S.*) Only the Anglo-Saxons created a genuine religious epic, a body of Christian poetry steeped in the popular consciousness of the Anglo-Saxon people" (*Ehrisman, Zum Germanischen Früh Christentum, Beitræge,* Vol. 35, 1909).

140.—5. LEAVE HATH GRANTED US LUCIS AUCTOR. The *Phœnix* poet, at the close of his poem, has adopted the peculiar device of linking together by means of alliteration Anglo-Saxon and Latin half-lines. In order to give the effect of this, the Latin half-lines have been retained in the translation. Rendered into English the passage reads: "Leave hath granted us the author of light, that here we might merit, by good deeds gain, joys in heaven; that so we men might reach the greatest kingdom, and sit in exalted seats, live in delight of light and peace; enter our home of blessed happiness, in bliss immortal; see our Saviour, without ending, merciful and mild; prolong his praises with laud everlasting, in bliss with the angels. Alleluia."

2. SECULAR LYRIC AND ELEGY

THE WANDERER

The elegiac note, so characteristic of Old English poetry, finds its most poetic expression in *The Wanderer*. "Wyrd biþ ful aræd," all unavoided is the doom of destiny,—this is the keynote of the poem. There is only a faint suggestion of the Christian hope in the first two lines. Over the body of the poem lie the shadows of fatalism, and a profound sense of the instability of the earth and its joys. *The Wanderer* is preserved in the Exeter Book, and probably belongs to the first quarter of the eighth century. For a discussion of the critical problems involved, see W. W. Lawrence, *Journal of Germanic Philology,* Vol. IV, 1902, pp. 460-480, and the edition of Old English Lyrics in the Belles Lettres Series.

140.—20. HUNTED BY WYRD. A free rendering of the Old English, Wyrd biþ ful aræd, Wyrd shall be fully accomplished. The fact that "Wyrd" and "God's Mercy" are mentioned together is nothing unusual (see *Gnomic Verses,* 155-14), and there is no need to assume that the introductory lines have been worked over by a Christian editor who

had before him an earlier pagan poem.—24. OFTEN ALONE
IN THE DARK BEFORE DAWNING. Cf. the Norse *Lay of
Hamthir*:

> "At the sad dawning, . . .
> When day is waxing
> And man's grief awakeneth
> And the sorrow of each one
> The early day quickeneth."
>
> —Morris' translation.

141.—12. SINCE LONG TIME AGO MY GIVER OF BOUNTY,
etc. For the other side of the picture, see *Widsith*.

142.—23. The following ten lines in the original text are
in the manner of the gnomic verses. Their omission from
the English version does not necessarily imply that the
translator considers them an interpolation, though their
counsels of worldly wisdom, prudence, and a safe mediocrity
certainly form a violent interruption to the uniform elegiac
mood of the remainder of the poem. If it be objected that
this is too subjective a test, the answer is that the value of
a book of selections and representative pieces depends after
all on the quality of the "subjective taste" with which it is
made. Where, as in the present case, there is good reason
to doubt that a poem has been transmitted in its original
form, the editor and translator, whose aim is literary rather
than critical and analytic, has a right to exercise the same
judgment in the elimination of parts of poems that he ex-
ercises in dealing with the body of Old English poetry.
The bracketed figures indicating the elision will enable the
critic easily to check the subjectivity of the translator. It
should be added that Boer considers the whole passage
57-87 an interpolation; but in this he is influenced by his
peculiar theory of the origin of the poem, and its relation
to the *Seafarer*.—31. DEAD IS THEIR REVELRY, DUST
ARE THE REVELLERS. This is the far-heard cry of medieval
poetry: "Ubi sunt qui ante nos in mundo fuere." Cf. Cole-
ridge's

> "The knights are dust, their good swords rust,
> Their souls are with the saints, we trust."

where the gray monotone of the Old English elegiac mood
is overlaid with the colors of romantic medievalism.

143.—2. SOME HAVE GONE DOWN IN SHIPS ON THE SEA.
Literally: One did a bird carry off over the deep sea. I have
followed Thorpe and Wuelker in interpreting "fugel" as
"ship," though I am by no means convinced that the old
poet may not have had in mind the same picture as Kipling:

> "Yes, the large birds o' prey
> They will carry us away
> An' you'll never see your soldier any more."

—13. WHERE IS THE WARRIOR, WHERE IS THE WAR-HORSE.
A thousand years later Thomas Carlyle expresses the same
mood in almost the same words: "That warrior on his
strong war-horse, fire flashes through his eyes; force dwells
in his arm and heart: but warrior and war-horse are a
vision, a revealed force, nothing more. . . . A little while
ago they were not; a little while, and they are not, their
very ashes are not." (*Sartor Resartus*).—15. THE DREAM
AND THE GLEAM THAT BRIGHTENED THE HALL. "There was
gleam and dream," says the Old English poet, in describing
the "seledreamas," or joys of the hall. "Dream" in Old
English meant joy. The modern sense is probably due to
Scandinavian influence.

144.—3. ALL THIS EARTH'S FOUNDATIONS UTTERLY SHALL
PASS. The classic expression of this mood in English literature is Shakespeare's:

> "The cloud-capped towers, the gorgeous palaces,
> The solemn temples, the great globe itself,
> Yea, all which it inherit shall dissolve,
> And like this insubstantial pageant faded,
> Leave not a rack behind."   —*Tempest.*

There follow five lines more in the Exeter Book, comprising
a few maxims of practical wisdom, and a conventional
Christian exhortation at the close.

THE SEAFARER

The *Seafarer* is a poem of 124 lines, of unknown date
and authorship, preserved in the Exeter Book. It probably
belongs to the eighth century. The first part, ll. 1-64, describes the joys and hardships of the seafaring life, and is
filled with high poetry. The second part contains practical

exhortations, echoed from the gnomic verses, and is full of dreary prose. This second part, omitted in the translation, is almost certainly a later addition, made by one or more monkish scribes. The German scholar Rieger first interpreted the *Seafarer* as a dialogue between an old sailor and a youth eager to go to sea. For the literature on the subject, and the divisions suggested by other critics, see W. W. Lawrence, *Journal of Germanic Philology*, 1902, Vol. IV, p. 461. The assignment of parts as given in our translation differs slightly from that of Rieger. Professor Lawrence agrees with Kluge that the latter portion, ll. 64b-124, is a pious appendix, but he tries to prove the first part the "lyric utterance of one man." It is clear that we have in the *Seafarer* the interplay of different and mutually exclusive lyric moods, suggested by life at sea. It is also clear that the same poet felt and expressed both moods, and that one mood is chiefly retrospective, based on experience, and the other prospective, based on anticipation. Whether the poet consciously dramatized these moods into an objective dialogue between an old sailor and a young man is a minor question. When a critic (Boer) says he cannot determine "whether the dialogue is carried on by two persons or whether a single man is talking with himself," we realize how perilously near to vain hair-splitting such a discussion may carry us. The main point is that the poem is lyric, not dramatic; it presents the interplay of lyric moods, and not the conflict of dramatic characters. The main, and perhaps the only justification for printing the poem in dialogue form is that so far from doing violence to its essential meaning and poetic values, it rather brings these into relief. For a precisely analogous dialogue of moods, compare Walt Whitman's "Give me the Splendid Silent Sun," where the mood inspired by life in the country alternates and conflicts with that inspired by life in the city.

Recently Ehrisman (*Beiträge*, 1909, Vol. 35, p. 212) has argued for a didactic unity of the whole poem. According to this interpretation, the pictures of the seafarer's life, with their contrasts of joy and sorrow, are introduced merely as a symbol of the Christian's life on earth, followed by the joys of heaven. It must be admitted that there is much in

Anglo-Saxon Christian poetry to encourage such a view, and
I have no doubt that the author of the religious appendix
understood the earlier sea-poem in this sense, and appro-
priated it to his symbolic Christian-mystical purposes, but
this is far from proving the unimaginative, unoriginal, un-
emotional, homiletic addition to have been part of the original fine sea-piece, and in fact its *raison d'être* and final purpose. Browning's sea-piece *Amphibian* is a good example
of a genuine blending of the real and the symbolic-mystical,
in a uniform poetic key.

144.—4. TRUE IS THE TALE, etc. This line has more alliterations than the strict rule permits.—14. HUNGER'S
PANGS, etc. Literally "Hunger from within bit to shreds the
courage of me sea-worried." Cf. *Job*. xviii: 12, "His
strength shall be hunger-bitten."—16. LITTLE HE DREAMS,
etc. The translation omits the preceding line and a half,
where there is an evident break or fault in transcription.

145.—19. THE TUMBLE AND SURGE OF SEAS TUMULTUOUS,
etc. This and the following line are an expansion of the
original "hean streamas, sealtyþa gelac," the high seas, and
the play of the salt billows.

146.—21. GIVE ME THE GLADNESS OF GOD'S GREAT SEA. I
have frankly taken a liberty with the original text here, and
the literalist will call my version perversion. Peccavi
fortiter! At this point the homiletic addition is welded on
to the genuine poem, and it is done in the following fashion:
"As for me the joys of the Lord are more pleasing than this
life-in-death, that passeth away on land." From here on to
the end, the depth of poetic feeling shoals rapidly, and the
rhythm breaks. The sympathetic translator who has felt
the heave and lift of the ground-swell under him thus far
is tempted to answer the pious homilist with his "dryhtnes
dreamas," in Kipling's words:

"Must we sing forever more
  On the windless glassy floor?
Take back your golden fiddles, and we'll beat to open sea."

THE HUSBAND'S MESSAGE

The somewhat enigmatic character of this poem has given
rise to various conjectures. Thorpe, the first editor of the

Exeter Book, recognizing the similarity between the opening of the poem and many of the riddles, interpreted the first portion (to l. 13 in the translation), as a separate riddle. Later critics perceived that the lines in question refer to the tablet of wood on which the husband's message is graven. Professor Blackburn (*Journal of Germanic Philology*, Vol. III) makes an ingenious hypothesis connecting riddle 61 of the Exeter Book with the *Husband's Message*, and combines them in his translation under the title *A Love Letter*. Professor Tupper (*Riddles of the Exeter Book*) shows that riddle 61 is a genuine riddle, and that Professor Blackburn's arrangement, while "pretty and ingenious," ignores the true solution of riddle 61 as a reed or reed-flute. In translating the *Husband's Message*, the original text of which is full of gaps, I have been aided by Professor Blackburn's version.

147.—21. EARNESTLY URGE THEE OVERSEAS. Old English: lustum læran, þæt þu lagu drefde. Professor Blackburn renders: "Earnestly to urge thee to sail the sea." The next four lines follow Professor Blackburn's version closely. The Old English has:

> "siþþan þu gehyrde on hliþes oran
> galan geomorne geac on bearwe,
> ne læt þy þec siþþan siþes getwæfan,
> lade gelettan lifgendne monn."

Literally: "When thou hast heard on the cliff's brow, the mournful cuckoo sing in the grove, do not thou then let living man sunder thee from the journey, hinder thee from going."

148.—18. In the original there follow five more lines, containing runes which are supposed to be a cipher or password known to the recipient of the letter.

III. CHARMS, RIDDLES AND GNOMIC VERSES

The specimens of Old English verse gathered under this head have more points of contact with medieval Latin literature, both in form and spirit than any of the poems in our collection; and yet, curiously enough, they afford us glimpses of the Germanic past, and pictures of the everyday life of the Anglo-Saxons, not found elsewhere in Old

English poetry: the ploughman in the field before sunrise, and the witch-doctor with his rheumatic patient, repeating incantations that remember ancient heathen deities, the house-wife kneading her dough, the gathering of the wild-honey into vats for the mead-brewing, the fisherman returning at night to his wife and home (an Old English "Meeting at Night"), the mother bending over her babe, the student over his book, the gold-smith over his ornaments, the oarsman over his sweep. The stateliness of the epic, the raptures of the religious lyric, the melancholy of the elegies are here supplemented by the homeliness of everyday life, with occasional touches,—in the riddles—of a real though coarse humor, rare in Old English poetry.

1. CHARMS

The two charms translated in the text are remnants of a kind of incantation whose origins must be looked for in the pagan past of the Germanic races. They are echoes of the solemn chant that anciently accompanied religious processions, and properly represent the earliest and most primitive strata of Old English poetry. In the form in which they have been handed down they are much overlaid with Christian lore, but it is not difficult to recognize the primitive mythologic strata. The Christian church made no attempt ruthlessly to eradicate all ancient beliefs and practices. Pope Gregory advised the English Christians to consecrate the places of pagan ritual to the new religion, but not to destroy them; to respect the ancient forest sanctuaries and sacrifices, and to proceed everywhere with restraint and moderation. This explains the strange medley of Christian and Pagan conceptions so common in Old English literature.

Cockayne's *Leechdoms, Wortcunning and Starcraft of Early England* (London, 1866) contains an interesting collection of charms, spells, cures, etc. On the subject of Germanic charms consult Gummere's *Germanic Origins* (Scribner's, 1891), pp. 372 ff. and 405 ff., where both of our charms are translated in full, and commented on; also Felix Grendon, *Journal of American Folklore* XXII, 105 ff.

The Ploughman's Charm

149.—1. ERCE ERCE. An unexplained term, probably the name of an ancient Earth-goddess. We are reminded of a famous passage in the *Germania* of Tacitus (cap. 40) where he describes the cult of the Earth-goddess Nerthus, as practised by the Ingvaeonic races of the North Sea Coast. "All of these people (among them 'Anglii') worship *Nerthus, i.e. mother earth*. They believe that she intervenes in human affairs, and visits the people." [In commune Nerthum, id est terram matrem colunt, eamque intervenire rebus hominum, et inveni populis arbitrantur.] Like the Norse Freyja, she is a kind of Germanic Demeter (Koegel), a goddess of earth and mother of vegetation. In the springtime she holds her progress, and is welcomed everywhere with eager joy, for in the tracks of her chariot drawn by cows, ancient symbols of fertility, rich harvests spring up. When she has blessed meadow and field, she returns to her underworld home beneath the surface of a lonely mere. Cf. Chadwick, *Origins,* Chap. X, The Cult of Nerthus.—17. HAIL TO THEE, EARTH, MOTHER OF MEN. According to Tacitus, the Germanic peoples believed mankind to be descended from Tuisto, whose mother was the earth. In Chaucer's *Pardoner's Tale,* the old man knocks with his staff on the ground, "which is my *moodres* gate" and says "Leeve *mooder,* leet me in," and it is quite possible that in the poetic figure there lurks a reminiscence of the old pagan notion of the earth mother of men. The next lines in the charm are pure pagan, and reveal the same conception that underlies the myth of Freyr and Gertha in the Icelandic *Skirnismal.* Freyr the Son of Njord (another form of the root found in Nerthus) is the god of the fertilizing rain, and then of fertility in general. He rides on the ship Skidbladnir (the cloud), which he can fold and slip into his pocket when his journey is done. His flashing sword is the sunshine, that comes after the rain to make the world green. His sword he gives to his servant Skirnir (the polisher, burnisher, cleanser), who is to woo for him the beautiful daughter of the giants, Gerd (the plant-world, released by the sunshine from the fetters of the wintry frost-giants). In the last lines the Christian coloring again predominates.

Charm for a Sudden Stitch

The rheumatism to be cured is thought to be caused by the darts of the "mighty women" that ride through the air. "Hexenschuss" (Hagshot), and "Hexenstich" (Hagstitch), are still popular names in Germany for rheumatism. It is possible that there is in this charm a faint reminiscence of the northern myth of the Valkyrias, the shield-maidens of Odin, who bring to Valhalla (hall of the slain), the heroes that fall in the battle.

In one of the Eddic songs we read of a band of Valkyrias riding through the air and led by a maiden with a gleaming gold helmet. "Their chargers tossed their heads; from their manes the dew dropped into the deep valleys." In an Old High German charm for the release of prisoners, three bands of "august women" are described settling down upon earth, and helping the warriors against the foe. With the introduction of Christianity, the "august women" and the shield-maidens of Odin degenerated into hags and witches who send their darts into the vitals of unwary mortals.

> "The hag is astride
> This night for to ride
> The devil and she together
> Through thick and through thin
> Now out and now in
> Though ne'er so foul be the weather."—*Herrick*.

151.—16. SHOT OF ESA, *i.e.* of the gods. The sing. "Os" is preserved in proper names, Oswald, Oscar, etc. In Old German the root appeared as "ans," preserved in Anselm (Ans-helm). The Norse pl. is Æsir. In the Eddas the Esir are specialized into war-sprites, while the spirits of nature kindly to man, like Njord and Freyr, are called "Vanir."—17. SHOT OF ELVES. In the Eddas "Esir ok alfar," *i.e.* gods and elves, are often mentioned together. The sing., Ælf, is preserved in Ælfred, *i.e.* the Elf-coun-selled, the Elf-wise, and in Alberich, *i.e.* the ruler of Elves. Originally friendly beings, they have become malicious sprites in our charm, together with the Æsir. In Scotland flint arrow-heads, relics of an earlier age, are called elf-arrows or elf-bolts, and they are supposed to be hurled not only at human beings, but especially at cattle.

"There every herd by sad experience knows
How winged with fate their elf-shot arrows fly."
—COLLINS, *Ode on Highland Superstitions.*

34. WITCH FLY AWAY. In old German, witches are called woodwives, and were supposed to inhabit the wild forest. We must not lay too much stress on the echoes of the Valkyria myth in our charm. Even before the introduction of Christianity, Germanic folklore had its wicked women and wood-wives, who had nothing to do with the shield-maidens of Norse mythology. The Norse had their "svart-alfar," black or wicked elves, as well as their "ljos-alfar," light or good elves. "The heathen Teuton saw all round him a varied race of demons (especially wood-sprites such as O.H.G. *haga-zussa,* O.E. *haegtes, i.e.* German hexe, witch, and Goth. *haljaruna,* O.H.G. *helleruna,* O.E. *hellerune*) in their several haunts, against whose malignant power his only resource was zealous devotion to witchcraft."—KAUFMANN, *Northern Mythology,* Temple Primers, p. 18. See note on hell-runes, Beowulf, 6-24.

In the *Havamal,* one of the Eddic poems, there is an interesting allusion to just such a "spell" as is preserved in our charm. The poet says:

"A spell I can work when witch-women ride
Speeding swift through the air.
My runes are strong. I can stop their flight
Hurry them naked home
Home with bewildered wits."

Other charms he claims to know which have the power of releasing foot from fetter, hand from haft, and of checking an arrow in full flight.

2. RIDDLES

In the Exeter Book is preserved a collection of some ninety riddles in alliterative verse. These riddles are descriptions or characterizations of objects, from which the object itself, which is not named, must be guessed. When the Old English poet, instead of naming the sea, called it the seal's bath, or instead of naming the ship, called it the ocean-stallion, he resorted to a familiar device of Germanic poetry known as the kenning. Now the Old English riddles are in essence expanded kennings: given the characteristics of an object, to guess what is meant. In the larger number of the riddles, the objects are personified and describe themselves, and many of them attain a high degree of literary excellence. Their scope is wide. "Nothing human is deemed too high or low for treatment, and all phases of Old English existence are revealed in these poems; so that they stand out as the most important contemporary contributions to the everyday life of their time." The reading and guessing of riddles of this kind seems to have been a favorite pastime with the Old English, and frequent references to the mead-hall in the riddles themselves make it likely that they were recited there along with lay and ballad. The Old English riddles have their parallels in Latin literature. A collection of one hundred Latin riddles, called the enigmas of Symphosius, was especially popular in England in the seventh and eighth centuries. Aldhelm (640-707), Bishop of Sherborne, imitated Symphosius in a collection of a hundred riddles in Latin hexameters. A third collection of Latin riddles is partly by Tatwine, who became Archbishop of Canterbury in 731, and partly by one Eusebius, of whom nothing is known except that he was an English Churchman and composed sixty enigmas, which with Tatwine's forty, made up the favorite one hundred of the riddle collections. While the riddles of the Exeter Book show the influence of these Latin models, they are in no sense mere imitations, but are full of fresh and close observation of life.

The English riddles, unlike those in the Latin collections, are not supplied with answers, hence their solution has long exercised the ingenuity of students of Old English. While most of them have been satisfactorily solved, the meaning of some is still in doubt. The theory that Cynewulf wrote the riddles has been effectually disproved. While no author is known, they show the workmanship of a single poet, and are not to be viewed as a random collection. For the whole subject of Riddle Literature, and the problems raised by the

Old English Riddles, see Professor Tupper's excellent introduction to his edition of the *Riddles of The Exeter Book* (Albion Series, Ginn and Co., 1910).

THE BOOK-WORM

151. No 48 of the Exeter Book. Perhaps more accurately, the Book Moth. The riddle is closely modelled upon No. 16 in the collection of Symphosius, which is given for comparison:

> "Litera me pavit, nec quid sit litera novi.
> In libris vixi, nec sum studiosior inde.
> Exedi Musas, nec adhuc tamen ipsa profeci."

The solution of the Latin riddle is given as "Tinea."

GNATS

152. No. 58 of the Exeter Book. This riddle has been variously interpreted as referring to swallows, or gnats, or starlings. The analogies from Latin riddles, quoted by Professor Tupper, seem to favor the solution "swallows." In that case we ought to read in l. 3:

> Dark-coated, dusky-winged, darting about,

and in the last line

> Gable-roofed towns! Now tell me their name.

THE SHIELD

No. 6 of the Exeter Book. "Illuminated Anglo-Saxon Mss. usually represent the warrior as armed with no other defensive weapons than shield and helmet. The shield, circular, or slightly oval in shape, is usually of linden-wood, sometimes covered with leather, with a metal-bound edge and in the center an iron boss, a small basin tapering at the top to a point and ending in a knob."—TUPPER.

BARNACLE

No. 11 of the Exeter Book. This puzzling riddle has been responsible for much ingenious guesswork. Among the answers suggested are the following: Ocean-furrow, Wake of a Vessel, Water-bubble, Anchor, Water-lily! Stopford Brooke (*E. E. L.*, p. 179, note) suggests "Barnacle-Goose" as the solution. Giraldus Cambrensis, a medieval writer, gives the following description of this mythical bird: "Barnacle geese are like marsh-geese, but somewhat smaller. They are produced from fir timber tossed along the sea, and are at first like gum. Afterwards they hang down by their beaks, as if from a seaweed attached to a timber, surrounded by shells in order to grow more freely. Having thus in process of time been clothed with a strong coat of feathers, they either fall into the water, or fly freely away into the air." Professor Tupper, in his note on the riddle, defends Brooke's interpretation; and the additional evidence adduced by him seems now to me conclusive in favor of the Barnacle-goose. My own interpretation, made before I had seen his article, I have allowed to stand as a suggestion, although it will probably be thought to be too fanciful. The "streamers of white," "Hwite wæron hyrste mine," were suggested to me by the way in which the green seas are churned into wavy lines of white foam by the barnacled undersides of a sailing-vessel when she heels to the wind. These "streamers of white" can be observed wherever the tide sweeps between the barnacled pilings of an old dock or bridge. On the other hand, the fact that "hyrste" is used of the feathers of the bird in the Swan riddle, favors the solution "Barnacle-Goose."

HONEY-MEAD

153. No. 28 of the Exeter Book collection. Professor Tupper, in his note to this riddle (p. 132), quotes a number of interesting analogues. "Honey was more important to the ancients than it is to us, for it constituted the chief ingredient of mead, the time-honored beverage of the Aryan peoples."—Sharon Turner (*Hist. of the Anglo-Saxons*, Bk. VII, Chap. IV) cites an Anglo-Saxon canon against drunkenness: "This is drunkenness, when the state of mind is changed, the tongue stammers, the eyes are disturbed, the head is giddy, the belly is swelled, and pain follows." (Both passages cited by Tupper.) Tacitus, long before, made the observation that the people of Germanic stock were addicted to the vice of drunkenness.

The Anchor

154. No. 17 of the Exeter Book collection. This riddle has a parallel in the Symphosius collection.

"Mucro mihi geminus ferro conjungitur unco
Cum vento luctor, cum gurgite pugno profundo.
Scrutor aquas medias, ipsas quoque mordeo terras."

(A double point is joined to me with hooked iron. With the wind I struggle, I battle with the surge profound. I scan the midmost waves, and bite the very bottom.) The Old English riddle offers a fine example of the way in which the poet's imagination vitalizes and dramatizes his object. The anchor has become a hero fighting desperately for the safety of the vessel committed to his charge.

The Plough

No. 22 of the Exeter Book collection. Professor Tupper has an interesting note on the ancient plough (p. 113), and gives references to pictures of ploughs in old Mss. "The illuminated Mss. are at variance regarding the form of the plough. In some the ploughs are of the rudest sort without wheels; in others they have wheels (so in the pictures of the Cædmon Ms.). All these ploughs are drawn by oxen, urged by a goad—usually in the hands of an attendant herd."—3. MY MASTER THE FARMER, OLD FOE OF THE FOR-EST. The Old English has simply, "Har holtes feond," hoary foe of the forest, which has also been interpreted as refer-ring to the ox that draws the plough.—10. A CURIOUS PRONG, etc. The coulter and share of the plough.

The Swan

155—No. 8 of the Exeter Book collection. See note on the "music of the swan," Phœnix, 132-32.

3. GNOMIC VERSES

Proverbial sayings, maxims of wisdom, reflections based on experience, were popular among the Germanic peoples from the earliest times, and were handed down in the tra-ditional alliterative form. Two compilations of gnomic verses are found in the Old English Ms. collections, one in

the Cotton Ms., comprising sixty-six lines, and given entire
in the translation, the other in the Exeter Book, comprising two hundred six lines, from which a few extracts are
given. But this by no means exhausts the store of "gnomic
verse," in Old English literature. We find both the Epic
and the Lyric verse of the Anglo-Saxons liberally interlined
with gnomic sayings, sober moralizing which to our mind
often interrupt the movement of the narrative or the flow
of lyric feeling. No doubt the cultivation of literature in
the monasteries emphasized this preaching tendency; but it
would be a mistake to suppose that wherever our taste is
offended by the intrusion of the gnomic genre, we are dealing with interpolated matter. In spite of the apparently
loose and haphazard manner in which the gnomic sayings
are strung together in our collections, there is a certain unity
of structure and design. The verses are closely knit together by alliteration and "enjambment," *i.e.*, the running
over of the sense from one line into the next, unlike, in this
respect, to the favorite distich or heroic couplet of eigh-
teenth-century didactic verse. The end of one "saying" and
the beginning of the next are generally locked together by
alliteration, but the alliterative line is rarely a thought unit.
It is interesting to observe how alliteration is thus made to
assist the memory in linking together a series of apparently
disconnected sayings. The need of some such help probably explains the large preponderance of "run-on" lines in
these gnomic collections. Here and there we seem to have
remnants of an earlier stanzaic form. In their swift pano-
ramic survey of life, and their delight in a huddled array
of concrete observation, there is a curious analogy between
these gnomic verses and some of the poems of Walt Whitman. (Cf. B. C. Williams, *Gnomic Poetry in Anglo-Saxon*,
Col. Univ. Press., 1914.)

156.—26. GIANT SHALL DWELL ON THE FEN. See the description of Grendel's haunt, *Beowulf*, ll. 1345 ff. (p. 13).

157.—8. THE WOLF SHALL HANG. An outlaw was called
a wolf. According to a widespread superstition, some men
had the power of changing themselves into wolves. Such
a man-wolf or "wer-wolf" was considered as especially
dangerous, and as late as the seventeenth century men were
tried in Europe for being wer-wolves.

IV. HISTORIC WAR POEMS

The Battle of Brunnanburg

This poem is in the *Anglo-Saxon Chronicle* for the year 937, and was evidently intended as a piece of historical narrative. Æthelstan, grandson of Alfred the Great, and hereditary ruler of Wessex, had been acknowledged overlord of Mercians, Danes of Northumbria, Britons of Strathclyde, and Scots. But in 937 a conspiracy against him was formed by Constantinus, king of the Scots, who joined with the Danes and Strathclyde Britons. The Norsemen of Ireland, under Anlaf or Olaf, aided their Northumbrian kinsmen, bringing their army over by sea from Dublin. The allies were defeated by Æthelstan and his brother at Brunnanburg with great slaughter. The site of Brunnanburg is unknown. Among several places mentioned, the most likely seems to be Bramber, near Preston in Lancashire, south of the Ribble. A great hoard of silver ingots and coins, none later than 930, was discovered near this place in 1847, and it has been suggested that this may have been the war-chest of the confederate army. (C. Hardwick, *Lancashire Battlefields*, quoted by Sedgefield in his introduction to the poem in the Belles Lettres Series.) Tennyson's fine version of the *Battle of Brunnanburg*, based on his son Hallam's prose translation, and the rhythms of the original, is well known, and is precious to all lovers of English poetry, as representing the effect which the old alliterative measure produced on the finest ear of the Victorian period. But Tennyson followed the prevailing custom of his day is considering the half-line of two beats, rather than the long line of four beats bound together by alliteration, as the metrical unit of the verse. As a result, Tennyson's version breaks up the alliterative scheme of Old English verse, and in so far fails to give the movement of the original. No one could undertake another version of Brunnanburg without showing the influence of Tennyson. Wherever I have been conscious of it, I have indicated it in the notes. The only reason for venturing on a new version of *The Battle of Brunnanburg* was to make it uniform in rhythm and alliterative plan with the other renderings of this series.

162.—5. EDMUND ÆTHELING. Three sons of Edward

the Elder reigned in succession: Æthelstan, 925-940; Edmund, 940-946; Eadred, 946-955.—7. BROKE THE SHIELD-WALL, HEWED THE LINDENWOODS. So Tennyson. The original has "bordweall clufon, heowan heaþolinda," clove the shield-walls, hewed the battle-lindens.—11. TRUE TO THEIR BLOOD. The blood of Ælfred the Great. Gardiner says of Eadred, the youngest of Æthelstan's brothers, "though sickly, he had all the spirit of his race."—12. THEIR HOARD AND THEIR HOME. Tennyson, "struck for their hoards and their hearths and their homes." The Old English has "Hord and hamas," hearth and homes.—13. BOAT-CREWS. The regular name for the Danish invaders in the *Chronicle* is "sciphere," *i.e.* ship-army.—17. CAME IN THE MORNING-TIDE GLIDING O'ER EARTH. Tennyson, "From when first the great sun-star of morning-tide . . . glode over earth." Old English, "Siþþan sunne up on morgentid, glad ofer grundas." "Till the glorious creature sank to its setting." So Tennyson. Old English, "Oþ þæt seo æþele gesceaft, sah to setle"; literally, "till the glorious creature, sank to setting."—21. SHOT OVER SHIELD. Old English, "ofer scyld sceoten."

163.—4. WHO CAME WITH ANLAF ACROSS THE WATER. *I.e.* from Dublin. Anlaf is the English form of Olaf. "There seem to have been two Olafs present at this battle: Anlaf Cuaran, son of Sihtric, Æthelstan's brother-in-law, and Anlaf, son of Godfrey, Sihtric's brother."—6. The Mercians formed part of the West-Saxon army. Edward the Elder had added the midland districts as far north as Chester in the West and the Humber in the East, to the West-Saxon dominion. His sister Æthelflæd, who aided him in making his conquest, was known as the Lady of the Mercians.—7. HAND-PLAY. Old English, "handplegan."—14. ON THE FALLOW FLOOD. Old English, "on fealone flod."—15. THE CUNNING CONSTANTINUS. Tennyson, "Also the crafty one, Constantinus." Old English, "se frode," the wise old man.

164.—1. DUBLIN TO SEEK. Dublin was the chief settlement of the Northmen in Ireland, and had been founded by the Viking leader Turgeis about 839 A.D.—164.—10. THE HAGGARD KITE. Literally, the greedy hawk-of-war.

It is possible that this is merely a descriptive epithet or kenning for the eagle. In that case we should translate:

"Leaving behind the white-tailed eagle
(Perched on the corpses), to prey on the carrion,
Greedy war-hawk, and the gray beast,
Wolf of the forest to feast on the slain."

Cf. Kipling's "Birds of Prey" March:

"The jackal an' the Kite
'Ave an 'ealthy appetite
An' you'll never see your soldier any more.
The eagle and the crow
They are waitin' ever so
An' you'll never see your soldier any more."

THE BATTLE OF MALDON

The fight commemorated in this poem took place in the year 991, and is thus described in the *Anglo-Saxon Chronicle*: "In this year came Anlaf with ninety-three ships to Stan (Folkstone), and laid waste the country round about, and from there he went to Sandwich, and so on to Ipswich, and harried all the country. And then he came to Maldon, where the ealdorman Byrhtnoth with his force came to meet him and fought against him. And they slew the ealdorman there, and were masters of the field of battle, and afterwards peace was made with them." The famous Olaf Trygvasson, celebrated in Longfellow's *Saga of King Olaf,* was the Norse leader. The site of the battle is described by Freeman (*Norman Conquest,* Vol. I, p. 268): "The fight of Maldon is the only battle of the days of Æthelred, of which any minute details are preserved, and every detail throws light on something in the manners or military tactics of the age. The battle took place near the town of Maldon (in Essex), on the banks of the tidal river Panta, now called the Blackwater. The town lies on a hill; immediately at its base flows one branch of the river, while another, still crossed by a medieval bridge, flows at a little distance to the north. The Danish ships seem to have lain in the branch nearest to the town, and their crews must have occupied the space between the two streams, while

Brithtnoth came to the rescue from the north. He seems to have halted at the spot now occupied by the church of Heybridge, having both streams between him and the town."

Byrhtnoth, alderman or ruler of Essex, under King Æthelred the Redeless, had been a benefactor of the monastery of Ely, situated not far from the scene of the battle. In a Latin chronicle of Ely, containing a somewhat legendary account of the fight, we are told a that the Abbot, "hearing of the issue of the battle, went to the field with some monks, and seeking out the hero's body bore it back to the church and buried it honourably, placing a round lump of wax where the head had been."

The author of our poem was in all probability one of the monks of Ely. He was either an eye-witness of the battle, or heard the details from one of the survivors. Though the beginning and the end of the poem were missing in the original Ms., there is no doubt that in the portion preserved, and fortunately copied before the destruction of the Ms. by fire in 1731, we have practically the poem in its entirety, and it is therefore misleading to speak of the *Battle of Maldon* as a fragment, in the sense in which *The Fight at Finnsburg,* and *Waldere,* or even *Judith,* are fragments.

For additional details see the introduction to W. J. Sedgefield's edition of the poem in the Belles Lettres Series (D. C. Heath and Co., 1904), H. W. Lumsden's article and spirited translation of the poem in *Macmillan's Magazine,* 55, p. 371, and Freeman's *Norman Conquest,* cited above.

165.—4. SHOWED THEM HOW THEY SHOULD HOLD THEIR SHIELDS. "The fighting men of the fyrd or militia had but imperfect ideas of military discipline, and needed the personal instruction of their general even as to the proper holding and use of their arms" (SEDGEFIELD).—7. LEAPED FROM HIS STEED. Freeman points out that battles were fought on foot in England before the Conquest, though horses were used to get to and from the battlefield. However, the ornamented saddle given by Hrothgar to Beowulf is called the "Battle-seat" of the king.—8. HIS HEARTH BAND, etc. His own retainers, or comitatus, who lived in his own hall, and were of his own household. Cf. *Germania,* Chap. 7; "non casus neque fortuita conglobatio tur-

mam aut cuneum facit, *sed familiae et propinquitates."*—
14. SEND THEM TRIBUTE. Æthelred the Redeless inaugu-
rated the bad custom of buying off the Danes who were
about to make raids. Money so paid was called Danegeld,
i.e. Dane Money.

166.—14. THE BREADTH OF THE STREAM. Below Maldon, the Blackwater opens into a sea-inlet, where a strong
tide runs.

167.—1. ON THE BRIDGE. The bridge probably crossed
only the deep channel, where the tide ran strong. The flats
on either side would be bare or nearly bare at low tide,
giving access to the bridge, but at high tide they would be
covered.—4. KEPT THE APPROACH, etc. Literally, "would
not make a flight of it at the ford." With Sedgefield I
understand the "ford" to mean the shallow flats between
either terminus of the bridge and the mainland. A ford is
a place where "the crossing is shallow." The spirited fight
on the bridge reminds us of Macaulay's ballad of Horatius.
—14. BYRHTHELM'S SON. *I.e.* Byrhtnoth.—WEST OVER
PANTA.—We should expect here "north over Panta," as
from l. 26 p. 168 it appears that the Vikings were south
of the English. If the main channel bent to the north at
the point of crossing, the Northmen charging from the
southern bank would be heading northwest, which the
exigencies of alliteration might easily make west.—22.
LINDENWOOD. A common kenning for shield. Cf. *Charm
for a Sudden Stitch,* p. 2, l. 5, and *Brunnanburg,* p. 82, l. 6.

168.—7. SON OF HIS SISTER. This tie of relationship was
considered in Germanic antiquity as more intimate and bind-
ing than that of "brother's son."—12. THE THANE, etc.
Literally, "bower-thane." The "bower" is the private sleeping apartment, as distinguished from the hall. When Beowulf fought Grendel in the hall, the Danes heard the noise
in the "bowers." "Bower-thane" is therefore equivalent to
the later chamberlain.—28. HE SHOVED WITH HIS SHIELD.
I.e. he caught the dart-point in his shield, but the shaft snap-
ping short, splintered and wounded him. This seems to
me a more, reasonable interpretation than Sedgefield's. In
the *Njals Saga* is a similar situation, when "Gunnar gave
the shield a twist as the sword pierced it, and broke it
short off at the hilt" (Chap. 30).

169.—10. Now ONE OF THE PIRATES, etc. With this passage, describing the death of Byrhtnoth, should be compared the killing of Douglas in the ballad of Chevy Chase. When Byrhtnoth, mortally wounded, no longer can grasp his sword, he still keeps encouraging his men. So when Earl Douglas is stricken in at the breast-bane, he cried:

> "Fight ye, my merry men, whiles ye may,
> For my life-days be gane."

—24. BROAD AND BLOOD-MARKED. Literally, brown-edged, —one of the conventional epithets for swords in Anglo-Saxon poetry and in the ballads. "Broad and brown-edged" is the sword of Grendel's dam in *Beowulf*. The epithets may refer to the rusty blood-stains purposely left on the sword-blade as marks of ancient valor and faithful service. Old English poetry is peculiarly sparing of color-epithets. Brown, gray, fallow, dun, are the only colors that appear frequently. Even in the ideal landscape of the *Phœnix,* and in the description of the bird's gorgeous plumage, the colors are suggested rather than described.—30. THE HOAR-HEADED WARRIOR. Probably more than a mere conventional epithet. In the *Life of Oswald,* Archbishop of York, written not long after the battle of Maldon, Byrthnoth's end is thus described: "With his right arm he dealt blow on blow, unmindful of *the swan-like whiteness of his head. . . .* With his left arm he defended himself, forgetting his bodily weakness, for his prayers and good deeds sustained him." The prayer of Byrhtnoth breathes the atmosphere of the monastery, rather than of the battlefield, and seems out of keeping with the warlike temper of the rest of the poem. The Chevy Chase poet knew better:

> "For Witherington my heart was sore
> That ever he slain should be,
> For when both his legs were hewn in two
> Yet he kneeled and fought on his knee."

170.—10. THE FIENDS OF HELL. It is not necessary to understand this of the Norsemen, though the epithet is one that the author would be likely enough to apply to the heathen Danes, whom the English monks had good reason to hate, and whom they may very well have regarded as "in direct league with the devil," as Sedgefield suggests. It would be more in keeping with the spirit of the poem if Byrhtnoth, like Beowulf, had thought of the fate of his people, rather than of his own soul, at this juncture.

171.—2. ÆTHELRED'S EARL. *I.e.* earl of King Æthelred, the West-Saxon ruler 968-1016.—11. REMEMBER THE TIME, etc. Cf. Beowulf's last fight, and the speech of Wiglaf.

172.—20. LEADERLESS, LORDLESS, etc. "A valuable survival of this taunting of men who broke the oath of loyalty is the cry of the sworn-brother in *Bewick and Graham:*

> "In every town that I ride through
> They'll say—'There rides a brotherless man.'"
>
> (Gummere.)

173.—2. ÆSCFERTH. He appears to have been an Englishman held by the Danes as a hostage. Managing to escape, he joined his own people against the enemy.—31. HE LAY BY HIS LORD, A LOYAL THANE. Professor Gummere (*Old English Epic,* p. 136) quotes an interesting passage from *Saxo Grammaticus,* illustrating the loyalty of thanes to their lord. Hialto says: "Sweet it is to repay the gifts received from our lord . . . let us do with brave hearts all the things that in our cups we boasted . . . let us keep the vows we swore." And Bjarki answers: "I will die overpowered near the head of my slain captain, and at his feet thou also shalt slip on thy face in death, so that whoso scans the piled corpses may see in what wise we rate the gold our lord gave us." Saxo's Latin prose, by his own account, is based on an old Danish song.

174.—4. WISTAN. He is called Thurstan's son, but in the next line he is referred to as "Wigeline's bearn," *i.e.* the child of Wigelin. There seems to be some confusion here. —174.—18. HEART MUST BE KEENER. These words of Byrhtwold contain the essence of old Germanic heroism: fearless valor and a loyalty that keeps faith to the end and prefers death to dishonor.

> "Men and houses
> Stand long enough if they stand
> Until they fall with honor."

THE END